Working Women and State Policies in Taiwan

Also by Fen-ling Chen

FAMILY POLICY (*in Chinese*)

Working Women and State Policies in Taiwan

A Study in Political Economy

Fen-ling Chen
Assistant Professor
Department of Sociology
Yuan-Ze University
Taiwan

First published 2000 by
PALGRAVE
Houndmills, Basingstoke, Hampshire RG21 6XS and
175 Fifth Avenue, New York, N. Y. 10010
Companies and representatives throughout the world

PALGRAVE is the new global academic imprint of
St. Martin's Press LLC Scholarly and Reference Division and
Palgrave Publishers Ltd (formerly Macmillan Press Ltd).

Outside North America
ISBN 0–333–80209–8

In North America
ISBN 0–312–23462–7

This book is printed on paper suitable for recycling and made from fully managed and sustained forest sources.

A catalogue record for this book is available from the British Library.

Library of Congress Cataloging-in-Publication Data
Chen, Fen-ling, 1967–
    Working women and state policies in Taiwan : a study in political economy / Fen-ling Chen.
        p. cm.
    Includes bibliographical references and index.
    ISBN 0–312–23462–7
    1. Women—Employment—Government policy—Taiwan. 2. Women––Taiwan—Attitudes. 3. Women employees—Taiwan—Attitudes. I. Title.
    HD6202 .C48 2000
    331.4'12042'0951249—dc21
                                                                00–027827

10   9   8   7   6   5   4   3   2   1
09 08 07 06 05 04 03 02 01 00

Printed and bound in Great Britain by
Antony Rowe Ltd, Chippenham, Wiltshire

Contents

List of Tables

List of Figures

Acknowledgements

This book is based on my doctoral study at the University of Bath in England. I would like to express my appreciation and profound gratitude to my supervisor, Professor Ian Gough. He has always been most generous with his time and attention; without his constant support and constructive comments over the past four years, the thesis would not have been possible.

I owe special thanks to my co-supervisor, Professor Jane Millar. She made many helpful comments and advised me on the best way of doing research. Thanks are also due to Professor Michael Hill and Mr Peter Cressey who kindly gave me useful suggestions in the final stage.

I am indebted to my interviewees who enabled me to develop my understanding of varied viewpoints towards the enactment of the Gender Equal Employment Act.

Many other people have contributed in various ways to this study. Among my friends, appreciation goes to Ching-yi Chiang for her kindness in collecting data in the Legislative Yuan, Shu-ching Chuang for providing me with the documentary data in the Council of Labour Affairs, Mieh-ching Liu for her arrangement of *interviews*, Yeun-wen Ku for his share of research experience. Huei-cheng Chen, Yu-ying Li, Steve Lin, Yun-jung Kim, Sung-jung Yi, Chien-ling Chang, Yueh-er Chang and Heng-cheng Kuo gave me friendship and assistance in Britain. The deepest appreciation also goes to my friend Heather Willes for her patient and careful proof-reading.

My parents give me unending love and financial support. No words can describe my thanks to them.

Finally, and most importantly, my thanks go to my beloved husband, San-lin Chung, for his love, encouragement, patience and discussion. Our daughter, Chu-ying Chung, has given us many wonderful times during the last year of my study. She also accompanied me to search for data at many libraries when I was pregnant. For this, I dedicate this book to them.

FEN-LING CHEN

List of Abbreviations

CEPD   Council for Economic Planning and Development, Executive
       Yuan
CLA   Council of Labour Affairs
DBAS   Directorate-general of Budget, Accounting and Statistics
DPP   Democratic Progressive Party
GEEB   Gender Equal Employment Bill
ILO   International Labour Organization
KMT   Kuomintang
LSL   Labour Standards Law
NHI   National Health Insurance
OECD   Organization for Economic Co-operation and Development
s.l.d. severe learning difficulties
UN   United Nations

1
Introduction

In recent years, feminist scholars have tended to think that patriarchy and capitalism should account for women's inferior status in the labour market. However, the emergence of welfare states has changed relationships between men and women. Women have to face not only a relationship with men and/or capitalism but also a new relationship with the state. Existing theoretical perspectives on social policy have ignored gender dimensions and have been criticized by women scholars. More scholars have begun to notice the importance of the state's role in relation to women's status in the labour market (Walby, 1986; Hernes, 1987). The more pessimistic among them, regarded the state's intervention in women's issues as a new form of patriarchy (Boris and Bardaglio, 1983), as a force controlling women's reproduction (Pascall, 1986), or as a drive to combine the oppression of women by patriarchy and capitalism (Cheng and Hsiung, 1994). Others have been more optimistic about state intervention due to women's access to welfare and state policies (Pillinger, 1992). Using working women as a focus, it is interesting to explore how far the state has used its policies to intervene in the utilization of the female labour force. How does the state deal with the conflict between capitalist development and the maintenance of the traditional family system? Can state policies transform systems of male or/and capitalist dominance to provide an environment of equal opportunities for women?

This study seeks to avoid the static conceptualization of the state as an invariable supporter of men's and capitalists' interests, but identifies the changing characteristics of the state through historical analysis. Since different states have different impacts on gender regimes and on women's opportunities to participate in the labour market, the study of developing and newly industrialized countries, such as Taiwan, could shed light on the understanding of the relationship between the state and women in an East Asian welfare regime. A study of non-Western experience could also provide a more comprehensive understanding of social policy and gender since the majority of existing theoretical approaches in this field are derived from the experience of Western societies.

Women's studies in Taiwan

It was not until the mid-1980s that the discussion of women's issues in Taiwan moved into the academic sphere. The early research on working women in Taiwan focused on the exploration of women's lives in factories and in rural areas (Kung, 1976; Huang, 1977; Diamond, 1979; Arrigo, 1980). More recently, scholars have become interested in the gender division of small-scale family businesses, and concluded that gender relations in the workplace reproduced those present in the family (Li and Ka, 1994; Lu, 1996). Some scholars also tried to find the causal factors of women's inferior status in the labour force in Taiwan. The majority of them employed quantitative method to retest existing theories. Economists had more interest in the explanation of wage differentials between sexes, and claimed that the human capital theory suited Taiwan's case (Lin, 1992; Kao et al., 1994; Lee, 1994), though few of them admitted the existence of gender discrimination in the labour market (Gannicott, 1986). Lu (1992, 1994) employed the Multinomial Logistic Model to analyze employment patterns of married women. Disagreeing with the emphasis of *Female Marginalization Theory* on the force of labour market, she found that gender division in the family accounted for the informal employment of married women. Wang (1995) used a survey method to find the causal explanation of women's work aspirations. Through logistic regression analysis, she found that the educational attainment and women's attitudes towards sex roles in the family were the most important factors affecting women's willingness to join the labour force. Other factors, including state policies on working women, family life cycle, levels of urbanization, and the accessibility of family support, had no significant correlation with women's work aspirations. In conclusion, the emphasis of the research on gender identity and the level of women's human capital was problematic. Gender relations and the inferior human capital of women could be a social, political and economic product. It is more important to find the underlying factors which dominate or lead to the current situation of gender division. It is also important to take political factors into account as politics construct gender and gender constructs politics.

Social welfare in Taiwan has drawn much attention in the 1990s. Regarding women's welfare, most research focused on the survey of women's needs, and was usually undertaken by the government (Chiang, 1990; Yang et al., 1991; Wang, 1992; Wang et al., 1994). As the government has paid more attention to women's welfare since 1989, there has been a feeling that exploring women's needs should be the first step in its action. Furthermore, the work of Hu and Chang (1995) explored public attitudes towards policies on women workers from focus groups, but here again the focus was on women's needs. Basically, these research works belonged to exploratory research rather than explanatory research. Recently, a few scholars have also begun to criticize the ways in which the social security system in Taiwan favours men, especially men in the labour market (Lee, 1994). Women have been incorporated into welfare through entitlements as dependents (Fu, 1995).

It has been claimed that the state has played an important role in exploiting women workers. Gallin (1990) found that, based on her field research and an interpretation of the literature, women workers in Taiwan lacked the class consciousness and the ability of collective action to change their working conditions. She indicated that the state played an important role in muting women's consciousness in Taiwan by inculcating traditional patriarchal ideology and restricting the functions of labour unions. According to the work of Cheng and Hsiung (1994), Kuomintang's policies, with capitalist and patriarchal ideology, led to the double exploitation of women as housewives and workers during the 1960s and 1970s. Using ethnographic data, they illustrated that the capitalists, the state and the international market benefited from exploiting women.

Without some consideration of time, these research works could only explain women's status in a particular period. For instance, Gallin's findings were unable to explain the emergence of the women's movement after the mid-1980s. The criticism of Cheng and Hsiung of state policies might be reasonable from certain standpoints, but it could not explain why, if women were just the victims of capitalist development, they had succeeded in gaining a positive change in their status. Therefore, we should avoid the static conceptualization of the state vis-à-vis women, and focus on the change of the relationship between the state and women.

In the past, historians in Taiwan have been interested in the status of women in mainland China. It was not until recently that historians began to explore women's experiences in early Taiwanese history, for example the excellent work of Yang (1993). Based on reports in 'Taiwan Min Pao' from 1920–32, she revealed the issues and history of the women's emancipation movement during Japanese colonization, and pointed out that capitalists, colonizers and patriarchal culture might account for the oppression of Taiwanese women. Yu's narrative of working women during Japanese colonization came to a more positive conclusion. During the colonial period, Taiwanese women did not have the same working opportunities as Japanese women in Taiwan, but women's status and social structure was changed by the increasing number of women entering the labour force (Yu, 1994).

Recent history has been dominated more by social researchers, such as Ku (1989) and Chang (1995) on the history of the women's movement in Taiwan. Moreover, Lin (1995) tried to explore the nature of social welfare in Taiwan using the traditional ideas and practices of charity in Chinese society. He explained the way in which state intervention led to the unequal distribution of welfare resource and the underdevelopment of Taiwanese welfare. Based on historical material Ku (1995) explored the development of state welfare through the interconnection between capitalism and state welfare in the developmental process, and his result echoed the basic analysis of the welfare state made by neo-Marxist political economists. That is, women have played no role in their 'welfare history.' Could Lin and Ku's theoretical approach explain women's experiences under the Taiwanese welfare regime? Analyzing the character of the Taiwanese welfare regime from a gender-critical perspective might lead to hidden aspects of welfare history.

Unlike in Western countries, women's studies in Taiwan are just taking off. Research on women in the labour market focuses on quantitative analysis and on social and economic factors, neglecting the influence of political power. Although there is some research on women's welfare and the implication of state policies on women workers, no one has tried to explore the relationship between the state and working women from a historical perspective. For a more comprehensive understanding, it is vital to place gender in a historical analysis of social policies. This book will discuss the relationship between state policies and working women in Taiwan through a historical review.

Placing gender in historical analysis

Scholars have increasingly placed value on the writing of women's history since the emergence of the feminist movement. Women's history has been neglected in the past partly because men have played active roles in the public sphere and dominated the definition of historical significance. Since women were regarded as having a limited number of stereotypical roles, historians were sceptical as to whether women's history could tell us anything new and what could be learned from it. Some regarded the writings of women's history, especially about the women's movement, as literature without a purpose. However, some feminist scholars gave emphasis to writing 'herstory' and to exploring women's lives in the private sphere even if it was just as they (feminist scholars) pleased, but most believed that they might produce new knowledge through gender-critical reflection on the processes by which knowledge had been produced. We might understand how a gender regime is produced and reproduced if we return to history.

Early discussion among feminists circled around a belief that women were an oppressed group. However, Gordon et al. stress,

> Analyzes of women based on static concepts such as caste or oppressed group renders history an external process, a force which presses against women's lives without a reciprocal interaction. Women become in the truest sense the objects of history, bound by their peculiar situation as victims of oppression. ... The dynamics of women's history occur along two interwoven threads: changes in the multiplicity of women's roles over time and across class, race and ethnic lines, and movement of women as a group toward consciousness of their common condition.
>
> – Gordon, Buhle and Dye (1976: 88–9)

One of the most meaningful values of placing gender in historical analysis is that we can examine the changes of women's roles over time. We are also able to identify which factors lead to a dynamic or unchanging gender regime.

Gordon et al. (1976) classified historical writing on women into four categories: (1) institutional histories of women in organizations, such as the history of women's movements, (2) biographies of important women, (3) histories of ideas about women and their roles, and (4) social histories of women in particular times and places. This last category was thought to expand our knowledge of women's lives. The other modes also influenced our conceptions of women's lives but were too narrow and limited to answer new questions over time. Social historians have insisted that women's roles and sphere have changed over time, and are concerned about the connections between women's roles in the home and work.

There are several strategies for writing gender into political analysis. First, to uncover women participating in major political events and fit them as a new subject into given historical categories. Secondly, to take evidence about women and use it to challenge received interpretations of progress and regress. Thirdly, to depart from the framework of conventional history and offer a new narrative (Scott, 1988: 18). Few women scholars would approve the value of the first strategy, as it is likely to replicate male norms. Research which employed the third strategy was criticized for isolating women as a special and separate topic of history. They usually reviewed different documents, employed different categories of analysis and did not have much dialogue with existing history and theories, so their contributions were easily consigned to a 'separate sphere.' Therefore, research of women's history has increasing tended to employ the second strategy and seek a new interpretation.

Since the 1960s, many theories have been drawn up to explain the development of the welfare state. Established approaches, however, have often ignored social policies targeted on mothers and women workers. What research there is on the origins of the welfare state has shown that the issue of maternity was a key theme in the policies of the rising welfare state (Koven and Michel, 1990; Bock and Thane, 1991; Cohen and Hanagan, 1991; Orloff, 1991; Skocpol, 1992; Skocpol and Ritter, 1995).

Norris's work, *Politics and Sexual Equality*, though it is not historical research, highlights the importance of considering social, economic, political and ideological factors in policy analysis of gender (Norris, 1987). Although some research into women and social policy includes the time factor, it usually focuses on one or two causal dimensions in the analysis of the past but fail to integrate other dimensions. For instance, Gauthier's book, *The State and the Family*, focusing on family policies in 22 countries over a time span of 100 years, tries to demonstrate the changing nature of the relationship between the family and the state, and the role which demographic developments have played in that relationship (Gauthier, 1996). This research contains both time and space dimensions and is informative on the development and contemporary face of family policies, but overlooks the active political character of policy and the policy making process. Another example is Skocpol's *Protecting Soldiers and Mothers*. Her 'polity-centred' analysis on the early development of US social policy underplays social and economic power as well as ideology. In the book, she emphasizes women's modes of practicing politics, through non-partisan membership organizations with the ability to mobilize local affiliates. The gender meanings of welfare strategies, non-institutionalized social care and employers' influence, which are also important for making social policies, are strangely absent from her political analysis. This neglect of other forces results in the exaggeration of women's contribution on the development to maternalist policies. Therefore, as a historical research focus on policy analysis of gender, it is important to incorporate various dimensions in our analysis.

As Skocpol (1992: 38) indicates, the perspective of gender identities and relationships cannot explain everything about the origins and development of social policies in a comparative perspective. However, any approach which tries to explain the history of social policies will certainly have to bring gender fully into the analysis. The analysis of gender could challenge established knowledge and bring a new interpretation. This study, therefore, will avoid a static analysis of women's history but examine the changes in women's roles over time, and incorporate social, economic, political and ideological factors in the historical analysis.

Methodological issues

The research design for this study employs historical documentary data in the analysis of a single country, with a gender-critical perspective. My motivation is to use historical analysis for understanding policy trajectories on women in the labour force and the causal factors which may determine them. The causal complexity and varying character of the causal factors in which I am interested encourage me to employ qualitative research to answer my research questions. Qualitative analysis is better for identifying relationship, processes and contradictions, and a historical approach is a proper method for understanding the relationship between working women and state policies. I have presented the importance of placing gender in historical analysis. In this section, therefore, I would like to discuss two methodological issues related to this study: the use of critical historical perspective and the possibility of single-country study. The discussion of methodology would help this study employ more rigorous data collection and research design.

A critical historical perspective

Critical social research is a way of approaching the social world. It is not limited by a single theory, nor by a research method. Basically, the perspective of critical social research regards social structure as an oppressive mechanism of one kind or another. This oppression reflects a dominant ideology, and the social structure is 'a particular historical manifestation.' Critical research is a process to reveal the nature of oppressive social structures. 'Critical analytic process is one of deconstructing taken-for-granted concepts and theoretical relationships by asking how these taken-for-granted elements actually relate to wider oppressive structures and how these structures legitimate and conceal their oppressive mechanism' (Harvey, 1990: 32).

Morrow and Brown (1994: 267–8) point out basic assumptions of critical methodology. 'Critical theory is dialectical in its recognition of the double hermeneutic of social inquiry, hence social structures are preconstituted by human agents.' As research is pursued in a society which is not ideologically neutral, it is legitimate to criticize rationally the definition of forms of research. In empirical practice, moreover, methodologies are differentiated as extensive and intensive; intensive methods are regarded as a primary way for understanding social phenomena in interpretive structuralist terms.[1]

To dig beneath the surface of social phenomena, a wide historical analysis is necessary. Historical analysis is useful for dealing with 'those [pieces of research] in which it is difficult to isolate variables, in which one must deal with numerous factors and few cases, require a high level of theoretical and methodological ingenuity' (Lipset, 1968: 52). In any analysis of social policy, we particularly need to take a historical approach to understand policy outcomes because there is no standard developmental sequence of policy-making but a variety of paths to qualitatively varying policy regimes (Skocpol, 1984).

In Harvey's account (1990: 26–8), reconstructing historical research is the result of an active interpretation of the available archaeological, documentary or oral evidence rather than just a matter of discovering the facts and events of history. Critical social research 'examines the historical genesis of a social system and shows how oppressive structures have emerged' (p. 27). It explores the relations between historical events and prevailing social practices, and the extent to which existing structures are sustained through them.

Feminism is based on arguing that gender is an oppressive mechanism. It implies a radical critique of reason, science and social theory which raises questions about how we know what we think we know (Ramazanoglu, 1989: 9). Traditional knowledge of social sciences has been challenged by feminism. Social researchers have provided a justification for the belief that social roles are natural; whilst feminist scholars argued that women's position within society was a social, political and economic product. Furthermore, as male researchers have dominated the realm of social sciences for a long time and important phenomena have been identified from a male perspective, knowledge of social research has been limited by the neglect of women's experience. For instance, Ann Oakley criticized the rule of 'disengagement' in interview as a 'masculine paradigm' of research attitude. According to her work, *From Here to Maternity*, she found that it was not reasonable to adopt this exploitative relationship with the women she interviewed since many of those women would ask for information (Oakley, 1990).

Feminist epistemologies criticized not only the assumptions of the traditional academic but also the methods that have been used to gather knowledge about women. But they do not always view science in the same way. *Standpoint feminism* considers that women's experiences are an excellent starting-point for a new social scene because of women's exclusion from the research realm. Since traditional empirical research, especially quantitative research, does not take place directly within life's processes but 'afterwards,' it never touches 'real life' (Hartsock, 1987; Mies, 1991). *Relativist feminism* rejects 'the ideal of any type of science for this would be just another way in which women's experiences are sequestrated by those who claim to be experts' (May, 1997: 22). They do not think that knowledge or 'truth' about women's position in society is possible, and believe that there can be no method or set of methods consistent with feminist values (Stanley and Wise, 1983: 26). Although the challenge of traditional scientific method is important, some women researchers think that it is now timely to move the focus of feminist methodology dialogue from definition to implementation. Adherents of *Empiricism* would like to not only follow more rigorously the existing rules and principles of the sciences, but also move away from their male-centred perspective and place women at the centre (May, 1997: 23).

Although the data from women's experience is important for new social knowledge, women's views are usually a social, political and economic product educated by the authority. For instance, the educational system and media spread the primary ideology of the government, scholars and politicians, which will affect women's views and experience. Therefore, it is doubtful whether we can get 'real' women's experience, especially when the research is focused on social policies. Ordinary women are not the experts of social policies, their expectations are largely affected by current social issues and limited by their knowledge. Even if 'real' women's experience is difficult to attain, I believe that each theory should be based on and tested by empirical data. Therefore, this study basically emanates from empiricism and makes an effort to place women at the centre of policy analysis. Besides, there are three principles of feminist research which are worth bearing in mind: research should contribute to women's liberation through producing knowledge that can be used by women themselves; should use methods of gaining knowledge that are not oppressive; and should continually develop a feminist critical perspective that questions dominant intellectual traditions and can reflect on its own development (Acker et al., 1991). This study will attempt to embody these principles.

A single-country study

Researchers observe that it is difficult to do comparative cross-national research on women's history because different issues have been raised in different countries. Historians of different countries may be interested in specific historical periods and questions, which makes the study with a comparative-historical approach more difficult when different countries have different trajectories of development (Bock and Thane, 1991: 2–3). Therefore, some books on women and social policies have chosen to study the histories or situations in several individual countries instead of doing comparative cross-national studies, but have tried to take one step towards comparative study in the conclusion.

There are various reasons why I have chosen a single-country study for this issue. First of all, comparative or comparative-historical research is more appropriate if the studies in all the comparison countries are well developed. However, we have less knowledge of the issue of gender and social policies in the case of Taiwan. It is more important to understand the situation in Taiwan as a basis. Secondly, the development of gendered social policies is formed by the complex interactions of social structures, economies and political institutions. Single-country studies permit the most thorough observation of policy-making processes, and deal with a full variety of evidence, such as combining the evidence from documents artefacts and interviews.

Case studies have been viewed as a less desirable form of inquiry for three reasons: they provide little basis for scientific generalization, they lack rigour, and they result in massive and unreadable documents (Yin, 1994: 9–11). Lack of rigour can be overcome by careful data collection and research design. The strategy of this study will be explained at the end of this section. Scholars with the third kind of prejudice often confuse this method with ethnography and participant-observation, but case studies do not depend solely on ethnography and participant-observer data. This problem can be solved by varying the design of report writing. First, however, I will discuss the generalization of a single-case study.

The contribution of single-country studies is challenged on the grounds that one cannot apply generalizations to other countries. However, the goal of a single-country study is to generalize its finding to 'theory' instead of generalising to 'other countries' (Yin, 1994: 30–2, 37). The findings of a single-country study are unlikely to represent the whole world, but surveys and comparative studies also face the same problem, no matter how carefully the sample is chosen and how large the sample is. For instance, Orloff (1993: 27) thinks that the ideal design is a comparison of a few 'carefully selected cases' if one is interested in generalization. However, in the field of gender and social policy, many comparative researches focus on the comparison of Western countries with similar welfare development or historical links (Britain and Sweden, see Ruggie, 1984; Britain and US, see Skocpol and Ritter, 1995; Britain, US, Sweden and the Netherlands, see Sainsbury, 1996). If comparative research only selects cases from Western society, a theoretical approach to gender and social policy is still unhelpful.

Moreover, Esping-Andersen's work on welfare regime demonstrates that welfare states are not all of one type but follow trajectories of development (Esping-Andersen, 1990). The concept of welfare regimes can be adopted not only in a comparative research but also in a single case study. We may, in some cases, discover an anomaly. The anomaly may lead us to consider the possibility of a fourth or fifth welfare regime. Taiwan is a 'newly industrialized country' and has special economic development experience. It has developed capitalism rapidly for forty years and caught up with the economic standards of industrialized countries. Within forty years, social values and state structure have been changing rapidly as well. Besides, under the influence of Confucianism, social values differ greatly from those in Western countries, so that state policies also reflect social custom. Therefore, it is worth exploring Taiwanese experience since we could learn from such a case study.

Stake (1994) suggests that case studies are suitable for refining theory, suggesting complexities for further investigation and helping to establish the limits of generalization instead of providing and advancing a grand generalization. However, many theoretical perspectives which still stand as a great contribution to the field of welfare-state research are from single-country studies, such as Gough on Britain and O'Connor on the United States. Some research works on gender are also based on data from single countries, such as Walby's *Patriarchy at Work* and Skocpol's *Protecting Soldiers and Mothers*. However, their theoretical perspectives become the vehicles for examining other cases and are important steps in gender research. The single case study is not an end in itself; on the contrary, it is an empirical resource for researchers to explore wider questions.

Strategies of this study

To avoid the accusation of 'naivety' or 'lack of rigour' of single-case studies, this study follows certain key principles of data collection and research design:

1.   *Ideas based on theoretical proposition*

The investigator has to draw some ideas from a theoretical proposition for the guidelines or hypotheses of a study, and needs guidance from existing theories to organize the collection of historical evidence (Ku, 1995: 62; Yin, 1994: 27–32). Additionally, the conclusion of the research has to be checked with existing theoretical propositions to explain the possible reasons for differences and similarities. This is especially important for a single-case study since it lacks other cases as a basis for comparison.

There are four factors included in the discussion of this study: patriarchy, capitalism, the state and women's power. The idea for the first two factors is defined from *dual-systems theory*, which presupposes that both patriarchy and capitalism account for women's inferior status in the labour market (refer to Chapter 2 for further discussion). However, the state is also central to the resolution of certain key conflicts between patriarchal and capitalist forces in the utilization of women's labour. Following the general trend of stronger direct state intervention, 'state feminism' focuses on the removal of formal barriers for women (Dahlerup, 1987: 116). Ruggie (1984) and scholars who pay

attention to the research of gendered welfare regimes, such as Ilona
Ostner, Jane Lewis, Diane Sainsbury and Julia O'Connor, claim that
different welfare regimes result in different opportunities for women to
enter the labour force. Consequently, the power of the state should be
included in the research of women in the labour market. Finally, the
impact of the women's movement is argued as a key factor in shaping
maternalist policies and other public policies in some Western countries (Freeman, 1975; Lovenduski, 1986; Bock and Thane, 1991).
Without some consideration of women's collective action, any theoretical approach which tries to explain the implications of modern state
policies for women would determine a pessimistic conclusion.

2. Use multiple methods of data collection (triangulation)

There is no one 'best' method, and each method has its strengths and
weaknesses. *Triangulation*, which used various procedures for data gath-
ering and explanation, is suggested by many social researchers as
reducing the likelihood of misinterpretation in single-case studies
(Bulmer, 1984: 28–33; Yin, 1994: 90; Stake, 1994; May, 1997). The
strengths of one type of method may be balanced against the weaknesses of another. One of the major strengths of case studies is their
ability to deal with multiple data and research methods so their conclusions can be more convincing and accurate. Using triangulation is a
growing trend in case studies. For example, Cockburn in her *In the Way
of Women* (1991) employs observation, documentary investigation and
in-depth interviewing by informal conversation and small-group discussion to explore the practice of equal opportunity policies within
four organizations.

Patton (1987) indicates there are four types of triangulation: data
source triangulation, methodological triangulation, investigator triangulation, and theory triangulation. In this study, I employ the first
two kinds of triangulation. Like most research using historical
method, this study depends primarily on the analysis of documentary data. However, the history of earlier periods is sometimes limited
to events in the 'dead' past and lacks contemporary sources of evidence. Interviews with key persons become a very crucial source of
knowledge with which to reconstruct latest events, especially in
Taiwan where most policies on working women have been
announced since the mid-1980s. Moreover, feminist scholars are
usually suspicious of the accuracy and completeness of the official
story due to gender bias and neglect of women's history. They particularly emphasize the value of interviewing (Folbre and Abel, 1989).

Finally, not all data is recorded by the written word. Women's actions, for instance, are seldom recorded systematically. In this study, interviews are mainly used to gather data related to the events leading up to the Gender Equal Employment Act and the operation of women's groups.

3.   *Choose material carefully and use multiple sources of evidence*

The foundation of scientific research is the quality of the evidence available for analysis. Using historical analysis, researchers should be able to distinguish between the kinds of bias inherent in the primary sources they use. They also need to note which documents are likely to be credible. Scott (1990) provides four criteria which can be used to assess the quality of evidence: authenticity, credibility, representativeness and meaning. Is the evidence genuine and of unquestionable origin? Is the evidence free from error and distortion? Is the evidence typical of its kind? Is the evidence clear and comprehensible? Most investigators would agree that much of the data available on women in the Third World is not only inadequate but provides a distorted picture of women's contribution. We should only select and cite the documentary data which fit the four criteria to avoid inadequate analysis.

Furthermore, as mentioned above, multiple sources of evidence can also increase the accuracy of historical analysis, providing that the researcher selects historical materials carefully. Researchers of social science seldom use only one source of evidence to pursue historical analysis. Marc Bloch also claims that every aspect of social life can be used as evidence (Chirot, 1984). Thus different kinds of materials will be collected in this study to understand the historical development of social policies and women's employment generally, such as legislation, administrative reports and plans, social survey data collected by the government, large-scale continuous surveys, publications of the opposition parties, parliamentary debates, political memos, reports in newspapers, scholarly research, private survey data, records of women's groups.

4.   *Maintain a chain of evidence*

To increase the reliability of the information, a researcher should maintain a chain of evidence for other researchers to review and to re-test. This is more important for case studies than other research methods since case studies are usually expected to provide equivocal evidence and biased analysis which influences the direction of the findings. Therefore, this study will describe the source of evidence clearly. In appendices, for instance, I also list interview questions, the background of interviewees and the characteristics of social surveys collected by the government cited at length in this study (Appendix 1), for further reference.

Plan of the book

The purpose of this study is to analyze how women's employment has been treated by the state in Taiwan. From the analysis, I attempt to observe the developing character of the Taiwanese welfare regime in a gender-critical way. This study will not discuss the implication of state policies on all kinds of women but focus on women in the labour market. Patriarchy and capitalism cannot fully interpret women's status in the labour force. To achieve a comprehensive explanation, one should also consider two other factors: the state and women's power. Therefore, the relationship between patriarchy, capitalism, state and women's power is discussed in this study to highlight the extent to which the development of capitalism has changed women's status in Taiwan, and how far the state has used employment policies and other related policies to intervene in the utilization of the female labour force.

In the next chapter, I present a review of key theories in Western countries which try to explain women's inferior status in the labour market, and the literature of the welfare state and welfare regime in a gender-specific way. Chapters 3 to 6 each discuss a factor of my theoretical approach respectively. At the beginning of every chapter, I will review the historical development of the factor, mainly following a chronological description, and then discuss some important issues. At the end of Chapters 3 to 5, the relationship between each factor and state policy will be discussed to explore how these factors affect the performance of the state. The review of history in this book will start from the Japanese colonization period, but remain flexible in design. For instance, the historical review of patriarchal ideology in Chapter 3 will include something of the early history of Chinese culture, but the discussion of state policies in Chapter 6 will only include the policies after the foundation of the Republic of China in 1912. In Appendix 2, a table of important historical development in Taiwan will be presented for reference.

Chapter 3 will focus on the relationship between patriarchal ideology and the state. Since the concept of 'patriarchy' is too abstract, this study employs 'family and gender ideology' to examine the patriarchal ideology in Taiwan. Many feminist scholars agree that patriarchal culture is a crucial factor when we discuss the causes of women's inferior status. Some scholars may not agree with the use of the term 'patriarchy,' but prefer to use 'gender relation,' 'gender regime' or 'gender ideology' as these terms are more neutral. Nevertheless, they all represent the force of culture on women's inferior status. Patriarchal ideology not only limits women from working outside the family but affects the direction of state policies. Traditional theories on welfare states, such as the neo-Marxist approach, do not regard ideology as an important factor in shaping welfare policies. Analyzing social policies in a gender-focused way, one cannot omit the factor of ideology. However, ideology should be regarded as one, but by no means the only, crucial factor in the research of gender.

Chapter 4 will explore the relationship between capitalism and women. The development of women's employment in Taiwan is different from the experience in Western society. For instance, Taiwanese women streamed into the labour market as a result of industrialization rather than wars. Since the reasons why women began to enter the labour market were different, those theories stemming from Western experiences could not be applied to the case of Taiwan. Theories emanating from experience in developing countries were no better. In focusing on women in the labour market, this study is concerned with the contribution of the capitalist mode of production. Although the presupposition of Marxist feminists, for example, that capitalism was a unique resource of women's oppression, was problematic, the capitalist mode of production has changed the form of gender division. This chapter will discusses the change of women's employment in Taiwan, the extent to which women's reproductive role has affected their working opportunities and the mode of gender inequality in the labour market which has grown in the wake of capitalist development. We will also discuss the influence of capitalist development on women's status and capital power on state policies.

In Chapter 5, the emergence of the women's movement and its influence are explored. Since the mid-1980s, Taiwan has experienced a dramatic change in social structure. Women have no longer passively accepted the arrangement of social systems but actively intervened in creating a proper social system for themselves. Skocpol (1992: 30) indicates that existing theoretical perspectives overlook the contributions of female-dominated modes of politics, some of which are not through parties, elections, trade unions or official bureaucracies. This chapter will discuss the impact of women's movement on social policies.

Chapter 6 will explore the implications of state policies for working women. As Taiwan has been ruled by the Kuomintang (hereafter KMT) government during 1949–May 2000 (at least up to the time this book went to press), this chapter will review state policies from the foundation of the Republic of China on the mainland in 1912. There are four kinds of social policies related to working women which will be discussed: welfare for women, employment policies, protective legislation and equal opportunities policies, and care policies. By analyzing the pattern of state policies, one can identify whether the state in Taiwan is keen to provide an equal opportunity environment for women, whether state policies encourage women to participate in the labour market, and how the state intervenes in using the female labour force. Although socialist and radical feminists regard the state as a new device of social control, the state's role in solving the conflicts between patriarchy, capitalism and women's benefits is worthy of discussion. This study will consider the state as an intermediary of other agents, and will discuss the possibility that the state has its own consideration beyond accumulation and legitimation.

Chapter 7 is an extended case study of the legislative process of the Gender Equality Employment Bill, which provides a good illustration of the relationship between the state, capitalism, patriarchy and women's power. The bill contains not only measures for the regulation of gender equal employment but welfare for employees with children. From the debates and actions engendered around the bill, one can understand the dynamics of the various influential forces on social policies.

In Chapter 8, a more comprehensive theoretical approach will be developed, which tries to combine the four factors of state, capitalism, patriarchy and women's power to interpret the phenomenon of gender inequality in the labour market.

2
Theoretical Perspectives

This chapter will discuss two theoretical perspectives, which will help to establish the theoretical framework for this study. One is theories of gender inequality in the labour market, which attempt to find a general explanation for the phenomenon of gender inequality in the labour market. The other is theories of welfare states and welfare regimes in terms of gender, which try to understand the main power behind the welfare state to uphold or change the relations between welfare states and women.

Gender inequality in the labour market

Gender inequality in the labour market is a global phenomenon. In Western countries, there are many theoretical approaches that try to explain it, but no single theory can be applied consistently to all working women, although particular explanations are appropriate in certain contexts. In this section, I want to sketch some of the main theoretical approaches and debate them. First, I will discuss the perspective of **human capital theory**, which focuses on the mechanisms of a free market. Women's inferior status in the labour force is regarded as the result of their rational choices and lack of human capital. **Dual labour market theory** throws light on the process of gender division in the workplace, and indicates that women are usually excluded from the primary sector in the workplace. The third theory is **Marxist feminism and the reserve army theory,** which emphasizes women's oppression under a capitalist system. Lastly, I will discuss the **dual-systems theory**, which argues that both capitalism and patriarchy may account for women's inferior status in the labour market.

Human capital theory

Human capital theory explains women's unequal treatment in terms of the characteristics of individuals. It assumes that employers' decisions and employees' wages depend on the levels of 'human capital (education, experience, training, and skill)' embodied in individuals: the more human capital and the greater amount of time spent in a job, the higher the wage. Therefore, women's low wages and inferior status in the labour force are regarded as the result of their lower levels of education, experience and training. Another reason why women are thought to be less valuable than men is the time they spend out of the labour force to bring up children, which results in a depreciation of their skills (Nanneke and Sinclair, 1991). Domestic differences between genders also lead to wage differentials. Women cannot do their jobs as efficiently as men because they are tired through doing the family's housework at night, while men come to their jobs fresh from their rest (Becker, 1965). Based on this viewpoint, employers often assume that women will have less commitment to firms than men, and consequently prefer to train male workers who will wish to work continuously.

Human capital theory also claims that occupational segregation between genders is down to women's choice. Women are thought to choose jobs that are easy to leave and re-enter, and require less education and training since they believe that they will spend fewer years in the labour market. Polachek thinks that two people with the same amount of work experience may have different wages since someone who has quit from the labour market has suffered more wage depreciation. Therefore, he assumes that women whose employment is often interrupted by marriage and bringing up children maximize lifetime

Figure 2.1   Polachek's hypothesis of occupational segregation between genders

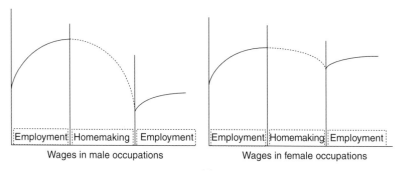

Wages in male occupations   Wages in female occupations

Figure 2.2   Zellner's hypothesis of occupational segregation between genders

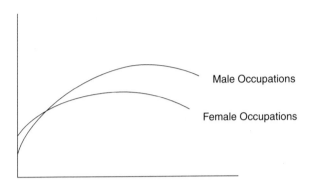

Male Occupations

Female Occupations

earnings by choosing occupations with low depreciation penalties during time spent at home (see Figure 2.1) (Mincer and Polachek, 1980).

Moreover, Zellner hypothesizes that many women do not work for enough years to allow an occupation's high appreciation rate to compensate for the lower starting wage, so women optimize lifetime earnings by choosing occupations with high starting wages but low wage appreciation (see Figure 2.2) (England, 1984).

Human capital theory is criticized for several reasons. First, the explanation that women's low pay and lack of promotion are the results of market mechanisms and rational choices of women workers is questionable. 'Choices' are in fact formed by culture and social expectation of sex roles rather than rational decision making. Secondly, this theory is challenged by empirical research since individual characteristics cannot explain the whole phenomenon of unequal pay and occupational segregation (Gannicott in Taiwan, 1986; Madden in America, 1987; Fillmore in Canada, 1990). Moreover, economic incentives, suggested by Polachek and Zellner, leading women to choose to work in traditionally female-dominated occupations are not obvious. England's empirical research showed that with parity of education and experience, women had higher lifetime earnings if they worked in predominantly 'male' occupations. Men had higher lifetime earnings in both 'male-dominated' or 'female-dominated' occupations than women, depending on their discount rate and accumulated experience at retirement (England, 1984; England et al., 1988). Duncan and Prus (1992) found that female-dominated occupations offer significantly lower starting wages and higher penalty rates in comparison to male-dominated occupations. Lastly, this theory has a major logical problem: it confuses the relation between cause and effect. It claims that women's low pay is related to their family roles (cause), but women's family roles (effect) are created by societies. Therefore, women's family roles should not be the real reason for their inferior status in the labour market.

The neglect of institutionalized power relations which create the unequal labour market lies at the heart of the failure of the human capital theory. Nevertheless, most of the factors that human capital theory use to explain why women are less valuable in the labour market come from women's family responsibilities. At least, the majority of employers believe so. Upholding the human capital theory, one can understand why employers have marriage discrimination, and why some feminists believe that the family system is the root of women's oppression.

Dual labour market theory

This theory has developed from 'economic segmentation perspective' economists in the United States, who principally criticize the notion of human capital theory. They argue that labour market discrimination is a structural product of industrial capitalism, not only restricted to wage discrimination but also discrimination in the demand for labour. The industrial economy is divisible into two mutually exclusive sectors, *oligopolistic capitalism* (core sector) and *competitive capitalism* (periphery sector), together known as 'dual economy theory' (Averitt, 1968; Harrison, 1974).

This theory was originally applied to racial segregation in the United States, and has been further developed into the 'dual labour market theory.' However, Barron and Norris (1976) adapted this theory to account for gender segregation. They think that dualism is a race issue in the United States, but a gender issue in the United Kingdom. They argue that the labour market is segmented into two main sectors. The primary sector offers highly paid jobs, good fringe benefits, working conditions and opportunities for advancement, and high levels of job security; the secondary sector is comprised of relatively low paid jobs, poor working conditions, less opportunities for advancement, and low levels of job security. Women often work in the secondary sector, and men tend to occupy the primary sector. Workers in the secondary sector are unlikely to be able to enter the primary sector. Nevertheless,

Beck et al. (1980) found that American women in the core (primary) sector suffered more discrimination than women in the periphery (secondary). The wage differential between men and women is lower in the peripheral sector than in the core sector, and 'credentials' (or human capital characteristics) were more equal between genders in the periphery than in the core.

Labour market segregation is regarded by some members of this school as an instrument to benefit capitalist hegemony. Gordon (1972) and Reich et al. (1973) stress that the gap between the primary sector and the secondary sector has been growing in the United States since the beginning of the twentieth century. The division between primary and secondary labour markets stems from employers' strategies in coping with two problems: first, the need to strengthen the stability of employees in certain jobs. Having limited resources, employers would rather retain their key workers by raising their pay and offering employment stability, but place the other workers in poor working conditions. Secondly, employers need to prevent the growth of class consciousness among certain sectors of the working class. Piore (1975) also believes that segmentation of the labour force can reduce the threat of general strikes and employees' pay bargaining power. Capitalists, by providing workers in the primary sector with certain privileges or benefits, ensure that those workers have some interests in common with them. If those workers want to keep their benefits, they have to help capitalists weaken the power of workers in the secondary sector. In the end, the workers in the two different sectors will think that they belong to the same sector.

Moreover, Reich et al. suggest that segregation gives employees clear job ladders. Each sector has different criteria for access. Employees, therefore, will limit their own aspirations for mobility, and have a clear goal to work towards. In this regard, labour market segregation results in a new class structure and social stratification. People are expected to play certain roles according to the economic sectors in which they work.

Occupational segregation has been described as one of the main reasons for gender inequality in the labour market in Western countries (Walby, 1986). This theory throws light on interpreting gender division in the labour market, and on the question of unequal promotion and different wage levels. Also, it emphasizes the contribution of social evolution rather than individual choice to women's inferior status in the labour force. Nonetheless, this theory has been criticized on several grounds. First, it fails to explain why women predominate in some specific occupations in the primary sectors. For instance, employers undoubtedly prefer to employ women in these occupations and this use of women as a preferred labour force needs to be explained. Moreover, this theory tends to be static and ahistorical. It suggests that discrimination is the product of industrial capitalism and the perpetuation of the inferior market status of minorities (Beck et al., 1980). In other words, it assumes that occupational segregation will exist forever and ignores wide country difference. Women will work in the secondary sector unless they can find other minorities to replace their positions.

Lastly, this theory does not emphasize who is responsible for creating the dual labour market. Although some scholars claim that employers do so, Hartmann (1979) emphasizes the role of men in creating and reproducing job segregation in the labour market. This job segregation can sustain men's superiority over women in both the labour market and the home, and poor working conditions can keep women from being men's dependents. Beechey (1987: 19) said: '(this theory) provides a loose classification rather than an explanation of the ways in which the labour process structures the organization of work in particular historical circumstances.' This theory is similar to the human capital theory in some respects and has the same drawbacks. Both describe only the existing phenomenon of gender inequality, and fail to explain the origin of gender discrimination, the main concern of feminists.

Marxist feminism and the reserve army theory

Unlike human capital theory or dual labour market theory, which only describe the existing phenomenon of gender inequality in the labour market, Marxist feminism tries to find the origins of women's subordination. Although Marx does not directly explain the reasons for women's oppression under the capitalist system in his work, Marxist feminists believe that Marx's paradigm can explain why the capitalist system causes the inferior economic position of women. They have attempted to emphasize women's roles in the capitalist system and have fitted it into Marxist theory.

Marxism presumes that women's oppression comes from women's reproductive and domestic roles. Engels argues, in *The Origin of the Family, Private Property and the State*, that 'family is the institution of private property that is the root cause of women's oppression.' Women's relatively inferior economic position is not a direct result of capitalism, but a result of the family system. Father patriarchy is reproduced via property inheritance, which perpetuates men's privilege. Engels predicted that women would become emancipated through participation in the labour force under socialism (Mallier and Rosser, 1983: Chapter 9). However, Engels's thought has been criticized for ignoring women's oppression in both the public arena and the private arena. Further, his assumption that proletarian families would not promulgate the subordination of women is clearly empirically incorrect (Walby, 1990: 71).

Marxists, who mainly focus on class conflict, do not regard women as a separate class. They believe that women are not oppressed primarily by men but by capitalism. In the labour market, both women and men are exploited by capitalists. Furthermore, housework is something within the capitalist system from which capitalists draw benefit. However, Harrison (1973) opposes this viewpoint, and argues that the notion of housework as part of the capitalist system has been confused with the idea that it is part of the capitalist mode of production. There are many modes of production within the capitalist system; housework is one and has its own form of surplus labour. Women may be both proletarians and housewives and their positions should be discussed separately; as such, we should pay attention to their exploitation in both the workplace and the home. In addition, both liberal and classical Marxist economic theory presume that the process of competition among cost-minimizing capitalists will finally eliminate discrimination in the labour market. The problem of this viewpoint is that it 'regards labour as an object rather than a form of social action embodying not only appropriate, but political, distributive and cultural practices as well.' In fact, discrimination against women is part of a viable divide-and-rule strategy for capitalist employers, and the competition among cost-minimizing capitalists is as likely to enhance it as to eliminate it because they can get benefits from the strategy of division (Bowles and Gintis, 1986: 110–11).

When they discuss women's status in the labour market, Marxist feminists mainly focus on capitalist relations. Women are treated as subordinate and cheap workers because employers see women's primary role as being in the household rather than in paid labour. Employers can make profits by exploiting them (Walby, 1990: 33). 'Much of Marxist feminist writing, therefore, focused on women as a distinct category of paid labour (in the sphere of production), and as playing an important role in capital accumulation through the bearing and upbringing of the future labour force (the sphere of reproduction)' (Rees, 1992: 26).

Based on Marx's discussion in *Capital* Beechey (1987: 43–5) points out that there are some advantages to capital of employing women workers. First, employing all members of a worker's family can lower the value of labour power. Marx suggested that 'the value of labour-power was determined, not only by the labour-time necessary to maintain the individual adult labourer, but also by that necessary to maintain his family.' It would be to an employer's benefit to bring the worker's wife and children into the labour force as well. The subsistence wage could then be shared among them. An employer could utilize the labour of all members of a family instead of just the head. Thus the labour power of the head of family is depreciated. Secondly, female labour is lower in value than male labour. Employers assume that a woman is partly dependent upon her husband's wages, so they often pay her a lower wage than that paid to a man. Thirdly, the circulation of commodities can benefit capitalists if they use female labour. After women work outside their home, domestic work, such as sewing and mending, could be replaced by purchasing ready-made articles in the labour market. This phenomenon can increase the circulation of commodities. Finally, in Marx's chapters on the labour process, the employment of women workers can undermine male workers' resistance to capitalist development that had existed in the manufacturing period. Male workers who struggle to maintain their privileged position will resist the employment of women and children. In this way, divisions within the working class are opened, weakening the power of male workers.

Reserve army theory

The idea of women as a reserve army in the labour market comes from Marx's concept of an industrial labour reserve. He described the reserve army of labour as a tool to prevent workers bargaining for their wages, and to meet labour shortages. In analyzing the rise of the female labour force during the world wars, researchers assert that employers employed women workers as the reserve army of labour (Beechey, 1977; Bruegel, 1979). While men were involved in war, women needed to earn money and were encouraged into paid work, especially in munitions factories. After the end of the war, women were encouraged to return home in order to let men have their jobs back. Furthermore, in the 1960s in Britain, once the state had initiated a policy to restrict immigration, woman became an important source of the industrial reserve army as capitalists needed a new cheap labour force to meet the labour shortage (Beechey, 1987: 49). The employment of married women was also regarded as an example of a flexible reserve army of labour. When the labour market needed them, they could meet labour demands, and quickly; when no longer required, they always had somewhere to go.

This approach is also used to analyze the situation in Third World countries. Nash and Fernandez-Kelly (1983) found that young single women in South-east Asia are employed on a short-term basis in electronic assembly work. Because they usually leave after marriage, companies do not have to pay for the costs of childcare and maternity leave.

However, some research only partly supports this approach. Fillmore (1990), on the basis of 1931–81 Canadian census data, argues that no single theoretical approach can explain the whole situation. Human capital theory, for instance, cannot explain the persistence of a wage gap between genders. Reserve army theory can only explain the presence of low pay in female-dominated occupations, and the dual labour market theory is suitable only to explain the exclusion of women from high-paid occupations. Additionally, Bruegel found that the impact of recession had fallen disproportionately on women in the manufacturing sector, but the service sector had mitigated the effects of the crisis on women's employment opportunities. Walby (1990: 36) argues that the reserve army effect is merely masked by the effect of job segregation between genders. Men were concentrated in the manufacturing sector and women in the service sector, so sex division in the labour market relatively protects women from loss of employment. Therefore, occupational segregation has become the chief feature in the labour market and needs further research.

Moreover, this theory cannot explain the phenomenon that women's labour force participation has increased since the Second World War in all Western countries (Rubery, 1988). Fewer women have left paid employment than men in three post-World War II USA recessions (Humphries, 1988), and in the British recession after 1979 (Rubery and Tarling, 1988; Walby, 1989) and in the mid-1970s recession in France (Bouillaguet-Bernard and Gauvin, 1988). The last criticism of reserve army theory is its internal contradictions. If capitalists like to employ women for low wages, they should retain low-paid women workers when they do not need so many workers. If they let women go before men, it will be against their interests and raise the labour costs.

The main problem of Marxist feminism is that it is too narrowly focused on the power of capitalism, so is unable to deal with gender inequality in pre- and post-capitalist societies. On the question of why women are in a relatively inferior economic position to men, and have an unfair share of domestic work, most feminists believe that the Marxist model alone cannot explain this situation. Therefore, some feminists introduce the concept of 'patriarchy' to analysis of gender inequality.

Dual-systems theory

Radical feminists define women's oppression as the result of patriarchal systems. The concept of *patriarchy* represents an important shift in feminist theory away from an exclusive focus on women's roles in reproduction to an understanding of how women's position in the family has shaped. Bowles and Gintis (1986) mention 'no more substantive statement can be made without a fully developed interpretation of the process of reproduction of patriarchal domination.' However, this approach is still problematic. Barrett (1980) argues that the term 'patriarchy' is ahistoric since it assumes that relations between men and women are unchanging and universalistic. She suggests that this often slides into a biologism that is unacceptable. Stanley and Wise (1993) also criticize the term as a kind of 'essentialism,' which indicates something old-fashioned, unsophisticated and irrevocably conservative. It seems that women's oppression is fixed across time and different cultures.

Nevertheless, dual-systems theory combines the idea of Marxist and radical feminist theory. It claims that both capitalism and patriarchy are important in contemporary gender relations, and the combination of the two systems creates a vicious circle for women as well as oppresses women in particular ways. Patriarchy was established before the development of capitalism and was carried over into capitalist forms of the labour process because men wanted to secure a privileged position for themselves. Through trade unions and a variety of other means, men used strategies to enable them to maintain their power over women within the waged labour system, with the result that sexual hierarchy was established. Moreover, capital was not all-powerful and was tremendously flexible. When capital accumulation encountered pre-existing social forms, it could either destroy them or adapt to them. The adaptation of capital could be seen as a reflection of the strength of these pre-existing forms to persevere in new environments (Hartmann, 1979, 1981).

Bowles and Gintis think that capitalism is not bound to reproduce patriarchy, but it might be so, perhaps reproducing another new form of patriarchy. Eisenstein (1979) thinks that the relationship between capitalism and patriarchy is symbiotic, that, capitalism cannot survive without the support of patriarchy. Patriarchy principally contributes order and control, while capitalism provides economic privileges.

However, Walby (1986: 160–1, 245) maintains that Hartmann's analysis underestimates the tension between the two systems. There is more tension between the two systems than Hartmann suggests, because the utilization of women's labour by one system is at the expense of the other. On the basis of British experience, Walby finds that there are two examples which interpret the tension between the two systems. First, when a lot of women entered factories in the early nineteenth century, male workers were worried that their job opportunities and wages would be affected by the entrance of low-waged women workers. Therefore, a cross-class patriarchal alliance sought via the Factory Acts to utilize the state to control women's employment opportunities. Secondly, the recruitment of women in munitions' factories was opposed by all-male engineering unions, such as the Amalgamated Society of Engineers, and the engineering employers because male workers wanted to keep their jobs. This conflict was resolved by state action. The state enacted legislation to secure the removal of women from 'male' work at the end of the First World War. Walby (1990: 40) also thinks that Hartmann insufficiently specifies the different structures of patriarchy. This dual-systems theory may be useful when we discuss women's oppression in paid work or in the family, but it gives very little analytic space to discuss other women's issues, such as violence and sexual harassment.

Additionally, Young (1981) argues that capitalism is completely responsible for the divide between the family and economy. Because of capitalism, dual-systems theorists incorrectly speak of the development of patriarchy in the family and of capitalism outside the family. There is no 'inside' to the family until capitalism created an 'outside' for it. Moreover, a separate-spheres model fails to specify the character of women's oppression outside the family. If working women are oppressed not simply as women or as workers but as women workers, then dual-systems theory is particularly unhelpful. Therefore, Young would rather use a 'division of labour' analysis, a unified-systems theory, to explain women's inferior status.

Basically, the discussion of women's status in the labour market transfers from the description of gender unequal phenomenon to the exploration of power which reproduces gender inequality. 'Women's choice' cannot explain women's inferior status in the labour market.

Some feminists believe that patriarchy and capitalism play important roles in women's oppression.

Welfare states, welfare regimes and gender

These theories which explain gender inequality in the labour market downplay the role of the state in reproducing or transforming a gender regime. It is clear that the welfare state has a strong direct and indirect influence on women's lives. The intervention of the state has been central to the resolution of certain key conflicts between patriarchy and capitalism, over the utilization of female labour. In this section, I will review three theoretical perspectives: explanations of the welfare state under capitalism, feminist perspectives on the welfare state, and welfare regimes. The review of these theories will help this study in its analysis of the relations between the state and working women.

Explanations of the welfare state under capitalism

First, the 'mainstream' theories of the welfare state, so called by feminist scholars, are reviewed. Although these theories do not point out gender-specific consequences of the welfare state, they can help us analyze the power which affects state policies towards working women. Many theories attempt to identify the key factors in the development of the welfare state. The **modernization theory** asserts that 'the welfare state is a product of successful political mobilization to attain full citizenship, in the context of industrialization' (Pierson, 1991: 24). Following a progressive-evolutionary logic, it regards the welfare state as a part of historical transition towards more complex and developed societies. Not only technological changes but also political revolution, especially the mobilization of the working class and the growth of full citizenship, lead to the rise of the welfare state. However, this theory, together with the logic of industrialism, assumes that the progress of the welfare state is inevitable, which describes the inconsistent political struggle between capital and labour. The **power resources model**, believing 'politics makes a difference,' focuses on the exercise of economic and political power. It claims that the welfare state is the product of a struggle between the political powers of social democracy and the economic powers of capital, and its further development could lead to the transition from capitalism to socialism. However, the political focus of the power resources model is too confined. Parties other than the social democrats have also supported the expansion of the welfare state, and the extension of the successful Scandinavian experience is not without problem. This model also downplays a possible characteristic of the welfare state as an instrument of social control of the working population in the interests of capital, which is pointed out by some neo-Marxists.

Rather than accepting the notion of the welfare state as an instrument of social control, some neo-Marxists point out the **contradictions within the welfare state**. O'Connor (1973) argues that the state has to fulfil two contradictory functions: accumulation and legitimation. The former refers to the process by which capitalism expands by employing labour to create surplus value in order to create new capital, which in turn is used to create further surplus value and further new capital leading to a continuous increase in the overall volume of capital. The latter refers to the process in which a state or political system successfully uphold a claim that they govern by right in accord with law, tradition and similar basis (Jary and Jary, 1991: 3, 363). Gough (1979) interprets the rise of the post-war welfare state as a response to the organized working class, and to the changing requirements of capital. To stabilize the capitalist system, the state has to restructure its policies to maintain the long-term accumulation of capital as well as to improve worker's welfare. The welfare state, therefore, is a 'contradictory unity,' with both positive and negative features for both capital and labour.

However, corporatists do not agree that the state is only an arena of capital and labour. Rather, the state creates bargaining arrangements with representatives of key interest groups. Although employers, labour and the state are the key actors in the policy-making process, policies are in fact introduced mainly for maintaining the state's own interests (Jessop, 1990). Additionally, Skocpol (1985) maintains that all Marxist theories about the state's role neglect state organizations and elite might acting against the long-run economic interests of a dominant class (also see Block, 1980). Skocpol brings up the concept of **state autonomy** where the state may have its own independent power in relation to policy–making. If the state were only acting to maintain the political dominance of a ruling class, it would not even be worth discussing states as important actors. Therefore, a meaningful theory of the state must be able to incorporate some element of autonomy. Nevertheless, state autonomy cannot be measured solely in features of states themselves, but also in the balances of state's resources and situation advantages compared with those of non-state actors.

Feminist perspectives on the welfare state

The 'mainstream' perspectives of the welfare state fail to recognize one of the most important aspects of power under the welfare state: its gender-specific consequences for women. Therefore, in recent years, many feminist scholars have made great efforts to analyze welfare states from a gender-criticized perspective. They have brought gender into the analysis by examining how social rights have been gendered and by focusing on the relationship between welfare states and women. They emphasize the interrelationships between the family, the state and the market in shaping the welfare state, and the interplay between the public and private spheres (Sainsbury, 1996: 34–7). Many dimensions of welfare states, such as caring, which have been ignored by mainstream welfare researchers have been emphasized by feminist scholars and have been proved to play an important role in structuring modern welfare states.

The attitudes of feminist groups towards welfare states are different, however. **Liberal feminists** think the welfare state provides a place for the extension of women's economic and social rights. They intend to reform the state and to change the current gender relations. **Socialist feminists** treat the welfare state as a social system which adopts policies to support the family system. They think that women should have access to social security benefits as individuals not as dependents of men. **Radical feminists** see the welfare state as a device of social control, which is operated by men; the aim of welfare policies is to retain men in a position of dominance and privilege. They mainly focus on gender relations with less regard for the economic and social context (Dale and Foster, 1986: 174–5; George and Wilding, 1994: 133–4). **Marxist feminists** mainly analyze women's relations to the welfare state by focusing on the contradictions between the labour market, the family and the state and between women's different roles as workers and mothers. Some Marxist feminists only emphasize the oppressive character of the capitalist state. Others focus on the new form of male domination in the public sphere and use the concept of patriarchy to analyze the modern welfare state (Siim, 1987).

George and Wilding (1994), however, think that it is possible to distinguish certain common themes in feminist analysis of the welfare state. First, ambivalence characterizes the feminist approach to the welfare state. For instance, although the welfare state reinforces women's dependence, it also helps women into the public sphere. Secondly, the welfare state has failed to take account of women's particular needs. Finally, the welfare state is the way in which social policies reinforce traditional family forms and gender roles.

For our purposes, I will focus on more recent debates about whether the welfare state constrains or benefits women. Some scholars claim the welfare state has offered women new opportunities for employment and has increased their independence (Brenner and Ramas, 1984). Piven (1984) recommends the welfare state as 'the main recourse of women.' She thinks that the benefits and services provided by the state reduce women's caring responsibilities, and let women survive without being wholly dependent on men. In Eisenstein's perspective (1983), the state is a mediator between conflicting class and gender interests. Women's struggles can vary under state intervention. Other scholars, some socialist feminists and most radical feminists, contend that the welfare state supports a certain family structure which enforces women's dependent role, controls women and keeps them in the private sphere (Wilson, 1977). They also claim that the state's intervention makes women more dependent on the state than on men, a shift from private to public dependence (Hernes, 1987). The state is an instrument of male control over women. State policies cannot change women's oppression but can create trade-off between family patriarchy and state patriarchy (Boris and Bardaglio, 1983). 'The power and control of husbands are replaced by the arbitrariness, bureaucracy and power of the state. Women's oppression changes from direct and personal to indirect and structural oppression' (Holter, 1984).

There is another new factor in that women are now economically more dependent on the state than on men. Increasing numbers of women are employees in the welfare sector as well as clients of the welfare system. Large numbers of women working in welfare agencies are one reason why the female labour participation rate has been increasing (Hernes, 1987; Pateman, 1988). The welfare state has created it has opportunities of employment for women and has increased their independence, but it has also created another form of women's dependence.

Nevertheless, Pateman argues that 'patriarchy' is neither replaced nor completely unchanged after the emergence of welfare states. She argues that those welfare states have changed the effect of patriarchy:

> There is one crucial difference between the construction of women as men's dependents and dependence on the welfare state. In the former case, each woman lives with the man on whose benevolence she depends ... In the welfare state, each woman receives what is hers by right, and she can, potentially, combine with other citizens to enforce her rightful claim. The state has enormous powers of intimidation, but political action takes place collectively in the

public terrain and not behind the closed door of the home, where each woman has to rely on her own strength and resources.

— Pateman (1988: 256)

Thus, women are not simply victims in the welfare state. They have been active in promoting and shaping the welfare state, and have used welfare policies for their own benefits. Women's intervention in the policies of the European Community was a typical example (Pillinger, 1992). Women's organizations have found a new political arena, the superstate, to influence nation-states' policies. Unlike mainstream research, research on women's policies and the welfare state emphasizes the importance of women's movements (or women's organizations) in shaping the modern welfare state (Bock and Thane, 1991; Skocpol and Ritter, 1995; Skocpol, 1992; Koven and Michel, 1993). Women have different ways to play the state. They may not affect state policies via political parties, elections or trade unions, but via social movements, bureaucracies, women-central organizations (Watson, 1990; O'Connor, 1993: 510; Skocpol, 1992: 30). Although male-dominated states had failed to solve women's problems, which only states had the resources to do, and only with respect to the state could women achieve the right to access to such resources.

Welfare regimes and gender

The welfare state does indeed have contradictory effects for women. These cannot be understood in one dimension. The images of different welfare states also reveal differences rather than similarities. That is why the research of welfare regimes becomes so valuable. In this section, I would like to discuss mainstream research of welfare regimes first, then review some recent work which tries to incorporate gender into the analysis of welfare regimes. Since different states have different impacts on gender relations and on women's opportunities to participate in the labour market, the study of gendering welfare regimes can shed light on the many areas of darkness created by attempts to understand the relations between the state and working women.

Among the existing welfare regime models, Esping-Andersen's model is one of the most original. He believes that the welfare state is not all of one type, and only comparative empirical research will adequately reveal the fundamental natures which unite or divide modern welfare states. His research tries to answer how far people are independent from selling their labour and how far welfare states intervene in the class system. He develops three dimensions (de-commodification, social stratification, and state and market) to cluster systematically eighteen OECD welfare states into three different regimes. The first cluster is the *liberal welfare state*. It uses means-testing to distribute benefits and encourages the market to provide private welfare services. Secondly, *corporatist welfare regimes* are used to maintain existing class and status differentials via social insurance. The state strongly intervenes in welfare services, so the market pays a marginal role in providing welfare. *Social-democratic regimes*, the third cluster, are characterized by principles of universalism, state service provision and de-commodification. Full employment and high taxation are central elements to maintain high standards of welfare (Esping-Andersen, 1990: 26–7).

These different welfare regimes have different implications for family and gender relations. In the liberal welfare regime, for instance, welfare relies on the provision of the market. Welfare provided by the state mainly goes to the low-income family or the family at risk. However, as a result, women are marginalized since the market usually fails to fulfil people's needs. In corporatist welfare regimes, the entry of married women into the labour market is discouraged and benefits tend to encourage motherhood, while collective forms of childcare provision are underdeveloped. The state intervenes in the family only when the family cannot solve the problems of its members. In social-democratic regimes, the state replaces some aspects of traditional family responsibilities, such as childcare, and so encourages women to work. The ideal of welfare does not focus on maintaining a particular form of family, but on encouraging individual independence (Esping-Andersen, 1990: 28).

Nevertheless, many scholars have not been convinced by Esping-Andersen's three model and have declared his ignorance of other welfare regimes. Langan and Ostner (1991) point out that only one regime proposed by Esping-Andersen in continental Western Europe is problematic. 'Latin Rim' countries in Europe should be an additional model. Those countries 'stress residualism, forcing people to enter the labour market under a line of laissez-faire condition while still relying on older traditions of self-help provided by traditional support systems and the church' (p. 133). Unfortunately, Langan and Ostner do not describe the characteristics of Latin Rim regime clearly, especially the difference between the Latin Rim and Bismarckian model. Moreover, Gough (1996) argues that Japan and some East Asian countries should belong to fifth regime.

Incorporate gender into the analysis of welfare regimes

Esping-Andersen's research has contributed significantly to the understanding of differences among welfare states. However, his study of welfare regimes is strongly criticized by feminist scholars because it overlooks gender factors (Sainsbury, 1994b; Borchorst, 1994; O'Connor, 1993). Also, he mainly focuses on the relation between state and market, whereas he does not take the family into consideration. Furthermore, the contribution of public services and unpaid caring work, which are chiefly done by women, is also neglected in his analysis (Bryson et al., 1994). In recent years, more scholars have also noticed the different treatment of women under different welfare regimes. They have found that women have different opportunities to participate in the public sector in different welfare regimes, because each welfare regime has its own gender and family ideology. Sainsbury (1994a) also points out that a weakness of early feminist studies was the lack of attention to the fact that women's situation are (were) different in welfare states. So, scholars have begun to bring gender into the analysis of welfare regimes. Some of them have re-explained mainstream theories from a gender perspective (O'Connor, 1993; Langan and Ostner, 1991; Borchorst,1994); others have preferred to create a new model in order to incorporate gender into welfare regime research (Lewis and Ostner, 1994; Siaroff, 1994; Sainsbury, 1994b, 1996).

Langan and Ostner (1991) reinterpret Leibfried's models from a gender perspective. They highlight the fact that Scandinavian countries offer a concept of citizenship based upon labour market integration. Those countries emphasize services rather than cash transfers, and regard women as individual wage earners. Moreover, they characterize the Bismarckian model as a *'gendered status maintenance model.'* The Bismarckian model prefers to provide cash transfers rather than services. Although the model emphasizes capitalist economic development, it relies on traditional notions of the family as a 'one heart one voice joint venture.' The Anglo-Saxon model stresses the equality of the marketplace, in which everyone is free to choose between working in the labour market and surviving in poverty. The family, however, still relies on the male citizen. State welfare emphasizes means-tested benefits, which may make women even more reliant on their male partners. Finally, Langan and Ostner characterize the Latin Rim societies as a *'mixed women's family support economy.'* A great number of women work in small firms and in the underground economy, but their wages are very low. Most women are not included in the social security system, and have to go back to their families when they need welfare.

Lewis and Ostner (1994) classify welfare regimes into three categories according to the strength of the male breadwinner, which is based on

Table 2.1   The 'breadwinner' and individual models of social policy

Dimension	'Breadwinner' model	Individual model
Familial ideology	Strict division of labour Husband = earner Wife = carer	Shared roles Husband = earner/carer Wife = earner/carer
Entitlement	Differentiated among spouses	Uniform
Basis of entitlement	Breadwinner	Other
Recipient of benefits	Head of household	Individual
Unit of benefit	Household or family	Individual
Unit of contributions	Household	Individual
Taxation	Joint taxation Deductions for dependants	Separate taxation Equal tax relief
Employment and wage policies	Priority to men	Aimed at both sexes
Sphere of care	Primarily private	Strong state involvement
Caring work	Unpaid	Paid component

Source: Sainsbury (1994b: 153).

the gender division of work. They suggest that most modern welfare states may be categorized in the '*strong male breadwinner model.*' In this model, men are expected to be the only waged workers in their families, and women should stay at home. There is huge gender division between the public and private spheres. Moreover, in France, an example of the '*moderate male breadwinner model,*' women are empowered as citizen mothers as well as citizen workers. In spite of the fact that patriarchal power was not absent in France, it was exercised at the individual level and had little impact on married women's labour force participation. The Scandinavian countries belong to the '*weak male breadwinner model.*' Women are not treated as dependents in this model. Marriage is seen as an optional relationship for two independent breadwinners.

The breadwinner model of Lewis and Ostner is criticized by Sainsbury (1994b; 1996: 43), as one-dimension and too simplistic. Too many diverse countries can be classified as strong breadwinner states. Building on the feminist critique, Sainsbury reconceptualizes the dimensions of welfare state variation (see Table 2.1). In this framework, the breadwinner model and the individual model are two contrasting ideal types. The breadwinner ideology means that 'the husband is responsible for earning a living and providing for the family, and the role of the wife is a caregiver.' The advantages of using this sort of analysis, she thinks, are its ability to formulate gendered welfare state analysis and its potential applicability, for use in analyzing the policies of any country over time. She also analyzes welfare states by women's entitlements to access benefits: as mothers, as wives, and as workers (Sainsbury, 1996).

The analytical criteria of Sainsbury's framework can help researchers examine the nature of welfare states relevant to gender. The weakness is that welfare in one country usually falls in both of the models: some dimensions belong to the male breadwinner model; others to the individual model. It is very difficult to identify which model a country should belong to.

The East Asian challenge

The focus of welfare regimes on the welfare mix between the family, the state and the market lies at the heart of the nature of welfare states. However, since all existing research of categorizing welfare regimes only focuses on Western countries or OECD countries, the possible forms of welfare regimes in other countries are neglected. Although the most important trait of some East Asian countries is Familism, for instance, Esping-Andersen (1997) claims that, using Japan as a case, there is little to indicate a distinct 'Pacific' model. Japan seems to combine elements of all three regimes. It shares with the social democratic regime a commitment to full employment; with the conservative regime, a status-segmented insurance system and Familism; with the liberal regime, a reliance on private welfare.

However, some scholars show that there may be a case for discussing an 'East Asian welfare regime,' which is different from the 'Western' pattern (Gough, 1996: 228). Some East Asian countries have similar economic, political and social backgrounds – for instance Japan, Taiwan, Hong Kong, South Korea and Singapore. These areas are also influenced by Confucian teaching. Confucian reading is still included in textbooks in these countries. Within the same influence from Confucian teaching these areas may develop their own characteristics of a welfare system, which is worth examining. Jones (1993) claims that Confucian teaching can explain the common patterns of economic success and welfare system among such East Asian countries as Japan, Hong Kong, Singapore, South Korea and Taiwan. Goodman and Peng (1997) observe that Japan and South Korea emphasize again on the family as a social welfare strategy to avoid the problems resulting from the rapid nuclearization of families. These countries would rather go back to their traditional cultural framework than adapt a Western pattern. Social welfare programmes in these countries can be regarded as 'piecemeal,' in response to current political and economic condition rather than following a long-term and overall plan. In a 'colonialist' analysis, Goodman and Peng regard Taiwan and South Korea as followers of Japan and call these three countries 'Japan-focused East Asian social welfare regimes.' However, in Taiwan's case, we know that early social policies and the principles in the Constitution employed Dr Sun Yat-sen's ideology, which was influenced by Bismarckian welfare states. The later development of residual welfare provision and charity service has been greatly influenced by America. There should be some reasons which cause their similarities, if any, but the influence of Japan is not an important one among them.

Goodman et al. (1998: 16–17, 20) argue that East Asian welfare systems are not homogeneous. Their experiences are of limited substantive relevance to the West. If they are relevant, it may be more to the West's past than to its future. 'Cultural' explanations – Confucianism – cannot explain the evolution of the East Asian welfare model. Public ideology of welfare may change over time, and new welfare concepts are being introduced after democratization. Welfare should be examined from political perspectives rather than ideological perspectives as the latter are often directed by a political elite.

In summary, some common elements of the East Asia welfare model share are pointed out by these scholars:

1. The social welfare system builds on the family and the community. Self-help is emphasized by the state.
2. Welfare expenditure is low. The state is not traditionally obligated; it is a regulator rather than a provider.
3. Occupational social insurance is status segregated and residual. Payments are too low to meet people's needs.
4. The main focus of state policies is economic development. Welfare schemes related to labour reproduction are well developed, such as education and health service.
5. Authoritarian regimes have been typical and conservative political parties have dominated political resources until recently; on the contrary, left-wing political parties and labour movements are comparatively weak in this region.

In conclusion, existing typologies of welfare states are not only difficult to apply to developing countries but cannot form an overall picture of the welfare state. Moreover, research into welfare regimes should incorporate the influence of ideology and culture factors into the analysis of welfare states, neglected by political economic analysis of welfare states (Castle, 1993). In the next chapter, we will begin our analysis of Taiwan's case with the influence of cultural factors on shaping the gender regime.

3
Family and Gender Ideology

Radical feminism presupposes that women's oppression results from the patriarchal system. Patriarchy, defined by Walby (1990: 20), is 'a system of social structures and practices in which men dominate, oppress and exploit women.' A patriarchal system not only has a particular ideology that limits women's performance in the public sphere, but also affects the direction of state policies and legislation. Therefore, the concept is important when discussing the relationship between state policies and working women. Nevertheless, the concept of patriarchy is too abstract to be applied in practice. In this chapter, therefore, the term family and gender ideology is employed to observe the patriarchal system in Taiwan.

Although mainland China and Taiwan have been separated for more than forty years, traditional Chinese gender and family ideology cannot be ignored in any study of the effects of patriarchal culture on women in Taiwan. Before the Ching Dynasty governed Taiwan, there were few indigenous people living there. It was only after this period (from the seventeenth to the nineteenth centuries) that intensive waves of Chinese people emigrated to Taiwan. Today, the majority of Taiwanese residents are of Chinese descent. Therefore, this chapter will not only review the modern history of Taiwan, but also the culture which stemmed in part from traditional China. I will begin with a discussion of traditional family and gender ideology in Chinese society, and attempt to clarify the changes in these two ideologies in modern Taiwan. Lastly, a review of state policies and family law can illuminate the extent to which the state maintains or transforms systems of male or/and capitalist dominance to provide an environment of equal opportunities for women.

Traditional family ideology in Chinese society

Chinese family ideology obviously limits women's achievement, reflecting the presupposition of Marxist feminism that women's oppression comes from the family system. Since China was dominated by imperialism for much of its history, Yang (1988: 97) observes, the majority of Chinese people (except the intellectuals) have concentrated on managing their families and have been regulated by Familism, paying little attention to larger collectives such as society and country. As a result, society has operated on a family-centred belief. In Western countries, the function of a family is to provide its members with a preparatory environment which can help individuals fit in with larger social institutions; in China, however, the main mission of the family is to continue the line and to enhance family welfare (Yi and Chang, 1994: 5).

Chinese society has been dominated by Confucianism. Confucianism, through its guiding principles of social relations and social behaviour, emphasizes status distinction (class, gender and age), obedience, familism, collectivism and mutual benefit. Confucian ideas were based on the principles of humanity and love. Through moral self-cultivation, Confucianism attempts to improve the social and political order. Confucianists want the family to be harmonious, the state to be well organized and the world to be at peace (Jayawardena, 1986: 170). There are five major human relationships, prescribed by Confucianism, as the yardsticks to guide social behaviour. Three out of the five relationships are related to family members: father/son, older/younger brother, and husband/wife. The other two are emperor/official and friends.

'Familism' is regarded as a significant Chinese trait. Familism, defined by Yang (1988: 97), is *'a set of values and their associated attitudes, beliefs and behavioural norms that are family dominated in the sense that people holding these values adopt the family as the basic social unit, not the individual; they share common property with family members; and family honours replace individual ones. The major goal underlying these values is to maintain the well-being and the continuation of the family.'* The central value encompassing familism is the concept of filial piety (*hsiao*), which emphasizes parents' authority and mutual dependence between parents and children. The Chinese family has certain characteristics as follows (Chang, 1976: 44):

1. The family is under paternal domination. The family follows the father's name, and the father has superior power inside and outside the family.

2. Chinese people prefer the extended family, where more than two generations live together.
3. The family is an economic unit. Family members work together or independently to maintain the family economy.
4. Obedience is emphasized within the family. The younger members should respect their elders; children should take care of their parents.
5. Women's status is inferior to men's.

Basically, the Chinese family is dominated by the father/son axis and the relationship between parents and sons is mutually beneficial. A son is able to inherit his parents' wealth, but is responsible for their welfare in old age; married couples without sons will face financial problems in old age. Additionally, a son must continue to provide for his parents in the spirit world after their deaths. He is also obliged to see that another generation is born to carry on the duties after his own death. In contrast, parents are unable to derive benefit from female offspring. A daughter is expected to belong to her husband's family and serves the members of that family in the future. All these factors have resulted in the Chinese family assuming boy-preference.

Traditional gender ideology in Chinese society

In Chinese history, it has not always been the case that women have been subordinate; this status was gradually formulated. Scholars believe China became a patriarchal society at about the time of the Shang Dynasty, with women's status worsening after the Sung Dynasty.[1] Although men have controlled the power of economy, law and religion for over 3500 years, women never questioned this situation until the twentieth century. After the foundation of the Republic of China, traditional patriarchy, the family and marriage system began to be challenged by intellectuals.[2]

Scholars believe that Confucianism may account for gender inequality in some South East Asian countries, such as Korea, Japan, China and Taiwan (Kim, 1996; Zhan, 1996; Jayawardena, 1986). According to Confucian teachings, the most important social institution is the family. Each person should fulfil his/her own role. In the home, the female role is to be an obedient daughter, faithful wife, devoted daughter-in-law and self-sacrificing mother. She is strongly discouraged from going outside the home. Women are troublesome and inferior to men. The ideology of Confucianism has cemented a patriarchal culture, which ensures men's superiority in and outside the family. In contrast, women are confined to subordinate roles and almost entirely excluded from the public sphere.

Under Confucianism, women have not been encouraged to study. It was a common belief that an uneducated woman has virtue. As a result of their lack of education, women were dominated by traditional norms and were unable to question their inferior situation. Chinese women are taught to obey and depend on men; they should obey their fathers in childhood, rely on their husbands after marriage, and depend on their sons after their husbands' death.[3] Traditionally, Chinese women have had no control of the household economy, depending instead on their husbands or sons. Usually, they will receive dowries on marriage, but they cannot inherit their parents' property in equal measure with their brothers.

An alternative view is put by Lai (1982: 388), who doubts whether Chinese women's inferior status was a common phenomenon in the past. Since the majority of historical documents were written by intellectuals, the lives of most people (farmers and other low class workers) are still a mystery. Commonly, the relative power, of the father as compared with the mother may have been proportional to the wealth of the family. In a farmer's family, where both men and women needed to work and contributed to the household economy, the father's power would not be so great. A woman's position in the family tree is important to her status since, in Confucian society, people are stratified not only by gender but also by age and class. Usually, if the eldest male in a family dies, his wife is supposed to inherit his power, but this power is regarded as the succession of the father's will and may not be permanent. A father's power is so much stronger than a mother's (Chu, 1978, quoted by Lai, 1982: 389). Therefore, even if women could control the power in their families, Chinese society is still patriarchal.

Family and gender ideology in change

Family and gender ideology in Taiwan has changed significantly during the period of industrialization. Education has proved to be an important factor influencing gender ideology in Taiwan (Lu, 1980; Kao, 1989). In the early stages of industrialization, parents expected their daughters to help them earn money in order to support their sons in higher education. As Taiwanese families ceased to suffer from poverty, they began to wish to invest in their daughters too. According to a survey in 1985, 93 per cent of people opposed the notion that girls were not worth such an investment (Taiwan Provincial Government, 1985: 86). Today, women in Taiwan have the same opportunity as men to participate in higher education, enabling them to find professional employment. Moreover, the decline in the birth rate makes it difficult to maintain the customary father/son axis. Traditional family and gender ideologies have to change under these circumstances. Is traditional familism still restricting women's performance? To what extend have the family and gender ideologies affected women's development in modern Taiwan? These questions will be addressed from six viewpoints: mutual dependence and living arrangements, economic autonomy, family power, boy preference, sex role attitudes and career attitudes among women.

Mutual dependence and living arrangements

Couples are supposed to live in the husband's home after marriage, later sharing this home with the husband's parents or other relatives. They may become a nuclear family after the parents' deaths. In 1980, 79 per cent of adults whose parents were still alive lived in their parents' house when they first got married (Yang, 1988: 112). In 1992, the paternalistic living arrangement was still significant. A high percentage of young married women lived with their parents-in-law, while few lived with their parents (see Table 3.1).

In the past, almost all parents expected to live with their sons in their old age. This attitude changed rapidly in the 1970s. According to a regular official survey, as shown in Table 3.2, the percentage of women who expected to live with their sons in old age dropped from 94 to 47 per cent between 1965 and 1985. The percentage of women who expected to be supported by children in old age also declined from 81 to 61 per cent between 1973 and 1985. Therefore, women had less confidence in being able to rely on their sons in old age, but this did not mean that they did not want to.

According to the same survey between 1965 and 1973, Coombs and Sun (1981) suggested that the extended family style would diminish in the next generation. Moreover, in every survey, the sample of people who have higher educational attainment tend to expect to live alone rather than live with their married sons. As educational opportunity has been improved in Taiwan, there is concern about whether the extended family arrangement has declined. It is true that the percentage of extended families has gradually diminished, but the majority of old people still live with or near their married children. Taiwanese families seem to have a strong adaptive ability to change their format to

Table 3.1 Living arrangements of married women in Taiwan

Data: 1992, number of sample: 2387, unit: %

Generation (birth date)	Living together	Not living together, but in the same city	Living in another city but maintaining frequent contact	Others	Total
The relationship with their parents-in-law					
1954–58	30	36	22	12	100
1959–63	35	30	24	11	100
1964–68	50	21	23	6	100
1969–73	58	19	14	9	100
The relationship with their parents					
1954–58	5	44	36	15	100
1959–63	5	47	34	14	100
1964–68	8	42	37	13	100
1969–73	9	52	23	16	100

Source: Calculated from the Ministry of the Interior (1993a: Tables 75, 77).

Table 3.2 Expectations of women aged 22–39 for living and financial support in old age in Taiwan, by education, 1965–85

Unit: %

Educational attainment	Live with sons in old age					Be supported by children in old age		
	1965	1967	1973	1980	1985	1973	1980	1985
No education	99	94	71	56	75	93	84	83
Primary	93	89	57	44	56	84	72	76
Junior high	82	63	37	37	43	58	59	58
Senior high or beyond	66	45	21	22	28	38	36	37
Total	94	87	56	41	47	81	65	61

Source: derived from Sun (1995: 38).

suit the environment. For instance, family members may not live together to form an extended family, but they may eat together and share common expenses; sons may fulfil their obligations towards supporting their aged parents through a meal rotation system.

In 1994, 67 per cent of elderly people over 65 years old lived with their children or next door (DBAS, 1995a: 15). Children still feel that they have an obligation to support their parents in old age and to ensure their health even if parents' expectation of their children's support is diminishing. In 1984, 85 per cent of the sample (88 per cent of the male, 85 per cent of the female) still thought that parents should live in their son's home, and 88 per cent of the sample would feel ashamed if their parents lived in a nursing home (Taiwan Provincial Government, 1985: 130, 134). Eighty per cent of students regarded the exercise of filial piety extremely important, and 98 per cent regarded it as the virtue of all virtues (Yang, 1988: 113). The results of the survey confirmed that the Taiwanese still retain a paternalistic living arrangement and tend to prefer a stem family.[4] Supporting elderly parents is still regarded as the responsibility of children, mainly sons.

Economic autonomy

Money is no longer entirely controlled by men in a family. According to the research of Yi and Chang (1994: 13), employed wives, regardless of occupational categories, tended to be responsible for household financial management. Moreover, asked about their attitudes towards inheritance, in 1983, 51 per cent of people agreed that the wealth of parents should be shared equally among sons, 47 per cent agreed it should be shared by all sons and daughters. In 1984, the percentages were 22 and 48 per cent respectively. In 1985, the percentages were 11 and 35 per cent (Wen, 1989: 6). Therefore, the culture of a male-dominated inheritance system is changing. More people think daughters have the right to inherit their parents' property. Although it does not mean that daughters and sons will inherit 'equally,' women have broken the taboo of possessing personal property.

In the past, married women could not have private property and they did not have an obligation to support their original families. Even if they earned a salary, the money was expected to be spent on their marital families. Nowadays some women also support their original families after marriage. In 1992, 15 per cent of married women claimed to shoulder the majority of living expenses of their parents-in-law; 30 per cent shouldered part of the living expenses. Three per cent of married women shouldered the majority of living expenses of their parents; 14 per cent shouldered part of the living expenses (Ministry of the Interior, 1993a: Table 82.3).

Family power

As far as power sharing in the family is concerned, this could be analyzed from three indicators: the decision-making model, the share of household duty and conflict resolution (Yi and Tsai, 1989: 115). In this study, by family power, I mean women's involvement in household decision-making. In a traditional Chinese family, parents usually control the decision-making in the household. Today, although parents are still respected, they have lost their total authority and real power.

Comparatively, women's status at home is supposed to be enhanced as more women have incomes and are able to manage their wealth. They have more economic power. Although some research in Taiwan supports this assumption (Yi and Chang, 1994; Chou, 1994), other research does not (Lu, 1983). Culture is seen as a more important factor than women's employment. For instance, after industrialization women in rural areas shouldered the burden of farmwork, but their domestic status and decision-making powers were still inferior to their husbands' (Gallin, 1984; Lu, 1983). A woman's income was considered subsidiary and was often lower than her husband's income, so it did not increase her status and power in the family. However, Yi and Chang (1994: 14) found increasingly that in couples in which the wife had professional employment, decisions tended to be made together. Yi and Tsai (1989) observed that the actual practice of family decision-making tended to be egalitarian if the wife had working experience, high educational attainment, a simple family style or lived in an urban area. Through these contradictory examples, it can be seen that participating in the labour market does not necessarily increase a woman's power in decision-making at home. Further discussion will take place in Chapter 4.

Nevertheless, all research, as mentioned above, claims that women in a nuclear family have greater decision-making powers than women in an extended family (Liu, 1976; Lu, 1983; Yi and Chang, 1994), and are more likely to control the household expenses (Yi and Chang, 1994: 13). On the contrary, married men tend to dominate the family decision-making in the extended family. Patriarchal authority is more likely to be sustained within the complex family, especially within a paternalistic living arrangement.

Boy preference

As mentioned above, in Chinese culture, having boys to continue the family name is a very important mission of couples. In 1976, 93 per cent of women and 89 per cent of men recognized the importance of having a son. The reason for their boy-preference was 'to continue the family name (50 per cent)' and 'to support them in old age (31 per cent).' If daughters took the mothers' name, 33 per cent of women and 31 per cent of men still approved the importance of a son. Even if the government had a good pension system for elderly people, 36 per cent of women and 29 per cent of men still thought that they had to have a son (Sun, 1995: 46).

Analyzed by generation, although more than half of married women wanted to have son and daughters in even numbers, many wanted to have sons more than daughters (see Table 3.3). In 1993, the proportion of the ideal number of children (the number of boys/the number of girls × 100) expected by married women was 1.24, and by single women 1.18 (DBAS, 1994a: 10). Therefore, it seems that women, especially married women, tend to have a boy-preference attitude, which may reflect pressure from their culture. Although the ideal number of children of married women has declined gradually and modernization pursued rapidly in Taiwanese society, the boy-preference attitude has not changed as significantly as expected.

Sex role attitude

The sex role attitude of men is more traditional than that of women in Taiwan (Chia et al., 1994a, 1994b; Chou, 1994). In comparison with American students, Taiwanese students held a more male-dominant attitude towards marriage. Taiwanese female students held a more egalitarian and liberal attitude than male students, and males expressed a desire to continue to play the dominant role (Chia et al., 1994a). In addition, some researchers believe that there is no variable which can interpret or predict men's sex-role attitude, so the effect of culture on men's sex-role attitude may be more important than any other factors (Kao and Yi, 1986).[5]

Although women can be economically independent and have improved their status within the family, they still respect the supposed superiority of their husbands and are willing to play a supportive role to their husbands. They would like to follow the traditional mother role and regard their subordinate role in the family as natural although they think their husbands should respect their opinions (Lu, 1980; Chang, 1986). With regard to the attitude of women towards house-

Table 3.3   Ideal number of children of married women in Taiwan, by generation

Data time: 1993, number of sample: 4491, unit: %

Generation (birth date)	1 boy +	2 boys +	1 boy, 1 girl	2 boys, 1 girl	2 boys, 2 girls	Others ++	Total	Average (person)
Before 1944	1	3	16	27	36	17	100	3.44
1945–49	1	3	24	34	27	11	100	3.05
1950–54	2	3	36	31	18	10	100	2.76
1955–59	3	3	42	29	16	7	100	2.60
1960–64	2	4	52	27	7	8	100	2.46
1965–69	3	2	61	24	4	6	100	2.34
1970–74	4	2	65	20	4	5	100	2.26

Note: + The percentage of girls only is under one per cent.
++ For the older generation, many of them prefer having more than 5 children.
Source: calculated from DBAS (1994a: Table 14).

Table 3.4   Women's attitudes towards housework and childcare, Taiwan Province

Date: 1992, number of sample: 4491, unit: %

Generation (birth date)	An honour and an achievement	Women's natural responsibility	Wife and husband should share the responsibility	A unfair burden for women
Household element				
Before 1922	7	55	46	3
1923–27	8	53	50	3
1928–32	9	43	60	3
1933–37	11	32	69	3
1938–42	11	31	70	7
1943–47	12	27	70	7
1948–52	11	22	78	5
1953–57	11	15	84	6
1958–62	11	10	90	6
After 1963	14	7	91	7
Childcare element				
Before 1922	9	52	51	1
1923–27	8	48	58	2
1928–32	13	38	70	1
1933–37	14	23	79	2
1938–42	13	22	78	4
1943–47	14	23	79	2
1948–52	13	19	83	2
1953–57	19	13	87	2
1958–62	19	9	93	2
After 1963	19	6	90	4

Note: Total of each column is more than 100; the samples can choose more than one answer.
Source: Taiwan Provincial Government (1993: Tables 66, 68).

work and childcare, as shown in Table 3.4, almost half the elder generation still believes that housework and childcare were women's natural
responsibilities. Most of the younger generation on the other hand
believed this work should be shared by both sexes. Obviously, younger
women tended to accept the notion of gender equality and denied the
gender division defined by culture.

Attitudes towards women's careers

In the past, the Taiwanese believed that women from good families did
not need to work; a job was for living instead of self-achievement.
Today, more women are willing to work even if they do not need the
income. A private survey on women's attitudes showed the changes in
attitudes towards women's employment to some extent. As shown in
Table 3.5, the younger generation of women tended to disagree that a
wife should not work if her husband earned enough money, while
older generations were in agreement. It seems that the ideology of the
male breadwinner is fading among the younger generation. For them,
having a job is not just about money. Educational attainment is
another powerful indicator. Women with higher educational attainment were willing to work even if their families did not have any
economic hardship (see Table 3.6).

When women had pre-school children, they tended to work when they
faced a shortage of money in the household, as shown in Table 3.7.
Seventeen to 29 per cent of couples still had highly traditional attitudes
towards women's employment, and considered that women with pre-
school children should not go out to work, even if this meant economic
hardship. Moreover, married women relatively respected their husbands'
opinions towards their employment. Only about one per cent of married
women expressed a view that women with pre-school children should
have absolutely autonomy to decide whether they can work. As regards
work patterns, 39 per cent of women agreed that women should interrupt
jobs if they needed to raise children, while 40 per cent thought that
women should not interrupt jobs for marriage or raising children.
Women with high educational attainment or who had professional or
administrative jobs tended to have a more aggressive attitude towards
their career. Those women upheld that working women should not deny
themselves career achievement or reduce the opportunity of social
contact in order to raise children (Kao, 1987).

Lu (1980) shows that the attitudes of Taiwanese women towards
their family role and career role may be independent. Their family
role is still the first priority and they accept their subordinate status

Table 3.5   Attitudes towards the concept: 'If the wage of a husband is enough for living, a wife should not go out to work'

Data: 1994, number of sample: 1010, unit: %

Generation	Agreed	Uncertain	Disagreed	Total
Before 1936	48	26	26	100
1937–46	28	28	44	100
1947–56	28	29	44	100
1957–66	17	28	55	100
1967–76	10	19	71	100

Source: calculated from Twenty-first Century Foundation (1995: 100).

therein. On the other hand, they express a great desire to participate in the public sphere and display their ability in society. Research on the attitudes of female managers also found that they put the family in first place although they disagreed with traditional women's roles and approved of their contributions to society (Adult Education Association, 1995: 239).

The state and the family

Between 1885 and 1945, Taiwan was governed by the Japanese. Before that, it had a long history as the territory of China. After the Second World War, the KMT, which was the ruling government in mainland

Table 3.6   The willingness of women to work in cases where there is no economic hardship

Data: 1988, unit: %

Generation	Will	Will not	Do not know	Total
Primary	46	10	44	100
Junior high	50	11	40	100
Senior high	49	9	42	100
College	72	9	19	100
University	72	11	17	100
Post-graduate	86	0	14	100

Source: Taiwan Provincial Government (1989: Table 57).

Table 3.7 Attitudes towards the employment of women with pre-school children, Taiwan Province

Data: 1988, number of sample: 4491, unit: %

Total	No need, even if they need money	Yes, if they need money	Yes, if the husband agrees	Yes, even if the husband does not agree	Others	
Employed women	17	40	38	2	3	100
their husbands	18	32	33	1	16	100
Non-employed women	24	40	30	1	5	100
their husbands	29	35	25	1	10	100

Source: Taiwan Provincial Government (1989: 100–7).

China, took over. In 1949, the KMT failed to defend its political authority in the civil war, then retreated to Taiwan. Since 1945, the KMT has
been the ruling party in Taiwan. Before the mid-1980s, the legal and
social systems in Taiwan have been completely dominated by the KMT
government. It was not until democratization in the mid-1980s that the
KMT lost its absolute political power. Social movements and opposition
parties began to intervene in the establishment of the legal and social
systems (refer to Appendix 2 for historical events in Taiwan).

As a revolutionary party, the KMT announced 'gender equality' as one
of its important policies before it came to power. Dr Sun Yat-sen, the
leader of the KMT, who is regarded as the father of the Republic of
China, criticized the fact that traditional culture oppressed women. He
said that the KMT would build a reasonable environment for women.
After the KMT came to power in 1912, 'gender equality' was written
into the KMT constitution. In 1924, the party declared gender equal
rights in law, economy, education and social life. In 1926, the party
announced its policy to introduce legislation to protect women's property rights, marriage and divorce rights and those who suffered from
domestic violence (Ma, 1992: 97). In 1931, the KMT government introduced a Civil Code that ensured women's property rights and allowed
freedom of choice in marriage and divorce by mutual consent.[6]
Generally speaking, in the period 1912–34, the KMT's policies tended to
transform the unequal social systems for women through the support of
male liberals and the pressure of women activists, although there were
also many male members who were reluctant to free women.

Nevertheless, the KMT's gender policy turned out to be conservative
after General Chiang Kai-shek took control. In 1934, Chiang Kai-shek
promulgated the *New Life Movement*, a neo-Confucian revival, which
emphasized rigorous self-discipline and obedience to the leader. The
attempt to restore Confucian morality in the New Life Movement was
criticized by Soong Ching-ling, the wife of Dr Sun Yat-sen:

> We must cleanse the Chinese mentality and free it from the
> cobwebs of Confucianist ideology which blocks our cultural devel-
> opment. Revival of Confucianism is pure reaction disguised as
> concern for social order.
> — Soong Ching-ling (1953) quoted in Jayawardena (1986: 192)

From 1950 to 1969, in the revised KMT Constitution, the party all
announced its policy to revive traditional ethics and morality and to
maintain the traditional family system.

In 1967, another attempt at reviving Confucianism was promoted by the KMT government. The *Culture Revolution* started by Mao Zedong in mainland China was criticized, so the KMT government introduced a parallel *Chinese Culture Revival Movement* to prove its legitimacy. In this movement, family values were emphasized; women were encouraged to practice traditional morality. The Central Women's Department of the KMT listed ten guidelines to teach women how to fit in with the movement. The guidelines were as follows (KMT Central Women's Department, 1968):

1. Fulfil filial piety obligations towards parents and parents-in-law.
2. Respect and take care of the elders in the family.
3. Have concern for relatives and neighbours.
4. Have good relationships with siblings and sisters-in-law of their husbands.
5. Teach children and youth how to behave well.
6. Urge husbands, sons and nephews to serve in the army for national duty.
7. Join and make a donation to the patriotic movement.
8. Serve the army during wartime.
9. Participate in general elections.
10. Join the research into traditional Chinese literature.

The guidelines of the movement show that, on the one hand, women's traditional role in the family was reinforced. They were encouraged to be carers in the family, and no positive role was encouraged. On the other hand, their responsibilities towards their marital families were emphasized, showing all the characteristics of the paternalistic family system in Taiwanese society. So, from 1934 to the mid-1980s, the traditional gender regime was reinforced by the ruling party.

After the establishment of civil women's movements in the mid-1980s, many state policies on women have been criticized. Taiwanese society is changing and is looking for a new gender regime. After the historical review of the state's role in the family and gender, in this section, I will examine the state's role in the educational system, welfare system and legal system, with particular reference to the Family Chapter in the Civil Code, to see how the state in Taiwan reinforces or transforms male-dominated culture.

Educational system

Before the development of modern schooling, children studied at private classes or were educated at home by guardians, and women seldom received formal education. Taiwan began to develop public schools during Japanese colonization. The Japanese government offered equal opportunity for both boys and girls to attend school but did not compel each child to do so. In 1917, the enrolment rate of young girls in primary schools was 4 per cent (boys 21 per cent); by 1943, it had increased to 61 per cent (boys 81 per cent) (Huang, 1992: 132). The reason the Japanese government developed schooling in Taiwan was to publicize Japanese and to enhance people's loyalty via education. The main purpose of women's education was to cultivate them to be 'Japanese-style' mothers, who could speak Japanese and educate their children in Japanese (Yu, 1994). Thus Japan's political power could really take root in Taiwan. Nevertheless, the educational system and courses for women were different from those for men. Moreover, in comparison with Japanese girls, Taiwanese girls received an inferior education. Courses for Taiwanese girls were only taught at primary level even if girls were in junior high schools. Also, the courses focused on teaching them how to be 'virtuous wives and good mothers,' which only encouraged women to follow their traditional roles (Yu, 1992). At this stage, education hardly changed women's status although at last they had the opportunity to attend formal education.

After the KMT government began to control Taiwan, it kept the public schooling system. However, the educational system was no longer segregated by gender. In 1968, the KMT government implemented nine-year compulsory education in Taiwan. More and more women have attended school since then. The original purpose of women's education under the KMT authorities was similar to that of Japanese colonization – cultivating women to be good mothers and wives. At the 1929 convention, the party declared: '*Women's education should focus on … the importance of maternity and promoting good family and social life*' (The KMT, 1976a: 112). At the 1935 convention, '*The development of women's education can cultivate benevolent, philanthropic, strong and knowledgeable mothers, which is the basis of saving the nation and the people*' (The KMT, 1976b: 286).' Besides, standard textbooks allowed the state to control the practice of education.

Nowadays women have the same opportunity to attend formal education as men, but the present courses are criticized for reproducing traditional sex roles and male-dominated culture. Courses for women and men are not the same. For instance, in high schools, boys take courses in military training, industrial arts and electronic wiring while girls have to learn nursing, cooking, sewing and handicrafts. In the past, in senior high schools, female students were forbidden to study engineering and science unless they could pass a special maths examination. Additionally, in set textbooks in primary schools, the father comes back from the workplace and reads a newspaper while the mother stays at home for the whole day, waits for her husband to come back and cooks for her family. Only six out of 214 illustrations in the historical textbooks of junior high schools are of women, and three of these are Madame Chiang who stands beside Chiang Kai-shek. In the textbooks of junior high schools, women's images are shy, beautiful, weak and dependent. Regarding women's occupations, the textbooks only show them as nurses and machine operators (Hsieh, 1995: 194). The bias of gender images in textbooks reflects the fact that the educational systems are mainly controlled by men, with the result of reinforcing gender division in the family and society. Because of the lack of positive identity for women in textbooks, women can have a lower motivation to achieve than men.

After opposition and petition by women's groups in the mid-1980s, female and male students in junior high schools were able to choose either industrial arts or household management. In 1997, the two courses were combined into one. Additionally, the number of women mentioned in the 1989 versions of standard textbooks has increased. However, the percentage of women in these new textbooks is still comparatively low (Hsieh, 1995: 193–5).

Mothers' classrooms

The 'Mothers' Classroom' is an adult educational system for married women, which has been highly promoted by the government since the late-1970s. According to the *Outline of Community Work*, one of the main purposes of Mothers' Classrooms is to promote the educational function of the family via lectures to enhance social harmony. Principally, this scheme wanted to utilize mothers as a medium to achieve the third goal of the 'Community Development Programme': improving ethics and morale. The Mothers' Classroom was promoted in a belief that 'to educate a woman to be a good mother is equal to educating the whole family' (Hsieh, 1985: 4). The government claimed that the foundation of our society was the family, not individuals, and that the mother played the primary role in the family. Therefore, in order to solve social problems and youth crimes, it was important to educate women how to be good mothers and wives in a changing society (Chao, 1985).

The government stressed that 'the primary activities of Mothers' Classrooms should fit in with government decrees, community work, national celebrations, folk festivals and educational purposes. Mothers' interests and needs were only a secondary justification (Chao, 1985: 10).' Thus the scheme was not designed for women's welfare, but for the state to control women for its own purposes. Through the scheme, the state attempted to educate women to follow the traditional sex roles and discipline them to serve their husbands, children and parents-in-law.

Welfare system

In Taiwan, the provision of welfare is mainly reliant on the family. The ruling party strongly emphasizes the importance of mutual help between family members. From 1982 to 1986, in the annual report on social administration, the Chairman of the Social Department of the Taiwan Provincial Government declared that the government's welfare measures would enforce the family functions (Taiwan Provincial Government, 1982–86). Moreover, according to the latest *Outline of Social Welfare Policies*, the fundamental guideline of welfare policies in Taiwan, the state will develop family-centred welfare policies, with the emphasis on family ethics, harmonizing family relationships and maintaining the welfare of family members via ethics teaching (Commission on Population Policies, 1995: 168–73). In 1998, at the conclusion of the 'National Social Welfare Conference,' the Premier announced that the government would develop social welfare towards familism and communitarianism (*Central Daily News*, 10/9/1998). It is clear that the state in Taiwan wants to develop a welfare system in which welfare is mainly provided by the family.

The state has also provided several programmes to improve family functions, such as the 'Scheme for Enforcing Family Education and for Promoting Social Harmony (1986–90),' the 1990 'Three Generations Living Together Scheme' and the 1992 'Harmonious Society Scheme.' In practice, the state has not provided any support to assist the family to fulfil its welfare function. All the schemes have tried to enforce the family role in welfare provision via the instillation of ideology. A strong family function in Taiwan is the best back-up the state has; the government has failed to provide family-support schemes, pension and housing until now. However, one thing should be borne in mind: under a familistic welfare system, women are more likely to suffer and to be restricted in the private sphere.

Legislation: the Family Chapter

After the foundation of the Republic of China, the KMT government adopted a modern European-style legal system. The concept that men and women are equal under the law was written into the Constitution and incorporated into the Civil Code (1930, revised 1985 and 1996). Although the KMT government adopted equality in law, in practice it did not have much effect on the patriarchal system. It should be remembered that Civil Code reform in 1930 was the result of a compromise between the KMT and liberals – it was not a KMT-led reform.

The original Civil Code had protected some women's rights in the patriarchal family system. Principally, it offered women three legal rights. First, they could possess and dispose of their properties freely without any undue restriction. Secondly, they had the same right as men to inheritance. Thirdly, a wife could divorce her husband in certain circumstances. Furthermore, the law also challenged the hegemony of parents. Parents were disempowered from making arranged marriages for their children. For its time, the law was radical and challenged traditional social values.

However, although equal rights for women was a stated aim of the Family Chapter, the law remained bound by traditional patriarchal spirit and to some extent protected the patriarchal family system, as shown in Table 3.8. First, it emphasized gender division in a family, for instance, by stating that the husband should be the 'breadwinner' (Article 1026). Secondly, it gave legal status to the culture of paternalistic living arrangement. A wife and children should take the domicile of the husband as their domicile (Article 1002 and 1088). Thirdly, it confirmed the superiority of the father in the family, with children treated as the possession of the paternal line (Article 1059). When parents had differences over children, the father's opinions took priority (Article 1089). Moreover, after divorce, the guardianship of children rested with the husband (Article 1084). Therefore, the role of the mother remained inferior in respect of teaching and guardianship of children. Finally, the law ensured the economic superiority of males; a husband was entitled to full control of any matrimonial property (Article 1018), even including the net income from to which the wife contributed property (Article 1019) and the wife's property (Article 1920). A woman had the right to own and manage her property, but she lost that right after marriage under the statutory 'union property' clause. In practice, before 1985, a wife could only dispose of her own property with her husband's agreement. The property (such as a house, land, etc) of the wife could not be mortgaged without the permission of her husband (Yu, 1993: 4). Upon divorce, the wife could lose any money and property, even those solely under her name. Therefore, under the original Family Chapter, women could only be the

Table 3.8 Comparison between the 1930, the 1985 and the 1996 versions of the Family Chapter of the Civil Code

Clause	The 1930 Civil Code	The 1985 Revision	The 1996 Revision
Rights of men and women within marriage	1. A wife shall take the domicile of the husband as hers (Article 1002). 2. In case the husband is insolvent, the living expenses of the household shall be borne by the wife out of her whole property (a man should be the breadwinner) (Article 1026). 3. A wife shall adopt the husband's surname as hers after marriage (Article 1000).	* A wife shall take the domicile of the husband as hers unless it has been otherwise agreed by the couple (Article 1002).	* The domicile shall be decided by the couple jointly (in 1998). * A wife and the husband can keep their original surname after marriage (in 1998).
Parents' rights over children	1. A child shall in principle adopt the father's surname except in uxorial marriage (Article 1059). 2. A minor child shall take the domicile of the father as his/her domicile (Article 1060). 3. The separate property of a minor child is managed by the father (Article 1088).	* A minor child shall take the domicile of the parents as his/her domicile (Article 1060). * The separate property of a minor child is managed by the parents jointly (Article 1088).	

62

Table 3.8 Comparison between the 1930, the 1985 and the 1996 versions of the Family Chapter of the Civil Code (*continued*)

Clause	The 1930 Civil Code	The 1985 Revision	The 1996 Revision
	4. The father and mother shall jointly exercise their rights and assume their duties to a minor child unless it is otherwise provided for by law. The rights shall be exercised by the father if the parents are not in agreement (Article 1089).		* The father and mother shall jointly exercise their rights and assume their duties to a minor child unless it is otherwise provided for by law. The rights shall be decided by the Court if the parents are not in agreement. The court shall consult the children, the authority and social welfare organizations before announcing a verdict (Article 1089).
	5. Members of a family council shall be selected from the following relatives ... among those of the same degree of relationship; the person in the paternal line comes first (Article 1131).	* Members of a family council shall be selected from the following relatives ... among those of the same degree of relationship, the person living in the same household comes first (Article 1131).	* Article 1051 is lifted.
	6. After divorce by mutual consent, the guardianship of children rests with the husband unless it has been otherwise agreed by the couple (Article 1051). 7. In the case of a divorce by		*After divorce, the

Table 3.8 Comparison between the 1930, the 1985 and the 1996 versions of the Family Chapter of the Civil Code
(continued)

Clause	The 1930 Civil Code	The 1985 Revision	The 1996 Revision
	judicial decree, the provision of Article 1051 shall apply in regard to guardianship of the children. But the Court may, in the interests of the children, appoint a guardian (Article 1055).		guardianship of children rests with one or both parties according to what is <u>agreed by the couple.</u> In the case of no agreement being made, <u>the Court may appoint a guardian</u> ... (Article 1055).
	8. Parents have the right and the duty to protect, educate and maintain their minor children (Article 1084).	* <u>A child shall be filial and respect his/her parents.</u> Parents have the right and the duty to protect, educate and maintain their minor children (Article 1084).	
	9. Parents may, within the limit of necessity, inflict punishments upon their children (Article 1085).		* Parents have an obligation to raise children which can not be affected either by divorce or marriage annulment (Article 1116–2)
Matrimonial Property +	1. The part of the union property which cannot be proved to be	* The part of the union property which cannot be	

Table 3.8 Comparison between the 1930, the 1985 and the 1996 versions of the Family Chapter of the Civil Code *(continued)*

Clause	The 1930 Civil Code	The 1985 Revision	The 1996 Revision
	property owned by either the husband or the wife shall be presumed to be the property contributed by *the husband. The husband owns the income coming from that property* (Article 1017). 2. The union property should be managed by the husband (Article 1018).	proved to be owned by either the husband or the wife shall be presumed to be the property contributed by the husband and the wife jointly (Article 1017). * The union property should be managed by the husband unless there has been a written agreement that the wife manages it (Article 1018).	
	3. The husband has the right to use and to collect net income from the property contributed to by the wife (Article 1019).	* The husband has the right to use and to collect net income from the property contributed to by the wife. The net income coming from the wife's property, after deducting the living expenses of the family and the cost for management of the union property shall fall into the ownership of the wife (Article 1019).	

Table 3.8 Comparison between the 1930, the 1985 and the 1996 versions of the Family Chapter of the Civil Code (*continued*)

Clause	The 1930 Civil Code	The 1985 Revision	The 1996 Revision
	4. The husband must have the consent of the wife for disposing of her property contribution, unless such disposition is necessary in the course of management (Article 1020). 5. The common property is managed by the husband (Article 1032).	* Upon termination of the relationship over union property (e.g. upon divorce), the net wealth, after deducting the liabilities, shall be equally distributed to the husband and the wife (Article 1030–1).	

Note: Underline indicates the main changes.

+ There are three types of matrimonial property regulated by the Civil Code: the union property, the community of property and the separation of property regime. The union property regime is the statutory regime.

dependents of their husbands. They could lose everything, including children and their own property, after divorce.

More than 50 years passed between the original enactment of the Civil Code and its first revision. Taiwanese society had changed rapidly during that time. Although the original Civil Code was regarded as a radical law when it was introduced, its patriarchal articles gradually began to be criticized by Taiwanese people. Hence, the 1985 Family Chapter was revised to be more flexible. Some male-superior articles were revised to ensure gender equality. Nevertheless, to avoid violation of the 'traditional family system,' many articles still remained the patriarchal principle (see Table 3.8). The husband still had priority in the family, controlling the wife, children and property. Although women were not satisfied with the 1985 revision, the government had no intention of revising the Family Chapter again. So, in 1993, a women's group, Awakening Foundation, began to review the patriarchal articles of the Family Chapter and introduced their revision to the Legislative Yuan. In recent years, women Legislators have also introduced their own versions of a revised Family Chapter to the Legislative Yuan. This action forced the government to provide a parallel revision (Awakening, 1995). The solicitors' groups of the Awakening also encouraged women victims to apply grand justice for interpreting the Constitution. In 1994, the judiciary announced that the priority of fatherhood in the case of divorce in the Civil Code violated the gender equality principle of the Constitution, so the government was forced to review the Family Chapter in the mid-1990s.

Women's groups and women Legislators also attempted to review the unequal articles, namely, those pertaining to in respect of matrimonial property and family name. In 1996, thanks to the opposition parties' Legislators, the Law Commission of the Legislative Yuan passed the first reading of the family name article; children could adopt either the father's or mother's family name dependent on their written agreement. The Ministry of Law exclaimed that they would use any possible means to stop the passing of the article since it would destroy the traditional social structure and family system. People would doubtless not accept such advanced legislation. The family name was not simply a legal problem nor a gender equality problem; it related to social custom, family blood system and the whole social system (*China Times*, 14/9/1996). Thus the reform of the Family Chapter in Taiwan met with opposition mainly from the ruling government.

Summary

Chinese gender roles, based on Confucian teachings, divided social life into the male/public and female/domestic spheres. Women's status was inferior and very limited in terms of economic autonomy and educational opportunity. The relationship between parents and sons is mutually beneficial. A son is able to inherit his parents' wealth, but has a responsibility to support them in old age and in the spirit world. *Family ideology* in Taiwan has slightly changed in recent decades, but the change is not as significant as might be expected. Familism and mutual dependence between generations are still notable Taiwanese traits. Although more women do not expect to live with and be supported by their sons in old age, in practice Taiwan retain a paternalistic living arrangement. New couples are supposed to live in the husband's home and a son has an obligation to take care of his elderly parents. However, parents gradually lose their superior power in the family; younger generations have more autonomy to arrange the family economy and family decision-making. But research also found that women had more power in the nuclear family. The traditional Chinese family style, the paternalistic extended family, would retain male-dominated culture.

In comparison with family ideology, *gender ideology* has changed greatly; younger and older generations hold very different gender ideology. Fewer women regard housework and childcare as women's natural responsibility; on the contrary, they hold a more egalitarian attitude towards marriage. More women have a positive attitude towards their employment. They do not think that women should work only when the family suffers economic hardship. However, the Taiwanese still tend to have a boy-preference attitude. Women still regard their family role as the first priority, and respect the supposed superiority of their husbands. The change of ideology is not always in the same direction; some ideology may change rapidly, others remain the same. As regards gender issues in culture, we should move on to discuss the state's role to see whether the state reproduces or transforms male-dominated culture.

Before the 1930s, as a revolution party, the KMT government challenged some traditional limitations on women, and ensured their equal rights in law. During the 1930s and the mid-1980s, the KMT revived Confucianism to encourage people to obey its authority. In Chinese history, Confucianism has been supported by many emperors and leaders since its principles emphasized obedience and status distinction which allowed the leaders to control people. Traditional family values and women's inferior roles have been emphasized during these periods. The educational system, welfare system and legal system all reflect the dominant ideology of the ruling government, maintaining the male-dominated family-centred culture and gender division. Under the old version of the Family Chapter, the husband was the breadwinner, with considerable power over his wife, children and property.

Since the mid-1980s, under opposition from women's groups and the challenge from liberals, the bias of gender images in education and the priority of fatherhood in law have been partly amended. The state has used women's activities as a means to transform the family and gender regime. However, the conservative nature of the current government has not changed; this government still seeks to reproduce the old male-dominated gender regime rather than to transform it.

4
Capitalist Development and the Female Labour Force

In the past forty years, Taiwan has performed relatively well in terms of national income when compared with other developing countries. Many scholars believe that women made a great contribution to Taiwan's 'economic miracle' (Huang, 1977; Diamond, 1979; Gallin, 1984; Liu et al., 1984). Traditionally, women were seldom involved in economic activities. The development of capitalism has provided a chance for women to join economic activities. In this chapter, the situation of the female labour force in the early stages will be reviewed to see the way in which women have begun to enter paid employment. The trends of the female labour force between 1966 and 1994 will be discussed in more detail since the pattern of women's employment has dramatically changed during this period. Moreover, rapid capitalist development has also brought out different forms of social problems, such as childcare. Childcare has always been regarded as the major obstruction for married women to stay in the labour market. This chapter, therefore, will discuss childcare provision and arrangements for working parents in Taiwan. In addition, Marxist feminists emphasize that capitalist development creates a new form of gender inequality. Under capitalist development, women have to suffer unequal treatment both in the family and in the labour market. It will be interesting to examine the extent to which women suffer unequal treatment and the changes in gender division in the labour market in Taiwan. The particular issue of whether women's status has improved under capitalist development is also discussed. Lastly, this chapter will review the possible influence of capitalists and business groups on the level of policy. As women's groups want the state to work for them, it is also important to research other possible actors in the political arena.

The female labour force in Taiwan: historical review

Capitalist development in Taiwan began with Japanese colonization. Originally, the Taiwanese economy was planned to focus on sugar and rice production only. In the 1930s, however, the Japanese government began to develop industry in Taiwan according to the wartime needs. During the period of Japanese colonization, some women in Taiwan joined the labour market. Some of these also worked outside the family as wage earners. It was estimated that 55 000 to 95 000 women did family handicraft work, and by 1923 one quarter of the labour force in factories were women workers (Yang, 1993: 264). Except for a few doctors, teachers and midwives, the majority of women workers were in the low-level service sector or worked as unskilled labour (Yang, 1993: 273). From 1905 to 1940, the economic activity rate of women was kept low and unstable, which might have resulted from the change in population structure. The population of women over twelve years old increased quickly, but the increase in 'active' women did not coincide with the growth in population. About 80 per cent of women workers were concentrated in the agricultural sector, mostly on family farms (see Table 4.1).

For those few women who worked in manufacturing, commerce or service industries, the firms or shops where they worked were small

Table 4.1   **Female population, activity rate and percentage share by industrial composition, 1905–60**

thousand persons, %

	1905	1915	1920	1930	1940	1951	1960
Population above 12 y	1028	1149	1225	1466	1830	2101	2824
Active population	314	478	456	418	625	885	1027
Activity Rate (%)	30.5	41.6	37.2	28.5	34.1	42.1	36.4
Agriculture (%)	83.8	82.0	82.8	80.0	75.7	57.6	52.6
Manufacturing (%)	5.8	9.6	8.0	6.9	7.1	6.7	14.1
Commerce (%)	2.2	2.6	2.4	5.2	3.8	7.9	10.4
Service (%)	1.0	1.4	2.4	4.4	5.9	+ 24.1	+ 18.6
Others (%)	7.2	4.4	4.4	3.5	7.5	3.8	4.2
Total (%)	100.0	100.0	100.0	100.0	100.0	100.0	100.0

Note: + includes public administration, social and personal services.
Source: 1. Data between 1905–40 is from Liu (1975: Tables 1, 15).
            2. Data between 1950–60 is calculated from DBAS (1994b: Table 88, 91).

family businesses. In other words, the majority of women who participated in economic activity during this period seldom worked outside
their families. The family was not only a consumer unit but also a productive unit. Moreover, the occupational composition of women
workers changed dramatically during 1940–51, as shown in Table 4.1.
Fewer women worked in the primary sector; on the contrary, increased
numbers of women worked in the service sector. Yu (1994) explained
the phenomenon by contesting that the Second World War has
created new working opportunities for Taiwanese women. According to
the statistics from newspapers in 1943, 93 per cent of employees in
companies were women.

In the 1950s, land reform and US aid led to a sharp rise in agricultural production enough not only to supply domestic need but also for
export. The prosperity in agriculture provided a base for industrialization. From 1952 to 1964, the state in Taiwan pursued a strategy of
import substitution. During this period, the percentage of female
labour in the primary sector declined to 58 per cent, while more
women worked in commerce and service industries (see Table 4.1). In
the late 1960s, highly paid domestic labour forced transnational
corporations in developed countries to seek cheap labour in developing
countries as part of their production line. The division of labour in the
world economic system provided an opportunity for Taiwan to develop
labour-intensive industry. The economy in Taiwan, therefore, had
developed fast during 1966–73 (Tuan, 1992: 55). A labour-intensive
export-oriented economy needs a great number of cheap labour to
support it. Labour from the agricultural sector rapidly streamed into
the industrial sector. In the 1960s, Taiwan focused on developing
textile and clothing industries. In the 1970s, transnational corporations transferred part of their production processes of electronics
industries to Taiwan. The increased labour among those light industries was suitable work for women, and stimulated women to join the
labour force, either to do family subsidiary work or to work in factories.
As an example, based on an official survey in 1970, 86 per cent of
employees in the clothing industry and 79 per cent in the textile
industry were female (Huang, 1977: 21).

To lower their costs, some medium-sized firms frequently subcon-
tracted some production work to home workers or family firms. Thus
the cities and rural areas in Taiwan were dotted with factories by 1973.
Over 90 per cent of firms in Taiwan were classified as small and
medium-sized businesses, and 53 per cent of firms had less than ten
employees in 1990. Many of them are family businesses, which means

that the majority of staffs are family members or relatives. In the family business, women, especially married women, are the principal labour force and often work as unpaid family workers.

During the early industrialization, unmarried girls who had just graduated from junior high school were the main targets of factories. In 1970, 57 per cent of vacant jobs in labour-intensive industries were specifically targeted on female labour (Huang, 1977: 21). The supply of young women fell short of demand during this period, while young men who had just left school even found it difficult to find a job (*China Daily News*, 2/7/1967). *Low cost* was the main reason why these unmarried young women were the preferred employees. The cost of labour was the most crucial factor in the survival of a labour-intensive industry, and employers needed cheap labour to make high profits. Moreover, women usually quit their jobs after they were married so their employers could save the cost of pensions, redundancy payments and increased wages along with their working experience. *High replacement rate of female labour* also allowed factories the chance to renew their labour since jobs in those factories were usually unskilled or semi-skilled. *Flexibility* was another important reason. A firm in the export-oriented industry could be vulnerable to international market fluctuations so it needed flexible labour, easily recruited and dismissed, in order to balance with the number of its trade orders. Many factories, for instance, saw a decline in their production under the threat of the energy crisis in 1974, and then many women workers left their jobs during this period. Those factories also preferred the *obedience* of young women. Women were used to being obedient in a patriarchal family; therefore, they were easy to be controlled and seldom asked for more benefits from their employers in comparison with male labour (Huang, 1977: 27–8).

In the meantime, society in Taiwan also changed dramatically. The birth rate declined from 0.466 per cent in 1952 to 0.153 per cent in 1994, while the life expectancy of women increased markedly from 55.7 in 1950 to 77.7 in 1994. Most married women do not have to spend many years bringing up children, and have more time to arrange their own lives after they finish the responsibilities associated with children. Besides, since more young women spend longer in school and postpone entry to the labour market in recent decades, factories face a shortage of labour. So, the government encourages those married women who have completed their childcaring responsibilities to join economic activities. Originally, married women who joined economic activities chiefly did family subsidiary work or worked as unpaid family workers. Nowadays, however, more married women have full-time jobs outside their families.

The educational reforms in 1968 let women have more human capital to find a decent and well-paid job. In the past, children were regarded as useful labour for household and fieldwork. Only children from the wealthy families had the chance to study. The average family was too poor to think about children's education. In Chinese culture, however, literati are the most respected persons. All parents want their children to study as much as they can, but boys are always the first to be educated when a family suffers privations. After a period of accumulating capital in the 1960s, the living standards of people in Taiwan were improved. The government also implemented nine-year compulsory education in 1967, which offered equal opportunity of education to boys and girls. More girls had the chance to receive formal education as the economy in their families improved.

Nowadays, the net enrolment rate of girls is higher than that of boys in any school age group (Ministry of Education, 1996: 5). Women are not the minority in higher education. The percentage of female students in universities and colleges was 13 per cent in 1952, but it rose to 44 per cent by 1989 (CEPD, 1990: 10). In 1994, 40 per cent of the female population had a university or college degree. In comparison with other countries, as shown in Table 4.2, Taiwanese girls performed well with regard to attend higher education. There is almost no gender

Table 4.2   The percentage of female students in each level of education, selected countries

unit: %

Country	Year	Primary edu.	Secondary edu.	Higher edu.
Taiwan	1995	49	49	50
Hong Kong	1987	48	49	(1992) 42
Singapore	1989	47	(1984) 50	(1983) 42
Korea, Republic of	1994	48	48	(1993) 36
Japan	1993	49	(1991) 49	(1991) 40
USA	1993	49	49	(1990) 54
Britain	1992	49	50	50
France	1993	48	50	55
Germany	1993	49	48	40
Italy	1993	49	49	51

Source: Ministry of Education (1996), *Statistic Indicators of Education in ROC*, 69.

Figure 4.1   **Numbers of employed persons in Taiwan, 1951–94**

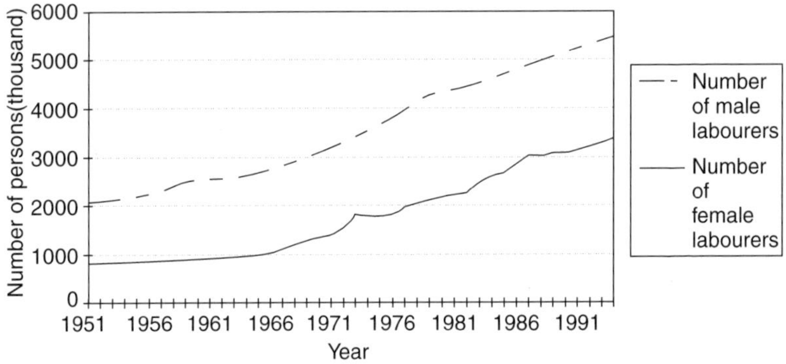

Source: DBAS (1994b), *Yearbook of Manpower Survey Statistics in the Taiwan Area*, Tables 1, 88.

difference in terms of the number of students in every level of schooling in Taiwan. Compared with men, however, women have to rely on their educational attainments to enter high-level occupations (Liang, 1988).

4.1.1   Trends in labour force participation: 1966–94

The number of employed women has increased rapidly since 1966 (see Figure 4.1). In 1951, there were about 821 000 women in the labour force; in 1994 it rose to 3 428 000 women. Many studies regarded 1966 as the starting point for discussing working women in Taiwan. After that date, the state changed its economic strategy and women streamed into the labour market. Thus in this section we will specially discuss the changes in the female labour force during the period 1966–94.

Employment and unemployment

In the past thirty years, the male labour force in Taiwan has decreased steadily. On the contrary, the female labour force has increased gradually but unsteadily. Some researchers explain this situation as female labour being easily affected by economic conditions (Kao, 1993). As shown in Figure 4.2, the female labour force participation rate grew sharply between 1966–73, from 33 per cent to 42 per cent, because labour-intensive export-oriented industrialization developed fast in Taiwan

Figure 4.2   Labour force participation rate by gender in Taiwan, 1966–94

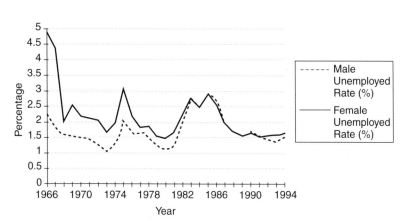

Source: as Figure 4.1, Tables 7, 89.

during that period. It fell slightly between 1974 and 1982. Liu (1984) thinks that the fall of participation rate was affected by two energy crises. However, it rose sharply after 1982 and reached a peak in 1987. In 1994, the female labour force participation rate was still only 45.4 per cent.

As more women join the labour market, the situation of men as the sole breadwinners has slightly changed. Twenty-seven per cent of

Figure 4.3   Unemployment rate by gender in Taiwan, 1966–94

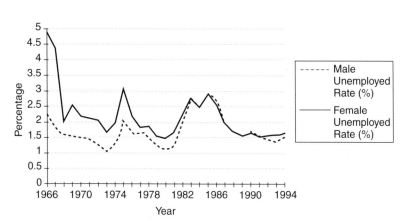

Source: as Figure 4.2.

Table 4.3   Female labour force participation rate in selected countries, 1994

unit: %

Country	Labour force participation rate	Unemployment rate
Taiwan	45.4	1.7
Hong Kong	47.1	1.7
Korea, Republic of	47.9	1.9
Singapore	50.9	2.8
Japan	50.2	3.0
Britain	71.0	7.7
USA	62.5	6.0
(West) Germany	61.5	14.7
France (1993)	59.0	12.0
Italy (1995)	42.9	16.2
Spain	35.6	31.4
Sweden (1992)	82.0	3.8

Source: 1. ILO (1995): *The 1995 Yearbook of Labour Statistics*, Table 1A.
2. OECD (1996): *OECD Economic Surveys*, individual booklets.

income recipients were female in 1976, but this figure rose to 35 per cent by 1994 (DBAS, 1996: 36).[1] More women have made contributions to the family economy.

The unemployment rate in Taiwan has remained very low in recent decades. The female unemployed rate was on average slightly higher than that of men, especially before 1982 (see Figure 4.3). Since then, the difference between the two rates has been small.

In comparison with other countries, the participation rate of women in the Taiwanese labour force was one of the lowest (see Table 4.3), but higher than that in Italy and Spain. Even if we only look at the participation rate of Asian countries which have similar economic systems to Taiwan (except Japan), Taiwan was the lowest.[2] The labour force participation rate refers to the percentage of people who have work aspirations. Therefore, it is clear that fewer women in Taiwan, for whatever reason, act to participate in formal economic activities. It will be interesting to see what kinds of influences have brought about this phenomenon.

Trends in labour force participation by age group

Nowadays, the pattern of the female labour force in Taiwan, as shown in Figure 4.4, seems more like the double peak pattern (M-shape curve).

Figure 4.4   Changes in female labour force participation rate in Taiwan by age

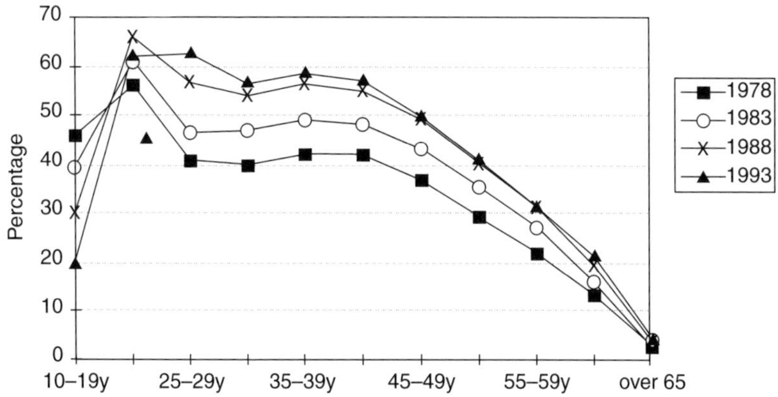

Source: as Figure 4.1, Table 10.

In the early years, women often entered the labour market in their teens, and many of them left the labour force at about age 25. However, in 1993, there were only about 20 per cent of women under 20 years old in the labour force due to the growth of educational opportunities. The number of employed women who continued working in the labour force after 25 years old was also much higher than the corresponding figure in 1978. Nowadays, fewer women leave the labour market after marriage or childbirth. Nevertheless, only few women in Taiwan have returned to the labour market in their middle-age after a career break.

Trends in labour force participation by marital status and with/without children

The labour force participation rate of unmarried women in Taiwan was higher than that of married, divorced, separated and widowed women. The labour force participation rate of unmarried women, shown in Figure 4.5, rose steeply between 1966 and 1973 due to the rapid growth of labour-intensive industries. However, since 1982, the labour force participation rate of married women has increased remarkably, while that of unmarried women has declined. Nowadays, increasing numbers of married women want to work.

Figure 4.5   Changes in the female labour force participation rate in Taiwan by marital status, 1966–94

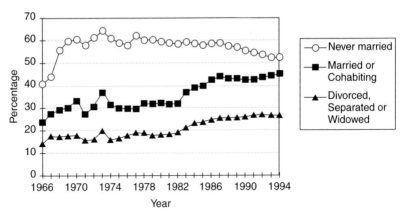

Source: as Figure 4.1, Table 8.

As far as married women with or without children are concerned, the labour force participation rate of married women without children is not much higher than that of other women, as shown in Figure 4.6. It seems

Figure 4.6   Labour force participation rates of married women with/without children, 1980–92

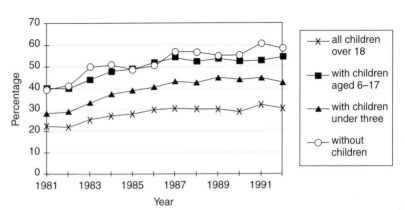

Source: DBAS (1995b: Table 2).

Figure 4.7   Changes in percentage share of female labour in Taiwan by occupational class, 1966–94

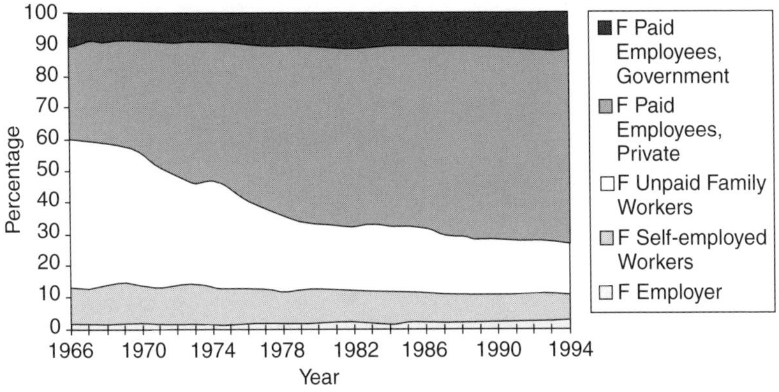

Source: as Figure 4.1, Tables 14, 92.

that childcare is not the only reason why married women do not want to work. Moreover, increasing numbers of women with children aged 6–17 and more women with children under three want to work in the last decade. This means that more families will need childcare facilities.

Changes in the range of women's employment

As shown in Figure 4.7, self-employed women workers and women employers have been very rare, and this situation has not changed over time. The unpaid family worker represents the most distinctive sex-typed category. Fewer men have worked as unpaid family workers, only 17 per cent in 1966 and 4 per cent in 1994 (see Figure 4.8). However, the historical concentration of women in this category has changed significantly. In 1966, half of the women who joined the labour force were unpaid family workers, but the percentage had decreased to 16 per cent by 1994, though it was still much higher than that of men.

Although Lu (1994) thinks that the problem of women working as unpaid family workers in informal sectors is serious, it seems that the tendency towards *proletarianization* is significant. From 1966 to 1994, both the percentages of men and women in paid work increased significantly. In 1966, 44 per cent of male workers and 37 per cent of women were waged employees; by 1994, the percentages had risen to

Figure 4.8   Changes in percentage share of male labour in Taiwan by occupational class, 1966–94

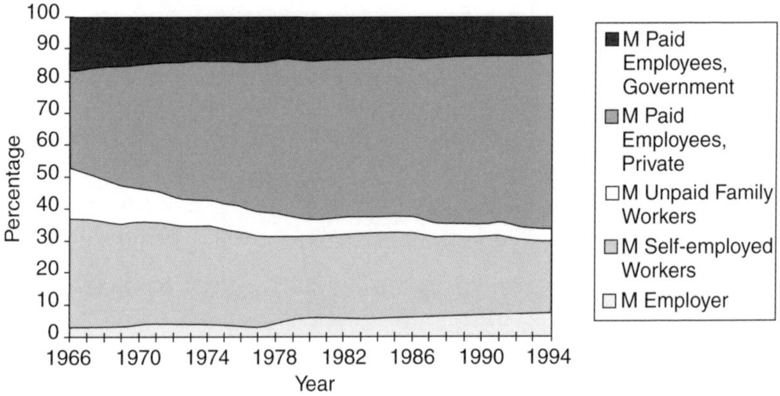

Source: as Figure 4.7.

66 per cent and 74 per cent respectively. In detail, by 1994, 74 per cent of women had worked for capitalists and the government, and 16 per cent of them had worked for their families or husbands as unpaid family workers. Only about 10 per cent of working women managed their own business. If more people rely on wages instead of land, family life and patriarchal culture may be changed. When a father no longer controls the tools of production, it is doubtful whether his authority can remain.

Changes in the occupational patterns of women's employment

As shown in Figure 4.9, in 1966, about half of women workers in Taiwan were concentrated in agriculture, animal husbandry, forestry and fishing work. After that, as we mentioned above, the surplus female labour on farms was absorbed by labour-intensive manufacturing industries. Since 1987, this kind of work has decreased sharply, probably because some labour-intensive factories moved abroad, especially to mainland China. On the contrary, the percentage of male workers as machine operators has remained high although the industry structure in Taiwan has changed in recent decades (see Figure 4.10).

Additionally, since 1977 the increase of women at professional levels has been remarkable. Increasing opportunities for attending higher education have allowed women to become skilled workers. However, it

Figure 4.9   Changes in percentage share of female labour in Taiwan by occupational composition, 1966–94

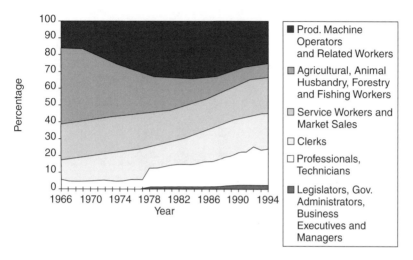

Source: as Figure 4.1, Tables 13, 94.

Figure 4.10:   Changes in percentage share of male labour in Taiwan by occupational composition, 1966–94

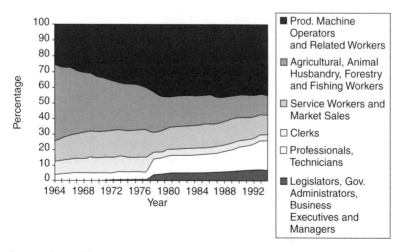

Source: as Figure 4.9.

Figure 4.11   **Percentage of women part-time workers by marital status in Taiwan, 1995**

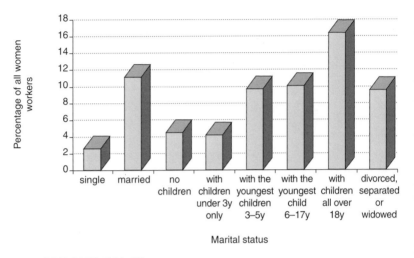

Source: DBAS (1995b: Table 20).

does not mean that these jobs are better than any others. Most 'skilled' women workers are teachers and nurses, jobs which have been occupied by women for ages. Moreover, women as managers and administrators have been noticeably rare; men have still occupied the managerial levels in the labour market.

Informal employment of married women

As mentioned above, more married women have joined the labour market in recent years. The majority of work pattern in Taiwan is now full-time. In 1994, 92 per cent of women workers worked full-time. However, the percentage of women working part-time has been higher than that of men over time, and married women have been more likely to work part-time than single women, as shown in Figure 4.11.[3] Lu's conclusions (1992) are inconsistent with the fact that women with young children (under 3) seldom worked part-time; while a higher percentage of women with adult children only (over 18) worked part-time. This may be because women quit their jobs to take care of their young children but some of them return to work part-time as their children grew up. Moreover, unlike in some Western countries, the manufacturing industry (not commerce) had the highest percentage of part-time workers in Taiwan. In the manufacturing industry, over 45 per cent of part-time workers were housewives, and the majority of part-time workers in small businesses which had less than 100 employees were housewives (DBAS, 1995c: 6). Small businesses usually provided less welfare to part-time workers than large businesses (DBAS, 1995c: Table 5). Thus, many casual and inferior jobs were filled by housewives.

Married women are also a pool of unpaid family workers. 22 per cent of married women workers were unpaid family workers in 1993. The percentage was much higher than that of male workers (4 per cent). Moreover, women's opportunities to participate in formal economic activities were affected by gender division of labour in the family. On average, married women spent 4.08 hours daily on housekeeping and caring, while married men only spent 0.22 hours per day (DBAS, 1995d). The burden of housework limits married women's participation in the formal economy.

Effects of marriage and childbirth on women's employment

In the early stage of rapid capitalist development, as we mentioned above, Taiwanese women usually quit their jobs after marriage and never returned to the labour market afterwards. According to an early official survey, 30 per cent of working women left their current jobs due to marriage and only 9 per cent of them due to childbirth or housework (Labour Force Research Centre in Taiwan Province, 1973: 105). Although an increasing number of women join the labour force today, there are still many married women who leave their jobs due to marriage or childbirth. In 1993, 48 per cent of women paid employees quit their jobs due to marriage or childbirth. Once women leave the labour market, it is difficult for them to return. Only 31 per cent of those women resumed jobs after interruption for marriage or being pregnant (DBAS, 1994a: Table 45). On average, it took 98.78 months for women who left their jobs for marriage to return to the labour force, and 75.93 months for women who left their jobs due to child-birth (DBAS, 1994a: Tables 48, 50). Analyzed by generation, we find that this situation has not improved over time, indeed, it has got worse (see Table 4.4). In addition, married women lacked work aspiration. In 1993, 92 per cent of married women who were currently jobless did not want to find a job. The principle reason was that they had to take care of their children (DBAS, 1994a: 224). Childcare is clearly the main obstruction to women working. It is interesting to see how Taiwanese parents manage their childcare.

Table 4.4   **Employment status of married women aged 15–64 who have been in paid work in Taiwan by generation, 1993**

number of sample: 4,109,505, date: 1993, unit: %

Generation	Job interrupted due to marriage and childbirth	Job interrupted due to other reasons	Never interrupted	Total
Before 1940	41	22	37	100
1941–50	44	11	46	100
1951–55	46	7	47	100
1956–60	51	5	43	100
1961–65	52	4	43	100
After 1966	54	3	43	100

Source: CLA (1995a: Table 50).

Welfare mix and childcare

According to the 1993 *Survey on Children's Lives in the Taiwan Area*, the mother was the primary person who took care of children under three during the daytime. Sixty-five per cent of children under three were cared for by their mothers, 23 per cent by other family members. With regard to children aged 3–6, 44 per cent were cared for by their mothers during the daytime, 13 per cent by relatives, 39 per cent by kindergartens and nurseries (Ministry of the Interior, 1993b: 18). Nurseries and kindergartens have shared the burden of parents with children aged 3–6, but children under three seldom stayed in institutions as parents thought that they needed personal care. Moreover, fathers were seldom the main carers for children in any situation (Fang, 1995: Table 4.19), which more or less indicates the male-breadwinner ideology in Taiwan

As far as the childcare methods of working women were concerned, as shown in Table 4.5, the number of working parents who cared for their youngest children by themselves has decreased sharply, especially since 1985. Childcare responsibility has shifted from parents to grandparents, mainly grandmothers. As grandparents often live in the same house or nearby and they usually have not been in paid work after marriage, they are the best alternatives for childcare. Also, they may want to show that they are useful labour, so that their children will not move them out. The number of children cared for by childminders has also increased. Childminding has become a new profession.

Table 4.5 Types of daycare arranged by married working women in Taiwan aged 15–64 for their youngest children

number of sample: 1 330 739, date: 1993, unit: %

Childcare period	Pay someone to take care of children (%)								Total	Average fee, NT $
	Self *	Parents	Others	Nanny	Child-minder	Nursery at work-place	Public nursery	Private nursery		
Before 1961	84	11	1	3	–	–	–	–	100	4 700
1961–65	69	21	2	5	2	1	–	–	100	3 042
1966–70	71	20	2	4	3	–	–	–	100	5 627
1971–75	64	26	1	2	6	–	0.2	–	100	4 729
1976–80	64	25	2	1	7	0.1	0.2	–	100	6 147
1981–85	54	33	2	2	10	0.2	–	0.7	100	6 825
1986–90	36	44	3	2	14	–	0.2	0.9	100	8 817
After 91	15	59	3	3	19	–	0.1	0.7	100	11 144

Note: * This data includes the interviewee herself and her husband.
Source: CLA (1995a: Table 45.6).

This survey also shows that a greater number of the younger generations of women have stayed in the labour force after childbirth. They might enter the labour market later than the older generations, but only leave the labour force when the number of young children is increasing. Women's employment patterns have changed; the reciprocal help between generation offers a solution for working parents.

Regarding nurseries, the first nursery in Taiwan was set up in 1928 for Japanese working women only. Since 1924, there have been some seasonal nurseries for women on farms during the harvest season (Shiu, 1992: 48). Generally speaking, there are three types of nurseries in Taiwan: public, private and neighbourhood nurseries. Nurseries accept children from one month to six years old, while kindergartens accept pre-school children above four. In practice, most nurseries only accept children aged 2–6. There are only 21 *public nurseries* in Taiwan, but their quality is usually the best. The original aim of public nurseries was to provide free day care for children in low income families so that their parents could go to work, but nowadays most children in public nurseries come from average-income families. *Private nurseries* are the main kind of nurseries in urban areas. In fact, the real number of children in private nurseries is much higher than the official data. Many private nurseries are not registered and the number of unregistered private nurseries is now higher than registered institutions. For instance, there were 589 nurseries in Taipei City in 1993, but only 142 of them registered (Feng, 1995). This phenomenon also made it difficult for the government to supervise the quality of private nurseries and to control the quantity of nurseries to meet the needs of childcare.

Lastly, *neighbourhood nurseries*, the main type of nursery in Taiwan, are regarded as quasi-public. They are non-profit organizations and in average 42 per cent of their income comes from government support. Therefore, they charge lower than the other two kinds of nurseries. They are usually set up through government support, but operated by city councils or community organizations such as farmers' associations, women's associations or citizen's service societies. Neighbourhood nurseries in Taiwan had been developed under the financial support of United Nations (hereafter UN) during the period 1963–74. After Taiwan was expelled from the UN, the state began to take charge of the neighbourhood nursery (Chang, 1988). Today, compared with other nurseries, the facilities in neighbourhood nurseries are often inferior, and the ratio of staff to children is low (see Table 4.8).

Workplace nurseries are not popular in Taiwan though they comparatively early to emerge. In 1950, there were only seven regular nurseries in Taiwan. All were set up by factories (Chang, 1988: 153). Nowadays, the actual number of workplace nurseries unknown since most of them are not registered and they survive in various forms. For instance, some of them cooperate with private nurseries and some also accept children of non-employees. According to an official survey in 1991, about 500 business units provided daycare service for babies of their employees, and 407 business units offered pre-school daycare for children. Seventy-two per cent of the former and 44 per cent of the latter were free, and they accepted 4284 children. However, data from the Council of Labour Affairs in 1993 showed there were 99 business units providing a nursery service for their employees, 50 of them attached to public firms and 49 to private firms. Private firms which provided a nursery usually had great numbers of employees, a high percentage of women employees and low average employees' age.

Nannies and childminders have been in Taiwan for a long period. However, childminders have not become popular until recently. The state was glad to see the increasing demand for childminders, and began to support childminding as a low-cost source. Since 1988, the state has entrusted some private organizations with the training and accreditation of childminders. Childminders are now highly approved of by the public. The state stressed that the childminder training scheme could 'utilize surplus labour in the family and increase employment opportunities for housewives.' 'Housewives will be able to improve their family economy as well as take care of their families.' (Pai and Kuo, 1988). Childminders who finish professional training courses will receive certification although untrained childminders can also do childcare work (*United Daily News*, 10/3/1994). Until now, there is no registration system to monitor the quality of childminders.

'Skills schools' (*Chai-I-Pan*) are a special and popular form of after-school care operated by private companies. These schools, with both learning and caring functions, either offer extensive school courses or offer extra-curricular activities, such as playing the piano, dancing, drawing and mental arithmetic. In Taiwan, 48 per cent of school children have attended these classes after school; they are even more popular in urban areas (Ministry of the Interior, 1993b: 24).

Current situation of gender inequality in the labour market

Childcare arrangements are not the only problem which followed on from capitalist development. The emergence of capitalism also brings new forms of gender inequality in the labour force, such as wage differentials and lack of promotion opportunities. As proletarianization is increasing and more people live on wages, unequal opportunity between genders is gradually attracting more public attention in Taiwan. In this section, the current situation of gender inequality in the labour market in Taiwan will be reviewed, including wage differentials, occupational segregation, unequal promotion opportunities, unequal welfare, and marriage and pregnancy discrimination. We will learn the extent to which women suffer another form of oppression after joining the labour market

Wage gap

As demonstrated in the early data from the Japanese colonial period, women workers in Taiwan have suffered from wage differentials since the early period of capitalist development. The earnings of Japanese were double those of Taiwanese, and men's earnings were double those of women's, both in the agricultural and in the manufacturing sectors (Yang, 1993: 261–315). From his research in the 1970s, Huang (1977: 53–63) concluded that men and women were paid differently since they did different jobs in factories, rather than being paid differently for doing the same jobs. He also pointed out other reasons why the salaries of young women workers were low. First, women workers in factories were younger than male workers. Originally, they were surplus labour in rural areas so they did not mind getting low wages. Secondly, their working experiences were limited. Thirdly, they usually had low educational qualifications. Fourthly, their physical strength and skills were lower than men's. Lastly, they were not family breadwinners so their earnings were not as important to their families. Under traditional patriarchal ideology, people believed that men's wages should be higher than women's. Therefore, employers would take this point into account when they recruited new employees. According to Huang's research, 79 per cent of women workers also believed that it was reasonable for male workers' wages to be higher than women's (Huang, 1977: 141–4).

In comparison with other Asian countries, only the wage gap between genders in Singapore was smaller than that in Taiwan (see

Table 4.6   Women's earnings as a percentage of men's earnings in selected
             countries, 1970–95 +

Country	1970	1975	1980	1985	1990	1993	1995
Taiwan				65	65	66	67
Hong Kong	–	–	–	77	70	63	61
Korea, Republic of	–	(76) 47	44	48	54	57	60
Singapore	–	–	63	–	74	72	73
Japan	(71) 52	56	54	52	50	–	62
Britain	61	68	70	69	70	71	–
Germany	–	–	–	73	73	74	74
France	(72) 78	79	79	81	81	81	–
Greece	–	–	–	–	78	80	80
Sweden	–	–	90	90	87	86	87

Note: (71) = in 1971, (72) = in 1972, (76) = in 1976. + for workers in non-agricultural
    activities.
Source: calculated from DBAS (1995b) and ILO, *Yearbook of Labour Statistics,* various years.

Table 4.6). The wage gap in Taiwan was much larger than that in some
Western countries, where legislation regulated equal pay between
genders. In Taiwan, the wage gap has not changed for the past 10
years. However, except Hong Kong, since the 1990s, wage differentials
between genders in other Asian countries have been improved.

When comparing the difference between men's and women's
earning in different industries, transport, storage, communication,
finance, insurance and property businesses tend to have the lowest
level of wage gap (as shown in Figure 4.12). The situation in mining
and quarrying industries is the most extreme, the average wage of
women workers being only about half that of male workers. If the job
level is taken into account, in almost every industry the wage gap
between genders at the supervisory level is smaller than that at non-
supervisory level. In industries, such as mining and quarrying, manufacturing and construction, which greatly depend on physical strength,
women's wages at the supervisory level are even lower than men's
wages at non-supervisory level

If the level of wage gap can reflects the situation vis-à-vis gender
discrimination, women's status in some industries, such as commerce, finance, insurance and real estate, and business services (in
supervisor level only), mainly in the service sector, has greatly
improved over time. However, the wage gap between men and

Figure 4.12 Wage differentials between genders in various industries, non-supervisory level only, 1977–93

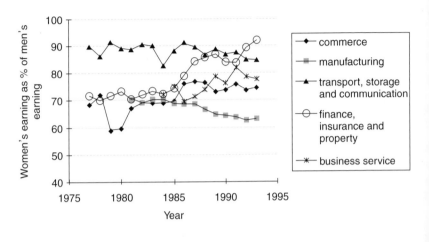

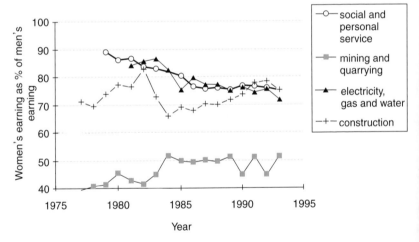

Source: DBAS (1994c: Table 13–4; 1987: Table 20–1).

women in some industries, such as community services, manufacturing, electricity, gas and water, and construction (in supervisor level only), has increased for the past years. It is ironic that most of these industries where the wage gap is larger have been regulated by the Labour Standards Law, with its regulations on equal pay for equal work. The gender wage gap in these industries even increased after the implementation of the Labour Standards Law in 1984. Therefore, although the law regulated equal pay for equal work, it was clear that the government and employers did not take it seriously.

Wage differentials between genders are often regarded, particularly by economists, as a powerful indicator to measure the level of gender inequality in the labour market. In Taiwan, most recent research on unequal treatment between genders has also focused on discussing the difference in earnings between men and women but the conclusions have been varied. Some researchers found that discrimination should account for the wage gap between genders (Gannicott, 1986; Lin, 1988); some found that lifetime work incentives are largely responsible (Kao, Polachek and Wunnava, 1994); others found that individual choice and human capital could account for it (Chiang, 1988; Kao, 1993). Additionally, although empirical research proved the existence of unequal pay between genders, they found that the effective coefficient of education on wages increased over time (Fei, 1982; Sheu, 1991). In 1993, the average earnings of women university graduates as a percentage of male graduates' earnings was 72 per cent; while the rate was 57 per cent at the level of primary school education only and 62 per cent at the level of junior high school graduates (DBAS, 1994c: 32). From this, we can deduce that education is an important human capital which is able to diminish the income difference between genders.

In the research of wage differentials, researchers usually put many factors into an equation to find out the degree of importance of each factor explaining the gender wage gap and which one is the most important. Those researchers usually choose the indicators which can be measured, but ignore the factors which are difficult to be calculated by computers, such as ideology and policies. However, the problem of these quantitative studies is that although many issues can be factored in to the equation, there will always be one or more factors which are left out or ignored; these may, of course, be very important therefore the resulting statistics would be flawed. Moreover, many of those studies have made unjustified assumptions based on linear causation, but a social phenomenon is more complicated than that. Furthermore, the wage differential between genders is only one phenomenon of different treatment between genders; it does not reflect the whole picture of gender inequality in the labour force. For instance, occupational segregation and different promotion and training opportunities could mask the seriousness of wage differentials. Men and women also have different opportunities to access jobs. For a full understanding of the situation of different treatment of men and women in the labour market, we should also take other phenomena into account.

Figure 4.13   Changes of the percentage of women employees in different
industries, 1977–93

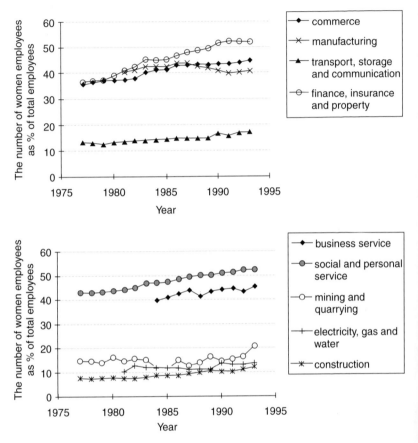

Source: DBAS (1994b: Tables 12, 91).

Occupational segregation

In Taiwan, a few studies had investigated gender segregation in occupations and this factor had been proved to be an important contributor to women's inferior status in the labour market. Based on the data during 1987–89, Lai and Chang (1993) found that the index of occupational segregation of genders was about 44 per cent in Taiwan. This meant that 44 per cent of women (or men) had to change their present occupations to make the percentage share of gender in every occupation the same. Most of the highly segregated occupations belonged to the manufacturing and mining industries, which relied on physical strength. Industries in the service sector tended to have low levels of gender occupational segregation. Women were only over-represented in few occupations, such as clerical work and nursing.

According to data from 1977 to 1993, there is no doubt that horizontal occupational segregation between genders still exists in Taiwan. Since 1977, there has been quite a rise in the percentage of women employees in all industries, except manufacturing. However, women have been greatly under-represented in transport, mining and quarrying, construction and the utilities, which have been labeled as male jobs. The concentration of women in commerce, business and social services, finance, insurance and property services has been remarkable, but women have not been over-represented in any of them (see Figure 4.13).[4]

As far as vertical occupational segregation is concerned, as shown in Table 4.7, the percentage of women in legislative, managerial and administrative positions has remained low, but women have increased their share in professional jobs. However, the definition of 'professional jobs' in official data is too broad. One cannot conclude that there have been more women in top jobs.[5] Moreover, in 1966 the proportion of women in clerical, service and sales work was broadly comparable to their contribution to the labour force as a whole; by 1994 these occupations had become typically 'female.' In

Table 4.7   Percentage of women by occupational composition, 1966–94

unit: %

Occupational categories	1966	1975	1980	1985	1990	1994
Legislators, administrators, business executives and managers	13	7	9	13	15	13
Professionals +	32	35	42	44	48	49
Technicians and associate professionals	–	–	33	38	42	39
Machine operators and related workers	21	35	31	31	30	28
Clerks	24	35	38	61	66	73
Service workers and sales workers	35	28	31	42	44	52

Note: + data of professionals before 1977 is combined with that of technicians and associate professionals.
Source: same as Figure 4.9.

Figure 4.14:   **Percentage of women in government departments by job position, 1980–94**

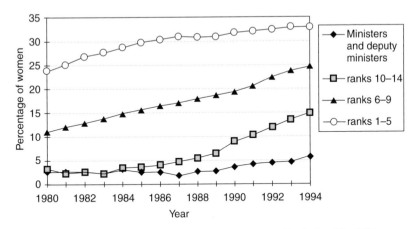

Source: Ministry of Personnel (1995: 34–7), *Statistics on Personnel in the Republic of China*.

government departments and schools, vertical occupational segregation between genders is still high. The proportion of women civil servants has increased from 24 per cent in 1973 to 36 per cent in 1994, and the growth rate of women civil servants was 5.67 times that of men within twenty years. However, in central government, only eight out of 145 heads of departments were women (*Freedom Times*, 28/8/1996). Nought point eight per cent of women civil servants were over 'rank ten' (usually high-ranking officers), compared with 2.7 per cent of men (Ministry of Personnel, 1995).[6] By 1994, under 5 per cent of Ministers and deputy ministers had been women. The situation is a little better in high-level job positions (rank 10–14), but only 15 per cent of these positions were held by women (see Figure 4.14)

Human capital theory maintains that occupational segregation is caused by individual choice. In other words, women usually choose to enter 'female-dominated' jobs. However, Lin (1988) found that it was difficult for women to enter professional occupations, but they had more chance to participate in traditional female-dominant occupations. Even if women have higher educational qualifications than men, they still cannot conquer structural obstructions to entering professional occupations. By analyzing advertisements in newspapers, Yu et

Table 4.8   Number of students in universities and colleges by course of
study

date: 1994, unit: person

Course	Universities		Colleges		F/M (%)
	Male	Female	Male	Female	
Art	1 598	3 612	1 105	5 382	333
Social science	12 266	28 139	1 421	4 809	241
Commerce and management	18 654	23 786	17 316	83 565	298
Natural science	9 498	3 541	396	462	40
Math. & computer science	14 368	6 218	5 260	12 456	95
Engineering	41 780	4 361	142 302	37 709	23
Medicine +	11 484	9 684	6 972	38 167	259

Note: + Courses of medicine in colleges focus on nursing.
Source: Ministry of Education (1995), *Statistical Indicators of Education in the ROC*, Table 13.

al. (1991: 34–6) found that many jobs were not equally open to both
men and women but limited to a single sex. It seems that many jobs
are labelled as men's jobs or women's jobs, so that job seekers do not
have much choice.

In Taiwan, the improvement of women's education does not change
the situation of occupational segregation between genders as we would
expect. On the contrary, the educational system may enforce gender
segregation in occupations. As shown in Table 4.8, the courses that students chose in universities and colleges were distinct between genders.
Less women chose to study engineering; they were concentrated in the
courses in art, social science and business. Sex roles and social expectation lead to the division of courses chosen by men and women as well
as the choice of occupation.

Unequal opportunity

Generally speaking, women have equal opportunities to enter government departments since the government usually employs examinations to recruit new staff. However, some public examinations are also
limited to a single sex, usually men. For example, women are not
welcome to attend the recruiting examinations of the Ministry of
Foreign Affairs because:

> Working abroad is a very tough job and workers often need to be
> rotated, so it is not suitable for women and will have a negative

influence on their marriage and families. ... Women often quit or refuse to work abroad after marriage. This phenomenon makes it difficult for our department to arrange work. ... Some areas, such as the Middle East, have conservative religions and customs. People do not accept women working outside of the family so we cannot arrange for women staff to work in these areas. Some areas have continuous wars and unstable politics and are too dangerous for women to work in (explanation by the Ministry of Foreign Affairs for their unequal recruiting policy).

 – *United Daily News*, 2/8/1993; *Freedom Times*, 9/6/1995

In 1996, under public pressure, some restrictions on women taking entrance exams were abolished by the new Minister of Foreign Affairs. The entrance examination for state enterprises is another case of gender discrimination. In 1989, women examinees were refused from 9 out of 30 jobs; 13 limited the maximum number of women who could qualify to pass the entrance exams and to become new employees. The State Enterprise Commission explained their policy of male preference as follows:

These jobs are not suitable for women since they are dangerous, and the transport systems to the workplace are not convenient ... these jobs often required physical exertion, to carry heavy materials, to work in a high pressure environment, to work in the field, to monitor buildings in the process of construction, to liaise with trade unions, and to deal with labourers' problems.

 – *United Daily News*, 6/6/1989

In addition, the Police Force also limited the number of women officers because they often complained about pressure and requested to transfer to office work. The entrance examination for environmental inspectors also limited the number of qualified women as the Environmental Protection Administration believed that too many women inspectors would affect work efficiency as a whole (*United Daily News*, 8/10/1989). The Ministry of Finance only granted male workers in insurance companies the right to receive further education abroad since it was a 'conventional policy.' The Ministry insisted that they had the right to choose what kind of person they wanted (*China Times Express*, 17/1/1989).

In comparison with the public departments, gender discrimination in recruitment for private firms is even more extreme. According to the research of Yu et al. (1991: 34), high-level jobs gave to men preference. For instance, 72 per cent of advertisements for managers requested male applicants only. Many advertisements for supervisors (50 per cent), professionals (65 per cent) and technicians (53 per cent) also wanted male applicants only. On the contrary, adverts for secretaries (88 per cent), accountants (77 per cent) and clerks (66 per cent) wanted women only. These jobs not only requested women applicants, but often had limitations on marital status or age as well. In most cases, they wanted unmarried young women

Women also have fewer opportunities to be promoted. The Bureau of Personnel even went as far as blaming the difficulty in finding suitably qualified people for high-ranking jobs in government on women workers, who were numerous. Also, they complained that too many women staff worked in the same jobs for ages, so that the qualification of personnel in government departments became lower (*China Times*, 1986). Nevertheless, Chang (1987) claims that the unbalanced proportion men and women in high-level job positions in government departments cannot be entirely attributed to gender discrimination. She thinks that this phenomenon will disappear as increasing numbers of women enter government service and the educational attainment of women is improved. In private companies, 74 per cent of employers admitted that a man would be promoted, even if a woman had the same capability (Yu et al., 1991).

General suspicion about women's key abilities leads men and women into two sectors in the workplace, upheld by 'dual labour market theory.' Women all too easily remain in the same jobs for long periods, without any aspiration to promotion. Lack of job satisfaction could affect women's working performance in the workplace or, sometimes, encourage them to leave the labour market.

Unequal welfare

'Workfare' is a way for companies to attract or keep their employees. In Taiwan, welfare provided by firms has been affected by traditional family ideology and the gender regime. In government departments, for instance, men are entitled to apply for food stamps for their parents in any circumstances, but married women are unable to apply for their parents unless they can prove that their brothers and unmarried sisters do not have enough income to support their parents.[7] In other words, married women are supposed to belong to the labour of their husband's families, and not to have an obligation to support their original families. Men are the main breadwinners at home. A similar situation can be found in private enterprises, where companies only offer marriage allowance, child allowance, dependent allowance or rent allowance to male workers (Yu et al., 1991: 72–81).

Marriage and pregnancy discrimination

Marriage and pregnancy discrimination is a popular issue in contemporary Taiwan. Many working women have been forced to resign after marriage or on becoming pregnant. Historically, this issue has been raised since the 1980s although many companies have had policies of marriage and pregnancy discrimination ever since they began to employ women. The possible reason why this was not a popular issue in the early years is that women themselves usually 'decided' to leave the labour force after marriage. At that time, married women belonged to the labour of their husband's families, so they could not decide whether or what kind of work they would do

In Taiwan, marriage discrimination is usually enforced by banks and museums, and pregnancy discrimination is common in the manufacturing, airline and transportation industries. Banks are especially notorious for marriage discrimination. This policy has been a social custom since Taiwan's colonial period, and almost all banks, including public banks, have followed this custom. The managers of these banks believed: *'the service attitude of single women is better than that of married women. Our customers would like to see young and vigorous women serve them.'* The manages also said: *'It is unbearable to see women workers with big bellies serving our customers'* (*China Times*, 1995). In fact, these banks wanted married women to leave because they hoped to keep vacancies open in case the relatives of their shareholders needed jobs and new staff might reduce their personnel costs. In the 1980s, some women workers began to go to court or to petition the government to protect their right to work. In Chapter 7, we will discuss how Taiwanese women struggle with marriage and pregnancy discrimination. Capitalist development has caused in some areas and forms of gender inequality, but it is still arguable whether the development of capitalism results in more oppression or emancipates women. We will discuss this issue in the next section.

Capitalism and women

Although Taiwan began to develop capitalism during the period of Japanese colonization, women in Taiwan streamed into industrial production after 1966, when the state led the development of the labour-intensive, export-oriented economy. The turning point for Taiwanese women entering the labour market was industrialization, while the turning points for women in many Western countries were the world wars. Although Taiwan also experienced wartime from the 1930s to the 1950s, and women were encouraged to play a more active role in the labour market, Taiwan was a peasant society at that time so the war did not push women to move outside their families. Moreover, employers needed female labour during the export-oriented stage not because male labour dried up but because female labour was cheaper. I doubt whether it is appropriate to apply the reserve army theory to the female labour force at that stage. A reserve army, according to Marx, was a tool to prevent workers bargaining up their wages and working conditions in times of labour shortages. 'Last in, first out' could contribute to the general situation of an industrial reserve army. However, as mentioned before, young women were the first target of employers, while young men found it difficult to find a job. Although the status of women workers remained inferior, women were the primary labour force of industrial production at that stage.

It is still an arguable issue whether the development of capitalism results in more oppression or emancipates women. Some scholars are optimistic about the changes in women's position after capitalist development because they claim that women have more freedom and economic power today. The reforms in legislation and politics subsequent to industrial capitalism have also improved women's status. On the other hand, pessimists, mainly Marxist feminists, think that women's status is even worse than before as they are now discriminated against both at home and in the workplace (Thomas, 1988).

It is also difficult to judge the impact of capitalist development on women in Taiwan because women's status is so very varied. In this section, I shall attempt to discuss this issue bearing in mind differences in marital status and working conditions (see Figure 4.15). Early on in the industrial period, parents in Taiwan sent their daughters to do unskilled and low paid work, sometimes far away from their homes, in order to support sons in the family through higher education (Arrigo, 1980; Gallin, 1984; Diamond, 1979). On the one hand, young girls were exploited by both capitalists and patriarchal families if they worked far away from their homes. On the other, they got a chance to escape the control of a patriarchal family. Although their status at home was still inferior to the males in the family, their contribution to the family economy let them win more

Figure 4.15   The changes of women's status by marital status and working condition

	Marital status	
Working condition	Single women	Married women
Work far from home	1. Their status at home does not change, but they have more freedom and autonomy 2. They have chances to receive more education and to make contact with the changing society. 3. They can control part of their earnings.	It is very rare for married women to work far from their families.
Stay at home, either as wage earners	1. Their status does not change and they do not have much autonomy 2. They cannot control their own income	1. Their status at home is higher than other married women, depends on how much money they earn. 2. They can usually control family economy and manage their own earnings.
Stay at home as unpaid family workers		Their status does not change.

autonomy and freedom, especially in decisions about marriage (Hu, 1985). They also had the opportunity to make contact with the changing society and to receive education in off-duty periods, which helped them find a better job as well as improve their status in the husband's family in the future. If single women stay at home, either working outside or remaining inside the family, their status usually does not change. They can control their own income only to a small extent. However, this situation has been changed recently since the economy in the average family has improved. More single working women can manage their own earnings. Even if they have to hand over their earnings to their parents, their parents usually transfer all the income into a dowry and even give them extra money to raise their marital prospects (Hu, 1985).

As far as married women are concerned, their ability to earn a salary beyond farm work enhances their status in marriage. In Taiwanese culture, married women are regarded as the labour of their husbands' families. In the past they had to hand over all their wages to their father-in-law, but nowadays most married working women can control their own earnings (Gallin, 1984). If a married woman works for the family business, she usually works as an unpaid worker. A lot of research has found that traditional division of the sexes was reproduced in family business. In a family business, the husband usually acts as the 'boss' who controls the power of decision-making and has to deal with buyers or main factories, while the wife usually works as a 'worker' or a 'secretary' who operates machines or deals with administrative matters (Lu, 1996; Li and Ka, 1994). The head of the family, either the husband or the father-in-law, controls all the labour in the family and all economic resource. It is evident that the status of married women at home has not changed much. On the contrary, they are now doubly exploited by both men and capitalists as Marxist feminists presupposed. Besides their traditional roles, such as farmwork, caring for the whole family and dealing with household matters, they have to sell their labour too. However, if a wife has more human resources, such as education, financial ability, transferable skills and work experience, she has more power in the decision-making process and is held in more respect by her family (Lu, 1996).

Thus the impact of the patriarchal family on women depends on whether they stay at home after participation in the labour market. In other words, women who work far from their families have more chance to get rid of the control of patriarchy. Moreover, although married women's ability to earn money is able to raise their status at home, they do not get as much benefit as single women do from industrialization. From this point of view, capitalist development and patriarchy can exist in tandem in some cases, such as married women. Conversely, the patriarchal family system may be fading for single women due to the development of capitalism.

The tendency to proletarianization in women's employment is significant in Taiwan, as shown in Figure 4.9. There is no doubt that more women in the labour market have to face a new relationship with capitalists. In peasant times, a father usually controlled all labour in the family. Since the whole family worked in the same economic unit, the father was able to control the family economy. Under such a situation, the father's authority was strong and other family members did not have much autonomy. Since industrialization, the younger generation no longer relies on income from farm work; they have their own income. Many fathers have relinquished their power over the family economy, and women's status has improved though their status is still lower than that of male family members (Hu, 1985). It seems that patriarchy is fading because of the development of capitalism, but some scholars are not so optimistic. Fan (1989) argues that the impact of export industries on women mirrors the approach presented by Elson and Pearon – women's inferior status in world market factors follows three steps: intensifying, decomposing and recomposing. After world market factories were introduced into Taiwan, women's economic value was intensified. Daughters were sent into factories as cheap labour under their father's authority, but they also got the chance to escape from the control of patriarchy. As the father's control decomposed gradually, another form of patriarchy was built up by managers in the workplace. After marriage, another form of patriarchy from their husbands dominates them again. Moreover, gender inequality and sexual division in the family seem to extend to the workplace. Women get different opportunities and treatment in the workplace, and their status is usually inferior to male workers

Many studies of female labour in Taiwan have focused on the export-oriented industries or the early situation in factories. However, the industrial structure has changed dramatically within the past thirty years. Many old industries, with poor working conditions and low wages, have been swept away to other developing countries. Today, half of all working women are employed in the rapidly growing service sector, and enter professional jobs in considerable numbers. Many of them have more autonomy in the workplace and a number even own their businesses. Women's status in the labour force is notably varied, and the impact of capitalist development on each woman is different. Moghadam said:

> For women, who historically have been the most disadvantaged social group, with a limited range of life-options, and an inability to act autonomously under long-standing patriarchal arrangement ... Development has differentiated women, but it has also provided them with a wider range of choices and activities.
>
> – Moghadam (1992: 246)

The development of capitalism usually lets a society accumulate wealth. Improving living standards among average people gave women greater opportunity and some expectation of receiving further education in order to accumulate more human capital, especially in a society like Taiwan where people respect education and literacy. Once women had more opportunity to make contact with the changing world and acquire knowledge to think more about their inferior status both at home and in the labour market, they have had more power to change their inferior status and have the state work for them.

In summary, this chapter has examined the relationship between capitalist development and women. Women in Taiwan streamed into the labour market after Taiwan developed its labour-intensive, export-oriented economy during the period 1966–73. At the commencement of industrialization, unmarried girls were the favourite labour of capitalists. Increased job opportunities offered women temporary work in factories before marriage. Married women seldom worked outside their families. Instead, some of them did family subsidiary work or worked unpaid in family businesses. After a period of rapid capital accumulation, living standards were improved. Women had more opportunities and for the first time an expectation of receiving formal education, especially after the state implemented nine-year compulsory education in 1968. Since the 1980s, more educated women have worked in the labour market as professionals or managers rather than as cheap labour. More married women have joined the labour force, and more women workers have flowed to the service sector.

Although the pattern of women employment has changed over the decades, there are two negative phenomena that we should bear in mind. One is the low labour force participation rate of women in Taiwan. A great number of Taiwanese women would not, or could not, join the labour force. The other is marriage and childcare, which is the main obstruction to women working. A great number of women leave their jobs after marriage or after having children, and married women's employment patterns are still very likely to be informal. Pre-school children are mainly cared for by their mothers. For the new generation, grandparents are the main substitutes for working mothers; childminders are also beginning to play more important roles. Other 'formal' types of childcare remain relatively unimportant; few firms provide childcare services.

The workplace produces another form of gender inequality. Women workers historically have lower wages and fewer opportunities for recruitment, promotion and receiving welfare than men in both public departments and private companies. The unequal treatment between genders has been directly related to the gender ideology. For instance, unequal welfare results from male breadwinner ideology; marriage and pregnancy discrimination are associated with male-dominated sexuality; fewer promotion opportunities are related to power models between genders. We may hope that the gender stereotype in work can be changed by the educational system. The improvement of educational opportunities has allowed more women to join the labour force and has reduced the wage differential with men, but it has not improved the situation of horizontal and vertical segregation between genders in the workplace. Men and women tend to work in different industries. However, it is doubtful whether women have enough autonomy to 'choose' their jobs, as upheld by human capital theory. In fact, many jobs are labelled as 'men's' or 'women's jobs' by employers, both in private companies and in government departments. Women can only 'choose' jobs that have been selected by employers

Women's experiences after capitalist development are not always the same, and depend on marital status and working condition. The status of married women has changed less than that of single women joining the labour force. The ability to earn money often let women have more autonomy at home, but this has not been the experience of women working at home. In addition to the discussion of capitalist development and the change in women's status, we cannot forget the increasing power of capitalism on the state machinery. Business is clearly an important actor in the government decision-making process. We should study the influence of business groups on state policies before moving to the next chapter.

Appendix: capitalists, business groups and state policy

Some corporatists take a negative view of business power as it may harm the achievement of a democratic government (Grant, 1987: 25). We cannot ignore the possible power of capital at this level of policy. Capitalists importantly depend on the structure power of the economy as discussed above, but also on the instrumental power of organized business. In this appendix, I do not attempt to prove how business groups affect public policies or their effectiveness. We will learn about this issue and about how the government responds to capitalists' demands from the case study of the GEEB in Chapter 7. My intention in this appendix is to show that business groups or businessmen have many formal and informal opportunities to express their opinions to the authorities. In addition, the complicated relations between the KMT government and capitalists should be observed as we focus on the relations between the state and working women.

To fully understand the current functions of business groups, we should start with the review of their historical background. In the Ching Dynasty, there were many commerce unions in Taiwan, with the power to control and integrate the economy. After Japan governed Taiwan, most of these unions were dismissed. During this period, business was controlled by a few big family firms and the Japanese government, so most Taiwanese were not interested in joining commerce unions. In the late-1920s, the Japanese government felt that it was necessary to organize firms and to control business for state development, so the government began to assist the setting up of commerce unions (Mei, 1993: 25–6). During this period, the political function of commerce unions was more meaningful than their economic functions. As far as the KMT government was concerned, when it controlled mainland China, it also led the foundation of business unions to mobilize businessmen. In 1915, the KMT passed a program which was called 'Promoting Businessmen's Movement,' that tried to organize businessmen to join the revolution (Mei, 1993: 20). In 1928, the KMT issued a resolution: people had freedom of organization, providing that it was under the instruction of the party and the supervision of the government (Ministry of the Interior, 1987: 294–5). After the civil war, most business unions stopped working. It was not until 1950 and the reformation of the KMT, that the KMT tried to organize business groups again. The former executive directors of business unions in China, who retreated to Taiwan with the KMT government, were assigned to set up the national **Business Promotion Association** (*Kung-Shang-Hsieh-Chin-Hui*). The two main organizers were the committees of the Business Movement Commission of the KMT party (Mei, 1993: 37–41). This group, with the purpose of fitting in with government decrees and being a medium between the government and people, was set up before the resurgence of the **National Industry Association** and the **National Commerce Association** and had been the leader group among business groups. By the late-1980s, many new capitalists had emerged and the leadership of those traditional business groups declined. Therefore, the KMT assisted another business group to set up, the **Business Research Association** (*Kung-Shang-Chien-Yen-Hui*), in order to maintain a close connection with young businessmen.[8] Generally speaking, after the Japanese colonization, major business groups have been set up for political purposes and under the control of the ruling government. These business groups have a diplomacy function, and share administrative work on business affairs with the government, such as export registration, quality inspection and overseas exhibitions. In 1981, for instance, the Premier also encouraged business groups to join the business affairs of the government: 'The government should reduce intervention in administrative trade work, which should transfer to business groups' (Ministry of the Interior, 1987: 315).

Capitalists also directly join the policy-making mechanisms, including the government and the ruling party. Thirteen out of 100 Presidential Consultants are heads of business enterprises, and three have a background in business (Journalist, 1996a: 91). In the new list of the Standing Committees of the KMT, there are three of business and two representatives of the economic departments. In comparison with one representative of labour, the executive director of the National Labour Union, capitalists can play a more important role in the policy-making process of the KMT (*Central Daily News*, 23/8/1998). Moreover, the Taiwanese negotiator, Cheng-Fu Ku, of 'China and Taiwan's Highest-level Meeting,' the highest level meeting between mainland China and Taiwan, is even a businessman.

In recent years, the way that capitalists intervene in the policy-making has become more varied. In the past, they primarily made contact with members of the Cabinet and leaders of the KMT. Since the political environment has changed, they have begun to give more consideration to the important roles of the Legislators. Business groups, such as the National Industry Association and the Business Research Association, have special commissions to communicate and to lobby Legislators. Many capitalists support candidates or join the electoral campaigns of Legislators. It is difficult to find out how many Legislators are supported by 'capitalists' from the data of Legislators. For instance, according to the records in the Legislative Yuan, we found that some famous millionaires registered their occupations as farmers. Nevertheless, according to the property lists reported by Legislators, 29 Legislators own property valued at over NT$100 m. Twenty-three of them are the members of the KMT, and six (out of 23) are designated by the KMT (Journalist, 1995a: 111). Many Legislators are members of business groups.

Business groups have many formal and informal opportunities to meet with the members of Cabinet. Formally, business groups will submit their suggestions to the government after their annual meetings. In the early years, this was a useful way for business groups to affect policies. Nowadays, business groups still provide occasional information and formal letters regarding special issues to the government to express their views (Chu and Hsieh, 1989: 81). Moreover, government departments often invite these groups to discuss new policies (Ku, 1983; *Central Daily News*, 28/1/1996). The members of Cabinet, especially economic officials, will attend the annual meeting of business groups. The National Industry Association also has a regular 'Lunch Meeting with Financial and Economic Ministers'.

Informally, businessmen have special 'Business Breakfast Meetings' (*Kung-Shang-Tsao-Tsan-Hui*) where all business groups will join together to exchange opinions. However, they usually invite the Vice-Premier, the Economic Minister and other important officials of economic departments to attend. These meetings have been a major bridge between the government and entrepreneurs for the informal exchange of opinions about policies (Journalist, 1996b: 97–8). Sometimes, individual business groups and large companies also invite or are themselves invited by economic officials to have 'breakfast' in order to discuss their investment cases. Sport is another method for businessmen and politicians to meet informally. There are many famous 'Golf Clubs' or 'Golf Competitions,' such as the 'Big Worm' (*Ta-Chung-Tui*), *Chih-Yuan-Tui* and the 'President's Championship' (*Teng-Hui-Pei*), which enable capitalists and politicians regularly to see each other (Journalist, 1996b: 98; 1996c: 71–2). Businessmen also own private clubs or luxury houses where they can chat with other businessmen and politicians in private. Some of these clubs and houses have become 'the information agency of politics' (Journalist, 1996d: 94) Through these informal activities, capitalists and politicians become friends, and sometimes support each other. In the 1996 President election, for instance, the Taiwan Plastics Business used advertisements to show its support for the KMT candidate, Lee Ten-Hui. The manager explained that 'I support him because we are friends, we often play golf together' (Journalist, 1995b: 76)

The relationship between capital and the ruling government is complicated. One of the reasons is that KMT itself owns many businesses; it is a large business enterprise. According to an official report, the net property of the KMT's businesses was NT$ 37 770 000 000, but the real value of these businesses is unknown. The KMT has a committee to manage these businesses. Many members of this committee are heads of big business enterprise in Taiwan and are in the list of 'Global Chinese Rich Men' (Journalist, 1995c: 14). Moreover, the principle of state capitalism introduced by Dr. Sun Yat-sen allows the state to own many businesses. In 1995, 16 per cent of all employed persons worked for state enterprises and government departments (Bureau of Small and Medium-sized Companies, 1996: 376). When a labour policy is discussed, the government will consider whether it can accept it. For instance, the Ministry of Personnel opposed the GEEB as the bill would affect the efficiency of civil servants (*Central Daily News*, 6/4/92). Lastly, blood ties make the relationship between capitalists and the ruling government more complicated. Many of them are relatives. In a society like Taiwan, which respects family relations, relations tied by blood make capitalists and politicians closer

   Judging by the background of business groups in Taiwan, their relationship with the KMT has been extremely close. They were not 'interest groups,' but 'external groups' of the KMT. The original purpose of their foundation was not to promote capitalists' interests but to promote the interests of the ruling party. Through those business groups, the KMT could control business for its own political purposes; simultaneously, capitalists can 'share' benefits by being close to political leaders. After democratization, the autonomy of these groups increased, so that they began to join various political mechanisms and express their opinions in various ways instead of contacting the Cabinet and the KMT only. We do not intend to measure the extent to which capitalists have affected policies. However, it is doubtful whether the ruling government can be an arbitrator between capital and labour as it owns a large business enterprise. Additionally, the friendship and blood ties between capitalists and the ruling party make the boundary between them blurred. Policy is not all about trade-offs between capital and government, but 'big business' is a privileged position.

5
Women's Movements and Women in the Policy-making System

Gender inequality has existed in Chinese society for over 2000 years, but women hardly ever questioned this situation until the twentieth century. Emerging in the 1970s, the civil women's movement in Taiwan has challenged gender regimes as well as women's policies. This chapter will review women's collective action and women's organizations after the establishment of the Republic of China, and focus on the history since the 1970s. As far as women's movements in Taiwan are concerned, there are two kinds of women's movements, which will be discussed individually, **official women's activities** and **civil women's movements**. In addition, we shall observe women's power in politics and the extent to which women's groups have access to the policy-making process.

Historical background

During the period of Japanese colonization, Taiwanese women already held collective actions. Historical documents show that women workers went on strike because of their inferior treatment. Poor working conditions, such as low pay, wage cuts and long working hours, were the major reasons for women workers to strike. Sometimes, the reason was bullying or sexual harassment from employers. According to reports in the *Taiwan People's Newspaper* (*Taiwan Ming Pao*), between 1921 and 1931 six strikes were started by women, and seven strikes by both men and women workers. Most of these strikes failed, except for two, which achieved their goals. The need for income usually forced the strikers to compromise with the capitalists (Yang, 1993: 263–315). However, four women strikers refused to make a concession to their employers after a united strike at six straw-bag factories in Kaohsiung. They established a straw-bag firm with the support of their families, and employed other unemployed women who had been bullied by their employers (Yang, 1993: 269).

As far as women's movements in mainland China under the KMT government are concerned, they were flourishing in the early twentieth century. Some women intellectuals joined the revolution led by Dr Sun Yat-sen, the father of the Republic of China. He promoted the 'women's movement' and encouraged women to devote themselves to the revolution. These women intellectuals set up women's organizations, issued journals, promoted educational opportunities across genders and organized women's troops. After the KMT came to power, women's troops were either dismissed or transferred to nursing work in the army. The original leaders of the women's troops began instead to promote women's political rights. In 1912, although Dr Sun Yat-sen had supported *gender equality*, the principle of gender equality was not written into the draft of the Constitution. The National Assembly also denied women's right to vote. So these women activists petitioned the President, Dr Sun Yat-sen, and led an attack on the Assembly for three days. After that, through the negotiation of Dr Sun Yat-sen, 'gender equality' was included in the draft Constitution (Pao, 1979: 292; Jayawardena, 1986: 182). At that time, the British Parliament was also discussing women's suffrage but did not approve it. British suffragettes sent their regards to their fellow women activists in China (Ku, 1988: 180).

In 1919, during the *May Fourth Movement*, a movement of cultural renaissance, the women's question became a national issue. Some feminists advocated that women should have an equal opportunity to participate in public spheres, such as education, the economy and politics. Many women's organizations were set up to promote women's political rights. They kept putting pressure on the KMT government to ensure that women's political rights were written into new legislation (Tan, 1952: 16–20). In spite of women's protests, political institutions still excluded women's representatives. For instance, the assembly election in Canton in 1913 was composed only of men (Jayawardena, 1986: 183). In 1923, the suffrage proposed was limited to educated men over 25 years (Ku, 1989: 103). At the national convention hold to discuss the Constitution in 1931, no women's representative was allowed to attend (Tan, 1952: 32).[1]

Although women's movements had been active in mainland China since the early twentieth century, there was no a systematic movement in Taiwan until 1987. As Taiwan had been a colony between

1895–1945, social movements have been forbidden under the circumstances. For instance, in 1925–27, Taiwanese women had tried to set up a women's group, but it was soon dismissed by the Japanese government. After the KMT government retreated to Taiwan, it became more conservative and authoritative in order to maintain social order. Since 1943, the establishment of non-governmental organizations has been restricted by the *Wartime Non-governmental Organization Law* (1943–86); social movements have been prohibited by *Martial Law* (1948–87) since 1948. These two laws have protected the absolute political superiority of the KMT government. After the limitations of the Wartime Non-governmental Organization Law were lifted, women's groups were able to be established formally and to march for their requirements legally. Since then, women's movements have become more systematic in Taiwan.

The effort of early feminists in mainland China are demonstrated in the Constitution, for example the article on gender equality and the reserved seats for women's representatives in elections. In Taiwan, some women activists asserted that women's movements in China had no connection with women's movements in Taiwan (*Taiwan Li Pao*, 20/3/1995). It is true that the emergence of women's movements in Taiwan was not an extension of women's movements in China. However, we should bear in mind that many women's rights in politics and law were the achievement of early feminists in China. Taiwanese women, for instance, have gained the right to vote without any movement. After the KMT government controlled Taiwan, its policies also had an effect there. Furthermore, current official women's organizations were extended from the KMT's experiences of organizing women when it controlled mainland China. These organizations have played an important role in ensuring the KMT's superiority, and have influenced women's lives before 1987. Before a review of civil women's movements in Taiwan, we should observe how the ruling party controlled women.

Official women's activities and organizations

'Official' women's organizations were established for the same purpose as the business groups. They were instructed by the ruling party, and could be regarded as 'external groups' of the KMT. In order to mobilize women during wartime, the KMT established a commission for women's movements in 1938, and assisted each level of local government to set up a women's association. In 1938, Madame Chiang Kai-shek also began to integrate women's groups. After the KMT retreated to Taiwan, a **Chinese Women against the Communist Party and Russia League** (hereafter **Women's League**) was established under Madame Chiang's leadership in 1950. Every city government, county government, school and organization was instructed to set up a branch, led by the wife of the leader of the institution. For instance, the wife of a mayor was naturally the leader of a branch. Every female staff and family member was invited to join the union. The main work of this league was service for the Army and their families (Fan, 1990: 41). Madame Chiang often led members of the Women's League to sew clothes for soldiers, to set up nurseries for soldiers' children, to help widows and orphans in military communities, and to send women's greetings to the army. After democratization, the Women's League faced a big challenge since more and more city mayors were no longer members of the KMT. The DPP (Democratic Progressive Party) mayors either forced the Women's League to move out of local government or asked the organizations to substitute their original leaders for their wives (*China Daily News*, 7/1/1990).

Another type of 'official' women's organization is the **Women's Society (Fu-Nu-Hui).**' In 1946, the **Taiwan Provincial Women's Society** was set up; each level of local government (including city, county, town, village, administrative division) was instructed to set up a branch, usually attached to local government. Each branch of the administrative division had a convener who had contact with and mobilized women in each household. Branch leaders were appointed by the ruling party. The activities of these women's societies were designed by the **Central Women's Department** of the KMT, and their funds for operation have been subsidized by the ruling party and local government. They were not set up for promoting women's rights, but as executive units of the KMT without any autonomy (Fan, 1990: 43). In 1984, the Women's Society was still the largest and most organized women's group, with over 300 branches and 200 000 members.

According to the plan of the Central Women's Department, official women's activities can be classified into four stages. The work aim of the first stage, from 1954–56, was to establish various women's organizations. The second stage, 1957–59, was to explore women's needs. In the third stage, 1960–61, the Department assisted local organizations to implement women's policies. In the fourth stage, 1962–67, the working aim was to extend women's organizations into the family and to mobilize housewives to join the push for national development (Chu, 1968: 58). The main work of the Central Women's Department was fitting in with the KMT's decrees, but it also led the Women's

Society to provide services for women, such as aiding adopted daughters and prostitutes, being match-makers, introducing domestic work or training women to do subsidiary work at home (KMT Central Women's Department, 1979).

The husbands of the leaders of the two official women's organizations usually held senior positions in politics or business, e.g. mayors, Ministers. These women's organizations were called *Ladies Clubs*. The leadership of the leaders did not come from elections, but from their husbands' power. Their members usually use their husbands' surnames as a symbol of respect, which is an unusual phenomenon in present Taiwan. These organizations mainly emphasized women's traditional roles instead of challenging male-superior culture. In addition to these two types of women's organizations, there were also other women's groups, including professional societies and branches of international organizations and churches, before the lifting of the Wartime Non-governmental Organization Law. However, they were women's clubs rather than pressure groups.

The emergence of civil women's movements

Official women's organizations had been used by the KMT government as a tool to prevent the foundation of civil women's groups. Under the regulations of the Wartime Non-governmental Organization Law, each area could only have one group with the same purpose. Official women's organizations had used to occupy the only 'quota.' Before 1987, none of women's organization for promoting women's rights had been allowed to establish themselves.

Official women's activities cannot be regarded as being part of the 'women's movement'. Taiwanese scholars claim that women's movements in Taiwan started from the 1970s, which is called **civil women's movements** (Ku, 1988, 1989; Chang, 1995). The civil women's movement in Taiwan can be classified chronologically into three phases: the pioneering phase (1974–79), the awakening phase (1982–86) and the post-martial-law phase (1987–present) (Ku, 1989) (refer to Table 5.1).

In the first phase, the pioneer, Lu Hsiu-Lien, tried to introduce the notion of gender equality to traditional Taiwanese society.[2] She developed a series of ideas and active strategies for women's movement, and then published a theoretical book, *New Feminism*, which was soon banned by the authorities on the grounds that it tried to violate social custom. As society could not accept feminism, she emphasized the labour division between genders and the need of the state to utilize the female labour force. Due to the limitation of Martial Law, she failed to

Table 5.1 Comparison of the three phases of the civil women's movements in Taiwan

	1st phase (1974–79)	2nd phase (1982–86)	3rd phase (1987–present)
Strategy	spreading ideas compromise	Symposia compromise	collective action legitimization
Membership	intellectuals	middle-class	middle-class + few working-class
Organization	failed	single organization, covering various issues	variety and specialization
Ideology	criticizing male-superior phenomenon	raising women's consciousness	various ideologies, but all concerned with women's rights
External environment	not accepted	suspicious	tolerant

organize women to join women's movements. After that, Lu found that it was useless to struggle for women's rights in a society that ignored human rights, so she gradually transferred to the democratic movement.

Although Lu did not let the women's movement in Taiwan become a systematic movement, her theory encouraged Taiwanese women to take action against their inferior status. **In the second phase**, Lee Yuan-Chen, one of Lu's followers, and some women elites have issued a monthly magazine, the *Awakening*, to 'raise women's consciousness, encourage self-development and voice feminist opinions' (Ku, 1988: 182). They adopted 'raising women's consciousness' as their main objective, and tried to get public support by holding many conferences to discuss new gender relationships but avoided using any feminist terms.

At that time, more and more people could not put up with the side-effects of industrialization. Well-educated women, especially middle-class housewives, were encouraged to join the new consumer movements and environmental movements (Hsiao, 1989). According to the research of Meyer and Whittier (1994), social movements often indirectly influence each other by way of their effects. In the Taiwanese women's movement, this seems to have been the case. Those women who were involved in the early stages of consumer and environmental movements later played an important role in civil women's movements. However, women activitists lacked both internal and external resources in this phase, such as financial support and participants, so that their achievements were limited.

In the third phase, people began to question the authoritarianism in Taiwan. The weakness of state autonomy, the universality of education, and the effects of international democratization prompted the emergence of social force in Taiwan. Social movements were established to push the government to solve social problems associated with autocracy and industrialization. Since 1987, after the lifting of Martial Law, many civil women's organizations have been established formally. Women's movements in Taiwan are no longer operated by a person or by a small group of women, and have transferred to a multi-organizational phase. 'Horizontal fragmentation' became a phenomenon among women's organizations, but there was no leading group. Each organization has its special work direction and attracts particular kind of members. These new women's groups usually shared personnel and took collective action in association with each other. The same phenomenon also happened among the official women's organizations. However, the two systems seldom cooperated with each other. Additionally, civil women's organizations seldom developed local branches, but had just one central organization which was often located in a city. One reason for the lack of systematic organization was the shortage of resource and personnel. As a result, women in rural areas seldom joined the campaigns of the contemporary women's movement in Taiwan. 'It seems that the roar of women's groups is loud,' said Solicitor Yu, 'but the number of members is extremely small.'

Different women's organizations also had different attitudes towards women's movements. For instance, the **Homemakers' Union and Foundation** opposes holding female-centred ideology for women's movements; whilst the **Awakening Foundation** insists this is the right way to pursue women's movements even in the early stages (Journal of China Discussion Group, 1988: 16–17).[3] Moreover, the **Progressive Women' s League** thinks that women's movements should not refuse to cooperate with men or be involved in politics; while the **Warm Life Association for Women**, which is composed of divorced women, asserts that men are always the chief enemy of women's movements.

In Taiwan, women's groups have been used by the political parties for their own interests. It was not until the emergence of civil women's movements that women began to bring their struggles to the political agenda. The ability of women to make the state work for them is an inevitable result of the sharing of political resources. The extent to which women in political and bureaucratic spheres will affect the gender senses of state policies.

Access to the policy-making systems

When we analyze women and political power, a preliminary categorization of these might be as follows (Eisenstein, 1990: 87–8):

1. Bureaucratic/individual: entering the bureaucracy of government at policy-making level.
2. Bureaucratic/structural: creating new structures within government to benefit women.
3. Legal reform: introducing new legislation, or revising existing legislation to benefit women.
4. Political participation in a leadership role: running for some form of political office. For example, seeking to become a mayor or member of a legislature.

5. Alternative structures: creating a feminist organization outside the mainstream of existing political and administrative structures, such as women's refuges or rape crisis centres.

In this section, based on the above categories, I will discuss the extent to which women have access to the policy-making process in Taiwan.

Women in the bureaucracy of government

In Taiwan, people can enter the bureaucracy of government by way of examination, recruitment, or appointment. At every level of the government, appointments, usually heads of departments, can be made by Ministers or mayors. Generally speaking, to become a public servant, one needs to pass national examinations. There are many kinds of examinations to recruit civil servants; two are very formal: one for non-commissioned officials (general examination), the other for commissioned officials (high-level examination). Only those who pass the latter examination can become heads of departments. As discussed in Chapter 4, more women have become high-level officials in recent years (see Figure 4.16). Also, the percentage of women who have passed the high-level entrance examination has increased sharply (see Figure 5.1). Although the proportion of women in high-level positions is much lower than that of men, it is expected that this proportion will increase along with the increase of women in government.

Figure 5.1 Women as percentage of those who passed the high-level examination of civil servants in Taiwan, 1966–95

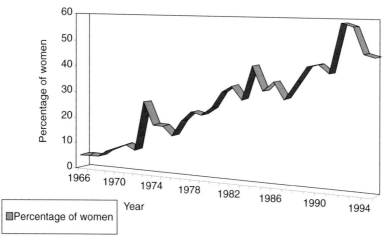

Source: Department of Examination (1996: Table 9).

As far as women Ministers are concerned, in 1990, the first women Minister, the Treasury Minister, was nominated in Taiwan. Since then, there have been on average three women Ministers in the Cabinet, including a women Minister of Health and Minister of the Interior. Today, although the Premier has mentioned the possibility of increasing the number of women Ministers, there are still only three women 'Ministers' in the Cabinet, one in the Commission of Culture, another in the Commission of Physical Education, and the other in the Commission of Fair Trade. Since the 1990s, when the Premier nominated new members of the Cabinet, gender has been a popular issue. So, under public pressure, the Premier had to consider the gender balance in the Cabinet. However, except in the Ministry of the Interior, women were seldom nominated to be heads of important departments. The female former Minister of the Interior was nominated after a series of crimes associated with women's safety. One hundred thousand people, most of them first-time demonstrators, marched on Taipei's streets to ask for improvement in public security. Therefore, the Premier nominated a women Minister of the Interior to stop the public outcry. After ten months, she was dismissed for no particular reason and before anything had been achieved, thus becoming the shortest term Minister of the Interior. This event reveals that the KMT government is reluctant to share political power with women.

Until now, there has been no special commission on women's issues in the central government. In the Taipei City Government, however, the *Commission for Promoting Women's Rights* was established under a DPP Mayor. Since 1995, each local government has also set up an *Evaluative Commission on Employment Discrimination*, which can deal with cases of gender discrimination in employment. Solicitor Yu, a committee member of the Evaluative Commission on Employment Discrimination in Taipei, observes that the new institute is noticeably effective in eliminating gender discrimination in the labour force. Many women's refuges and women's advice centres are being established.

Political participation

In the early twentieth century, women sought political participation through women's suffrage. Suffrage was regarded as a tool for women to enter the political system and to affect policy-making. However, the majority of women voters in Taiwan have not used their voting rights to affect policies. According to Liang's reports, more women (73 per cent) were unconcerned about the results of election than men (61 per cent). More women did not go to vote, or try to understand candidates' political views (Liang and Ku, 1995: 108). Furthermore, women were more easily affected by their husbands and families with regard to voting behaviour. They were too easily affected by vote buying (Liang, 1988: 8). Research on women's voting behaviour demonstrates that more women are unconcerned about politics. They lack political knowledge and experience, and fail to show their power through the ballot box. However, there is no difference between voting behaviour of men and women who are young, unmarried, with high educational attainment and in the white-collar class (Liang and Ku, 1995: 109). Since the educational achievement of women has been improved in recent years, there should be more women voters showing independent and rational voting behaviour. Politicians in Taiwan need to pay more attention to these women. Moreover, it is not surprising that more political manifestos mention caring issues since this is a common problem among married career women, who are more concerned about politics and know how to use their electoral power.

Concerning women candidates in elections, the Constitution declares that representative elections should reserve a certain percentage of positions for women.[4] The reserved proportion of women representatives in each election varies, from ten to 25 per cent. In the early stages of democratic politics, this system was extremely important in term of encouraging women to enter the political arena. In the 1940s, the number of female nominees was never more than that of reserved representatives. From the 1950s to 1970s, the number of female nominees was slightly higher than that of reserved representatives, but the percentage of women winners stayed at around 15 per cent in every election. Women won elections that had no proportion reserved for women (Chou, 1987: 18). In the 1980s, increasing numbers of women stood for election, and more women won elections without the protection of the proportional representation system. Women also began to stand as magistrates and in mayoral elections. In 1985, two mayors were female. In the 1990s, the increase in female candidates has been noticeable partly because more representatives were needed. However, the number of female nominees has not increase as much as expected (Ministry of the Interior, 1993d: 278–81). Today women are still the minority in the political arena (see Table 5.2). In 1997, the Revised Constitution regulated that 25 per cent of non-elected party representatives of the National Assembly should be female. Women's groups, including the *Central Women's Department* of the KMT, tried to increase the proportion of reserved representatives from ten per cent to 25 per cent in all kind of elections during the discussion period leading up to the Revised Constitution but they were unsuccessful (*Central Daily News*, 19/2/1997).

Table 5.2 Women nominees elected in Taiwan in the 1990s

unit: person

Year	Items	Total	Women	Percentage of women	No. of reserved representation
1991	Members of the National Assembly	325	42	12.9	19
1992	Legislators	161	17	10.6	10
1994	Members of the Taiwan Provincial Assembly	79	16	20.3	9
1994	Members of the Taipei Municipal Assembly	52	12	23.1	5
1994	Members of the Kaohsiung Municipal Assembly	44	6	13.6	5
1994	Magistrates and Mayors	23	1	4.3	0
1994	Members of Hsien and City Councils	824	128	15.2	94
1994	Heads of villages and towns	309	6	1.9	0
1994	Representatives of villages and towns	6 317	937	14.8	0

Source: derived from Liang and Ku (1995: 100).

As far as the different political parties are concerned, women politicians in the opposition parties are more active. For instance, the DPP has three female mayors; while no female members of the KMT have become mayors. The number of female candidates nominated by the KMT has usually only equaled the number of reserved representatives in each election (Liang, 1988: 11). Moreover, it was not until 1993 that the KMT nominated one female candidate to join the mayoral election. Furthermore, in 1997, the DPP passed an article that 25 per cent of party nominees should be female.[5] In comparison with the opposition parties, the KMT tends to be conservative in terms of promoting women to participate in political systems although it has more political resources to achieve this.

Women activists of civil women's groups, unlike businessmen, seldom stood in elections by themselves. Until now, no female candidate has stood for election in the name of civil women's groups. In the National Assembly election, there is a quota reserved for representatives of women's groups, but these places are dominated by official women's organizations. Although there are two women's groups and one women's political party which especially focus on political participation, they are inactive in the current political arena. In 1989 and 1992, women groups issued their own manifesto. In 1991, some women's groups announced their support for a female candidate in the National Assembly election (Liang and Ku, 1995: 118–19). In recent years, some liberal female Legislators also cooperated with the action of women's groups. However, compared with businesses, it seems that women are only in the peripheral sector of politics.

Lastly, in Taiwan, many women politicians who stand for election come from political families. They stand for election for the continuation of the political power in their families. Many women politicians of the DPP are the wives of male politicians who are or have been in the political wilderness and cannot join political action. Their husbands have great influence on their performance in politics. Therefore, these two types of women politicians still play a dependent role. Few women have stood for election on their own initiative and platform.

Legal and system reform

In Taiwan, legal reform has been the main method adopted by women's groups to intervene in the policy-making process. Since 1984, women's groups have tried to directly affect the enactment of legislation (see Table 5.3). In the second phase of civil women's movements, women's groups only petitioned the Legislative Yuan to monitor the

Table 5.3 Important activities and consequences of civil women's movements in Taiwan

Time	Women's groups	Methods	Issues	Consequences
1984	*Awakening* and other 6 women's groups	Petition	The passing of abortion articles in the *Eugenic Protection Law*, especially in cases where the pregnancy will jeopardize the mother's mental health or family life.	Partial success
1985	*Awakening* and YWCA		Reviewing the patriarchal articles of the Civil Code	Failure
1987 1988 1993	*Rainbow Project* and different kinds of non-government groups	1. March 2. Jog (1993)	Protecting child prostitutes	The problem has become a public issue. Special action has been launched.
1990	*Awakening*	Drafting legislation	Introducing the *GEEB*	Proceeding
1990 to 1997	*Women's Rescue Foundation* and universities' societies	Various activities	Against sexual harassment and sexual violence	In 1997, the *Preventive Law for Sexual Crime* was issued. In 1998, the *Preventive Law for Family Violence* was issued.

Table 5.3 **Important activities and consequences of civil women's movements in Taiwan** (*continued*)

Time	Women's groups	Methods	Issues	Consequences
1993 to 1998	*Awakening*	Drafting legislation	Reviewing the patriarchal articles in the Family Chapter	Partial success, except matrimonial property
1994 1995	*Pink Collar Union* and other women's groups	1. March 2. Petition 3. Making a stand	Against marriage and pregnancy discrimination in the workplace	Partial success though such discrimination is still going on

enactment of the Eugenic Protection Law, which protects unborn children. In the third phase, women's groups were positively involved in the policy-making process. The *Awakening* began to introduce new legal systems for women by way of drafting the GEEB and the family law revision of the Civil Code. Some issues raised by civil women's movements have never been discussed in public, such as sexual harassment and gender equal employment. Other issues have existed for many years but the state has never tried to solve them – these include the problem of child prostitutes and unreasonable articles in family law. It is, of course, difficult to measure the impact of women's movements at the level of policy. However, the most important thing is that women's movements have raised some important issues, and the state has had to consider women's policies under pressure from women's movements. Moreover, women's groups as pressure groups express their requests during the enactment of legislation. Legal systems are no longer dominated by men.

It is difficult to define the impact of social movements at the level of policy. In Western countries, many policies (such as gender equal pay and equal treatment, maternity rights, and the provision of childcare service) coincided with the demands which made by women's movements. However, Lovenduski (1986: 100) claims that similar policies have also been adopted in countries where no women's movement has existed, such as Sweden and the USSR. It is possible that the changes in the pattern of women's employment and the demands of working women alters women's policies sooner or later, even without pressure from women's movements (Lovenduski, 1986: 284). Many scholars in Western countries believe that the major effect of the women's movement in the 1970s is a change in consciousness. Affected by this change, new policies have been introduced (Charles, 1993: 243; Gelb, 1990). In Taiwan's case, the women's movement is a touchstone to push state action. Further discussion takes place in the case study of the GEEB in Chapter 7.

Trade unions: an alternative?

Traditionally, research has emphasized the roles of trade unions in promoting women's rights in the labour market. However, in the case of Taiwan, it is unclear whether trade unions have been important actors in terms of promoting equal employment between genders. Trade unions have been developed for political purposes, similar to the establishment of women's groups and business groups. Since 1950, the KMT government has positively assisted in the establishment of trade unions for the purpose of social control and political stability. Setting up trade unions needed the ruling party's permission. Otherwise, the government would not dare to issue them a licence; it would delay issuing a licence to self-organized union and instruct the employer to bring forward a parallel application (Lee, 1992: 117).

> In a trade union election, the sub-branch of the party should provide a list of the candidates for directors, supervisors, executive directors, and executive supervisors to the party. On the approval of the party, the administrative department and the employer, the list should be submitted to the chief committee member. (The procedure of cadre election.)
>
> – The Trade Department of the KMT (1976: 41–2)

In short, the top ranks of the trade unions are under the control of the ruling party, the administrative department and the employer. In addition to the function of controlling labour movements, trade unions also have economic and diplomacy functions. They discuss with employers how to increase work efficiency, and have contacts with international labour organizations (Lee, 1992: 64). During elections, they are also an important source of votes for the ruling party.

When the KMT government still ruled China, the Communists developed their power through trade unions. After the KMT government retreated to Taiwan, it employed restrictive policies towards unions to hinder their ability to unify workers in order to ensure political superiority.

> The establishment of labour unions should be under the control of the party. Otherwise, the same story [the experience of losing China] will be repeated.
>
> – The Trade Department of the KMT (1964: 127)

First, under Martial Law, strikes were not permitted. Unions could not organize workers to take action against their exploitative working conditions and win concessions. Secondly, legislation regulated the number of workers required to set up a trade union. All workers were made to join trade unions, which made it impossible for large numbers of workers to improve their situation through collective bargaining. Thirdly, the establishment of area unions is prohibited. This regulation isolated labour in individual factories, making it difficult for workers to realize their common positions (Gallin, 1990: 188). Fourthly, the top ranks of trade unions were occupied by workers who were close to the employer or the KMT. Many joined trade unions for their own political purpose rather than for improving workers' benefits. Finally, many workers did not trust their trade unions. In a survey, 73 per cent of workers felt let down by their trade unions' executives (Lee, 1992: 126). Another survey showed that 50 per cent of workers would solve their conflicts with employers by themselves; only 22 per cent would ask their trade unions for help (Lin, 1987: 8).

Since the mid-1980s, more self-organized unions have been established, and the ruling party has lost the control of some trade unions (Lee, 1991: 48). More 'external system' labour organizations have been established. Moreover, more unions have adopted collective action to improve their working conditions or to get reasonable wages and redundancy payments. However, almost none of the action was to improve gender discrimination or focused on gender issues. To sum up, trade unions in Taiwan have been established under the control of the ruling party for political purposes. The legislation has also limited the development and functions of trade unions. They have had weak autonomy in terms of promoting workers' benefits, and could not get their members' trust.

In conclusion, this chapter reviews the history of women's movements in Taiwan and their influence in state policies. Although gender equality was trumpeted by the revolutionary party before it came to power, even after the foundation of the new government, women still needed to struggle for their political and legal rights. The efforts of early women activists in China allowed Taiwanese women to gain suffrage without collective action. The network of the *Women's Society* and *Women's League* allowed the ruling party to mobilize the majority of women, especially during elections. They could be regarded as the product of politics and patriarchy. No serious women's issue has been touched upon, they only emphasized the value of feminine virtues and encouraged women to sacrifice themselves for the state. Since the 1980s, civil women's groups began to ask the state to respect their rights and take action to challenge male-dominated culture. In recent years, they gradually transferred, involving themselves in the policy-making process and becoming pressure groups in the political arena. We have also found several phenomena in terms of women in politics:

1. It is expected that more women will become the heads of government departments as more women pass the top-level entrance examination for civil servants. New structures within government for

women's benefits have been created; reform is mainly in local government. Moreover, the number of women Ministers is extremely low, and they are often in less powerful departments.

2. Since the 1980s, more women have stood for election, but the total number of female nominees has not increased as much as expected. In other words, women's participation in elections has been limited even if more women are interested in politics. One possible reason is that many women are unconcerned about politics. Their voting behaviour is easily affected by their families and vote buyers. They fail to show their power through the ballot box, and to pressurize candidates into concern about women's issues. Women activists of civil women's groups seldom stand in elections by themselves, but in recent years they have tried to increase the quota reserved for women representatives to 25 per cent in every election, which ought to improve women's political participation.

3. Civil women's groups mainly focus on legal and system reform. They would like to act as pressure groups rather than have access to the legislature. Many issues that they have raised have caught the public's attention, and some get state support.

4. Trade unions are historically weak in Taiwanese society. They have been controlled by the employer, the administrative unit and the ruling party, with limited functions. Since the mid-1980s, more self-organized unions have been set up, and some trade unions have no longer been controlled by the KMT. The reform of trade unions is taking off, but women have been absent in the reform.

It seems that Taiwanese women only participate in the peripheral sector of politics. They do not stream into politics even after democratization. To make the state work for them, women's groups usually cooperate with women politicians to achieve their goals. They also tend to use their power vis-à-vis the media to put pressure on the state and to influence the political agenda. However, women still lack the political experience and training to demonstrate their power. After reviewing the power of patriarchal culture, capitalism and women's collective action, we should move on to discuss the changes in state policies under the influence of women's power.

6
Social Welfare and State Policies

> Gender relations cannot be understood apart from the state, politics and policy. Welfare has been a key area for their [scholars'] investigations of the state's role in reproducing gender order.
>
> – Orloff (1996: 3)

As discussed in Chapter 2, the intervention of state policies has a strong direct and indirect influence on gender relations. Nowadays, women must face a new relationship with the state, especially those women in the labour market. Therefore, it is interesting to see how far state policies intervene in the utilization of the female labour force and how the state copes with the traditional patriarchal family system under the development of capitalism. Since different states have different impacts on gender relations and on women's opportunities to participate in the labour market, this chapter aims to discuss the changes of state policies on working women, which will lead to a better understanding of the relations between the state and women.

As far as women's role in the labour market is concerned, there are four kinds of policies which affect women's opportunity to participate in the labour market. First, **the provision of social welfare for women**. Socialist feminists regard the welfare state as a social system to support the family system; radical feminists think that the aim of welfare is to keep men in a position of dominance and privilege. We can consider this issue from an analysis of welfare provision in Taiwan. Secondly, **employment policies** indicate how the state utilizes the female labour force and whether it encourages women to participate in the labour market. Thirdly, the state may have **protective legislation and equal opportunities policies** for women workers. The emphasis on the former is placed on protecting women as weak workers and mothers, while the latter seeks to provide equal environment for both male and women workers. Lastly, **care policies**, including policies on childcare and care for other family members, also affects women's opportunity to participate in the labour market. The last policy helps working women reconcile their roles in work and at home. In the following sections, I would like to present the operation of these policies in Taiwan.

When considering each kind of policy, except the first policy, we will analyze the change of state policies in chronological order. The analysis of policy will include legislation, the pronouncement and constitution of the KMT government, and related measures. Secondly, the policies of the two main opposition parties in Taiwan, the DPP and the New Party, are examined. The DPP, founded in 1986, was a representative opposition group even before the lifting of Martial Law. This party has to some extent affected state policies in the past ten years. The New Party, which split from the KMT in 1994, is a conservative party and on the far Right. Compared with the DPP, the structure of the New Party is not so mature. The 'White Paper on Policies' of the New Party represents the stand of the party, but is not a constitution and cannot be regarded as a definite commitment to the future action of the party. The opposition parties, however, play a more important role nowadays, as the KMT no longer holds an advantageous position in the Legislative Yuan.[1] So it is necessary to take the policies of opposition parties into account when we review state policies on working women. Finally, practical actions taken by the state, including their output and outcome, are discussed in this chapter as a supplementary indicator. 'Policy' usually means a proposal or a set of proposals carrying commitment to future actions (Levin, 1997: 20). Nevertheless, it would be easy to come to an incorrect conclusion if we only take account of policies on paper. The state in Taiwan may have fruitful policies but often fails to put the policies into practice. Even if the state actually implements some policies, only few people benefit from them. The analysis of policy may represent the changing ideology of the state, but may not be a good evidence of past, present or future actions.

Welfare provision for women

Welfare provision for the family and working women is important in analyzing the extent to which women can choose to stay at home as full-time carers or join the labour market as workers, although the welfare system in Taiwan is severely underdeveloped. Feminist analysis of the welfare state has seldom focused on welfare expenditure, while mainstream research usually downplayed services. In this section, therefore, analysis will cover social insurance schemes, welfare expenditure and service for women to form a picture of women's access and women's entitlement to benefits.

To begin with, it may be helpful if we briefly present the characteristics of the Taiwanese welfare system to see if women are able to get their fair share of society's resources. We shall start with a review of occupational welfare. We may find that employment-based welfare offers the best benefits in Taiwan. One strategy of feminists is to promote gender equality through financial independence. However, can women have equal access to benefits if they join the labour market? It is worth finding out. Moreover, welfare expenditure on women has increased sharply in recent years, but it is also important to examine what the state's means by 'women's welfare.'

Occupational welfare

When discussing whether state policies offer women enough flexibility to choose between paid and unpaid work, there are two kinds of welfare provision we should consider: those which support women to stay at home and to take care of their families, and those which attract women to join the labour force. Research in Britain and other European countries has often used various indicators to evaluate the degree of family support by the state, such as family allowance and child benefit. However, it is difficult to use those indicators to evaluate welfare provision in Taiwan since few of them have been adopted. As discussed in Chapter 3, the state's action to sustain the family system and to keep married women at home has been through the educational and legal systems instead of the welfare system. The only universal welfare scheme available to people in unpaid work is National Health Insurance (hereafter NHI). Apart from that, there is no child benefit, childcare allowance, care allowance, lone parent benefit, non-employment maternity benefit, etc.

Although 'women's rights to welfare are based on their roles as mothers,' as stated in the Constitution, the reality does not follow this basic national principal. On the contrary, occupational welfare is developing well. Social security system is based on industrial contribution and covers family dependants. Women can approach welfare with entitlements as workers or as dependants. In this section, the main forms of occupational welfare for women workers will be discussed: social insurance, maternity benefits, parental leave and family leave.

Social insurance

In Taiwan, the lack of universal non-contributory benefits makes social insurance benefits the only alternative to social security. The benefits from social insurance are particularly important because of the insufficient provision of state welfare in Taiwan. Through social insurance, women can get maternity pay or free medical treatment during childbirth via their entitlements as workers or as wives. They can claim old age benefits as workers, and widows' benefits or pensions as wives.

Social insurance and employees' benefit systems in Taiwan are complicated. Workers are required to join different insurance systems according to their occupation. This requirement could be regarded as a means of restricting the mobility of workers, with an element of social control.[2] Thus, occupational benefit systems in Taiwan encourage employees to work for the same employers. For example, workers in private companies are eligible to claim old age payments from their employers only if they have been in service with the same employers for over 25 years. Also, employees' working history and the benefits accruing cannot be split between two insurance systems. For instance, if civil servants transfer to private firms, their working experience in public departments cannot be accepted by the Labour Insurance system.

There are two ways in which government employees, military servicemen, teachers in public schools and labourers can claim disability, death, or old age benefits: one from the insurance system and the other from the employer. As shown in Table 6.1, before the three principle insurance systems were introduced, Labour, Military, and Government Employees' Insurance, government employees, military

Figure 6.1   Women's entitlements under social insurance systems in Taiwan, 1994

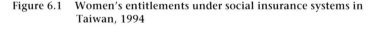
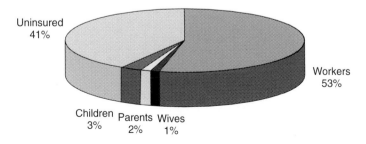

132

Table 6.1 Histories of social insurance and employees' benefit systems, women's entitlement and the percentage of the female population covered in Taiwan ++

Insurance systems and kinds of benefits	Start year	Women's entitlement	Percentage of women population covered, 1994
Government Employees' Compensation Law (D)	1943	dependant	–
Government Employees' Retirement Law (O)	1943	worker	–
Teaching and Administrative Staffs of Public Schools Compensation Law (D)	1944	dependant	–
Teaching and Administrative Staffs of Public Schools Retirement Law (D)	1944	worker	–
Military Servicemen's Compensation Law (D)	1949	dependant	–
Labour Insurance (MHIOD)	1950	worker	42.54
Military Servicemen's Insurance (IOD) +++	1950	+	+
Government Employees' Insurance (MHIODF) +++	1958	worker	2.11
Retired Govern. Employees' Insurance (MHIDF)	1965–85	worker	–
Insurance for Teaching and Administrative Staffs of Private Schools (MHIOD)	1980	worker	0.22
Health Insurance for Govern. Employees' Dependants	1982	wife	1.22
	1989	parent	1.48
	1992	children	2.73
Labour Standards Law (IOD)	1984	workers	–
Health Insurance for Retired Govern. Employees, and their spouses	1985	worker / wife	+

**Table 6.1 Histories of social insurance and employees' benefit systems, women's entitlement and the percentage of the female population covered in Taiwan ++   *(continued)*

Insurance systems and kinds of benefits	Start year	Women's entitlement	Percentage of women population covered, 1994
Health Insurance for Retired Teaching and Admin. Staffs of Private Schools and their spouses	1985	worker wife	+
Farmers' Insurance (MHID)	1985	worker	8.40
Representatives' Insurance	1989	worker	0.08
Health Insurance for the dependants of Teaching and Admin. Staffs of Private Schools	1990	wife	0.04
	1991	parent	0.06
	1992	children	0.13
Total			59.01

M = maternity benefits, H = health benefits, I = disability benefits, O = old age benefits, D = death benefits or widows' benefits, F = dependants' funeral benefits.

Note: + The numbers are very small.

++ There are some other insurance systems for special occupations excluded from this analysis.

+++ The insurance systems have their own hospitals which provide free or reduced-fee medical services for the workers and their dependants.

Source: 1. Calculated from Bureau of Central Trust (1995), *Statistics of GEI.*

2. Bureau of Labour Insurance (1995), *Statistics of Labour Insurance.*

servicemen and teachers could already claim old age benefits and widows' benefits since the 1940s, paid by the state instead of through insurance contributions. Before the operation of the NHI, their dependants could also join the health insurance scheme. In the past, many women got benefits as dependants of employees in these special occupations.

Nowadays, 59 per cent of women are covered by insurance. 53 per cent of women have joined insurance schemes as workers, 1 per cent as wives, 2 per cent as mothers, and 3 per cent as daughters (see Figure 6.1). However, the percentage overestimated the situation of women's entitlements as workers in social insurance. In 1994, 60 per cent of housewives joined the Labour Insurance Scheme and 16 per cent of them joined the Farmers' Insurance Scheme in order to be covered for medical services (Fu, 1995). Since the establishment of the NHI in 1995, the percentage of women covered by Labour Insurance has declined since all housewives are now eligible to join the NHI as dependants. In 1995, the NHI in Taiwan covered about 92 per cent of people (Department of Health, 1996: 104).

There is no gender discrimination in terms of joining social insurance system and the access to insurance benefits, but a large difference between the various social insurance systems.[3] The coverage of the three main social insurance systems is presented in Table 6.2.[4] Generally speaking, the social insurance systems for government employees and military servicemen are more generous than the others. For instance, the death benefits for dependants of those workers are considerably more generous. The income of dependants is hardly affected by the death of the breadwinners.

Besides, old age benefits are usually paid as a lump sum in Taiwan, but senior government employees and military servicemen can choose pensions offering 75 per cent to 100 per cent of final wages. The state also offers special interest rates to them (e.g. an annual rate of 18 per cent) for saving for old age benefits. As discussed before, the majority of them were men so the best social insurance system was taken up by male workers. Only 2 per cent of women were covered by Government Employees' Insurance; while 43 per cent were covered by Labour Insurance. However, women workers in the Labour insurance Scheme seem to receive more benefits than those in the Government Employees' Insurance in terms of maternity payments because the former receive two kinds of benefits for childbirth, one to cover the medical costs associated with delivery and the other for expenses for the newborn baby.

Table 6.2   Comparison of three main social insurance systems in Taiwan

From insurance systems	Government employees' insurance	Labour insurance	Farmers' health insurance
Maternity leave	42 days	8 weeks	none
Maternity payments	In kind, free medical care, including employees' spouses	In cash, childbirth fee: 1 month wage ++ childbirth benefit: 1 month wage Pay 15 days wage if male employees' spouses give birth ++	In cash, 1 month wage (fair rate) including farmers' spouses ++
Average maternity payments, 1994	NT$ 17 290 (average medical cost of maternity)	women workers: NT$ 25 046 spouses of male workers: NT$ 24 651	
Minimum maternity benefits, 1993	free medical care	women workers: NT$ 26 700 spouses of male workers: NT$ 6675	NT$ 13 350
Death benefits	30 months death benefit + 5 months funeral benefit +	30 months survivor's benefit + 5 months funeral benefit	15 months funeral benefit (fair rate)
Retirement conditions (age)	join ins. over 5y, and 60 years old or working for the government more than 25 years	male: 60, female: 55, or join ins. over 15y +55 years old, or work in the unit and join ins. over 25y	none
Old age benefits	maximum 36 month	maximum 45 month	none

Table 6.2 Comparison of three main social insurance systems in Taiwan (continued)

From employers	Government employees	workers
Death benefits	death benefit + food payments (inc. payments for dependants) +++	30 months death benefit + 5 months funeral benefit
Old age benefits	as a lump sum or as pension	as a lump sum ++++

Note: + Data from 1992.
++ This benefit became free medical care instead of payment after the establishment of the NHI in 1995.
+++ The insured who work for the government less than 15 years are paid lump sum death benefits; those who work over 15 years receive both lump sum payments and pension benefits for dependants. The parents, children and widow of the insured have the first priority to share the benefits equally.
++++ This benefit required 25 years of service with the same employer, or 15 years of service, but the recipient must be more than 55 years old.

Table 6.3   Labourers' old age benefits: gender differences

Genders	In labour insurance, 1992		In the LSL, 1991	
	Number of payments (%)	Average payments (NT$)	Number of payments (%)	Average payments (NT$)
Men	71.17	472 193	84.5	990 349
Women	28.82	245 565	15.5	536 740

Source: Lee (1994: 43).

Although social insurance schemes are gender-neutral, in practice, men and women are unlikely to receive the same amount of benefits. The major problem is that almost all benefits are paid based on the level of earnings, and women's wages are on average lower than men's. Women usually receive fewer benefits than men from insurance systems, though their contributions are also lower. For instance, women workers' old age benefits are only about half of men workers' (see Table 6.3). Theoretically, through labour insurance women workers can receive four times more maternity payments than spouses of male workers, but the average maternity payments among the former are almost equal to those among the latter (see Table 6.2). In other words, women workers actually receive fewer benefits as a result of earnings differentials between genders.

Moreover, benefits are dependant upon one's employment history. In jobs covered by social security, workers, such as women, with interrupted employment records, are disadvantaged. For instance, by 1988, an insured person who interrupted his or her Labour Insurance for more than six years had to start a new record of insurance. Many women, even though they have worked for several years, fail to meet eligibility requirements for old age benefits since they left the labour market early. It is unfair for these women since they have paid insurance fees for many years but cannot get benefits. As shown in Figure 6.2, in the past few women have been eligible to claim old age benefits in comparison with men, though partly because more men participated in the labour force. Workers with longer employment histories have special bonus of benefits, such as old age payments under Labour Insurance, and can receive more benefits. Women have usually had a shorter employment history.

Finally, many women, especially married women, work in informal sectors, such as part-time work, family subsidiary work and child-

Figure 6.2   Old age benefits, 1966–94: gender differences

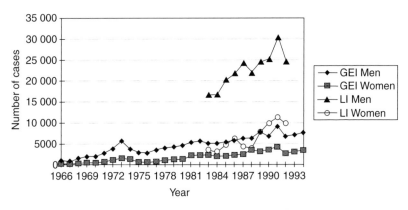

Note: GEI = Government Employees' Insurance; LI = Labour Insurance.
Source: 1. Derived from the Bureau of Central Trust, 1966–94, *Statistics of GEI*.
             2. Lee (1994: 12).

minding. They are usually outside the protection of social insurance. In 1995, only 3 per cent of part-timers were covered by old age benefits; only 0.8 per cent of firms with less than 30 employees offered old age benefits to part-timers (CLA, 1995b).

Being absent from the labour market and as a disadvantaged group, women have all too easily to become financially dependent in old age. In 1991, 27 per cent of men over 65 depended on their old age benefits living expenses, 38 per cent of them depended on their children's support; while only 3 per cent of women over 65 relied on their old age benefits for living, and 69 per cent have to ask living expenses from their children (DBAS, 1992). In a country like Taiwan where social security is mainly based on employment achievement, joining the labour market has become an effectual way to basic social security. For women, however, it is a different story.

Maternity benefits

Maternity benefits developed as labour protection schemes to reduce hazards to the health of working mothers and their babies, and to compensate for loss of earnings during leave, paid by social insurance schemes or employers. In some European countries, maternity benefits are paid by the state. Since 1929, eight-week maternity leave with pay has been a statutory right in Taiwan. Between the 1950s and 1995,

Table 6.4 Implementation of maternity leave and maternity pay by industry in Taiwan

unit: %

Occupations	Industries not covered by the LSL (%)			Part-time workers (%)		Industries covered by the LSL (%)
	Commerce	Finance, insurance, property and business services	Social and personal services	Indus-tries not covered by the LSL	Indus-tries covered by the LSL	
Duration and pay						
Duration						
Over 8 weeks	29	15	13	51	45	84
6–7 weeks	22	38	36			
4–5 weeks	42	38	44			2
Others	3	4	4			14
No leave	4	4	4	49	55	
Pay						
Full earnings	76	86	71	68	61	52
Basic	17	9	20			38
Half	1	0.2	1	+13	+12	3
No pay	3	1	4	16	19	2
Others	3	4	4	3	9	5

Note: + reduced wages.
Source: CLA (1992: Table 34, 37); (1993: Table 10); (1995c: Table 10).

social insurance covered the hospital costs of childbirth or paid earnings-related benefits for the medical costs of childbirth. Since the establishment of the NHI, the costs of childbirth have been covered by the NHI. In Taiwan, there is no universal maternity allowance. Only working women are able to receive full earnings for maternity leave in the form occupational welfare provided by employers, which is generous in comparison with the regulations in some European countries.[5]

Since 1984, maternity leave and pay have been regulated by the Labour Standards Law. Many occupations in the service sector, which accounts for half of working women, have been outside the protection of the law.[6] Analyzing the results of implementing maternity leave and pay, there was no significant difference between the industries covered by the law or those not covered by the law. Many offered shorter periods of leave than the statutory periods, and part-time workers received inferior benefits. Among the industries covered by the Labour Standards Law, 34 per cent offered statutory maternity leave and pay. As shown on Table 6.4, 15 per cent did not offer maternity leave and only 52 per cent paid women workers full pay during their leave. On the other hand, among the industries not regulated by the Labour Standards Law, only 21 per cent offered statutory maternity leave and pay. Although only 19 per cent offered the statutory length of leave, only 4 per cent did not offer maternity leave and 78 per cent paid full pay during leave.

Parental leave and family leave

According to women activists in Taiwan, parental leave is seen as an important way of reconciling career and family responsibilities. However, research on the effect of parental leave in Western countries found that parental leave had negative effect on women's promotion chance and their job satisfaction. If fathers can also apply parental leave, it is expected to increase men's involvement in childcare but will not suffice for equalizing women's and men's employment situations (Calleman and Widerberg, 1984, quote from Haas, 1990: 416).

Parental leave has been implemented in Taiwan since 1990, but only civil servants and teachers in primary and junior high schools can apply for it (nurses and policewomen are excluded). Originally, the period of leave was one year for caring for children under one. In 1997, a period of leave has been extended to women civil servants who needed to take care of children under three years old, their parents and parents-in-law, or sick partners and children. The maximum period was two years and could be extended to three years if necessary. The organizations, however, have the right to decide whether their female staff can take the leave.

In comparison with selected Western countries, the state in Taiwan provides a generous length of leave for its employees, especially family leave (see Table 6.5). It is probably because the Taiwanese often need to take care of their parents and other old relatives; Western countries have other support systems to take care of older people. The lack of economic support during leave is the major problem. In reality, every civil servant in Taiwan already has nine days per year on full pay to deal with family emergencies, which is comparable to so-called 'family leave' in France and Germany.

It is interesting that the Cabinet opposed the application of family leave to civil servants when they discussed the GEEB. However, it began to implement parental leave even before the passing of the bill, and the offer was more generous than the original proposal by women's groups. In fact, the government had allowed women teachers in public schools to apply for parental leave between 1975–77. The policy was cancelled as too few women teachers had applied.

Women are still not keen on applying for parental leave today. According to a survey by the Executive Yuan in 1993, only 388 people had applied for it; about 7 per cent of qualified women civil servants. The survey upheld that women did not apply for the leave for several reasons. First, they had other family members or childminders to care for their children. Secondly, they would not be entitled to government employee insurance during their leave, but they needed medical services especially after childbirth. Thirdly, they would face economic difficulty during parental leave since there were no wages or allowances during leave. Finally, the policy did not guarantee right of re-engagement in the same job upon return to work. So, women civil servants were not keen to apply for parental leave. They were afraid that their jobs would be changed, and that leave would affect their opportunities of promotion in the future (Chang, 1994).

State welfare in Taiwan

In Taiwan, welfare provision from the state has been too low to meet people's needs; only education, public health and social insurance have been properly achieved. Since they are closely related to labour reproduction and social investment, their development has seldom met any political obstruction. The percentage of expenditure for social welfare has appeared to increase greatly in recent years. In 1995, 24.5 per cent of general government expenditure was spent on social welfare, community

Table 6.5 Comparison of parental and family leave in selected countries

Country	Parental leave			Family leave		
	Statutory	Paid leave	Length	Statutory	Paid leave	Length
Denmark	Yes	10w = maternity benefit + Other = 80% unemp. benefit	10–52w	No	N/A	N/A
Sweden	Yes	12m = 75% earnings + 3m = flat rate pay	18m	Yes	Yes	60 d/y
France	Yes	Flat rate pay	up to 3y	Yes	Yes	1–4 d/y
Germany	Yes	Flat rate pay	up to 3y	Yes	Yes	10 d/y
Italy	Yes	30% of earnings	6m	No	N/A	N/A
UK	Yes	6w = 90% earnings + 12w = flat rate pay	14–29w	No	N/A	N/A
USA	No	N/A	N/A	Yes	No	12w/y
Taiwan +	?	No	2–3y	?	No	2–3y

Note: + The policy is applied to civil servants only.
Source: Equal Opportunity Review (1996: 22–9).

development, environmental protection and pensions (13.8 per cent on social welfare); in 1966, it was only 4.7 per cent (Ministry of Finance, 1995: 70–1). However, many items which did not belong to the area of social welfare were included in welfare budget. Analyzing the expenditure of central government for social welfare in 1990, for instance, 24 out of 117 items were not for social welfare, but they represented 59 per cent of all welfare expenditure (Chan, 1989).

Moreover, the distribution of welfare has been severely unbalanced. Social welfare has been mainly directed at particular occupations, such as civil servants, teachers in public schools and military servicemen, to maintain the state's own benefits. In the central government budget for social welfare in 1990, 34 out of 117 items were for people in the three occupations mentioned above and their dependants (Chan, 1989). In 1991, about 74 per cent of welfare expenditure was spent on these same three occupational groups (see Table 6.6). Money spent on the disadvantaged, who really needed support from the state, has been extremely low.

Furthermore, welfare expenditure spent on women was the lowest in comparison with other items; each woman only received one NT dollar per year from the state on average (see Table 6.6). Some male politicians and officers refuted the criticism of low expenditure on women's welfare. They stated that since welfare expenditure did not even contain an item for 'men,' the state had treated women very well. However, if we analyze welfare expenditure from a gender dimension, military servicemen and veterans, who received over half of the welfare resources, were almost all men. Therefore, the distribution of welfare in Taiwan has been very unbalanced in terms of gender.

State welfare for women

Documentary data about women's welfare is very deficient. In the past, there were mainly two kinds of welfare services directed at women: retraining for disadvantaged women, and 'Mothers' Classrooms.' The former began in 1948 and was targeted especially at adopted daughters and prostitutes, to give them new working skills to find jobs (Taiwan Provincial Government, 1966: 6).[7] The latter schemes were for ordinary women to teach them working and household skills.

In the mid-1980s, the government began to think more about women's welfare. Welfare expenditure on women has been listed as an independent item since 1985, while much new work began in 1989 (see Table 6.7). According to the Ministry of the Interior, it was because 'the state understood the direction of society.' The increase in welfare

Table 6.6 Welfare expenditure per capita, by the Taiwanese central government, 1991

unit: NT$ 1000

	Expenditure	No. of persons	As percentage of welfare expenditure	Benefits per head
Retired members of national parliaments	1 015 664	275	0.64	3 693.324
Military servicemen	12 512 880	484 000	7.90	25.853
Government employees and teachers	17 169 005	607 692	10.85	28.253
Veterans	87 864 758	593 744	55.50	147.984
Farmers	14 257 645	1 600 000	9.00	8.911
Labourers	1 297 636	6 557 852	0.82	0.198
Fishermen	89 955	212 803	0.06	0.423
Children	1 031 744	4 407 406	0.65	0.234
Youths	276 842	2 258 999	0.17	0.123
Women	56 169	5 942 733	0.04	0.001
Elderly	2 001 769	653 602	1.26	3.063
The disabled	1 281 377	149 080	0.81	8.595
The poor	410 268	148 492	0.26	2.763
Total			100.00	

Source: Ku (1995: 135).

Table 6.7 The allocation of welfare expenditure on women of the central government and Taipei city government

unit: NT$ 1,000

Item	year started	Ministry of the Interior				Taipei City (1993)
		1993	1994	1995	1996	
Service centres for women +	1989	40 000	55 000	15 000	80 000	–
Activities	1989	9 500	11 500	50 500	26 500	365
Mothers' Classrooms	1992	5 200	6 200	15 000	7 000	–
Measures to protect disadvantaged women +	1989	41 000	55 000	60 000	70 100	3 740
Including disadvantaged women allowance	1992	–	–	–	2 644	381
Subsidy to local government	–	–	–	–	140 718	–
Training, publicity and surveys	1992	5 922	6 500	2 718	6 574	892
Medical subsidy for rape victims'						249
Flats for single women						841

Note: + Expenditure on these items was mainly for setting up new institutions and improving facilities.
Source: 1. DBAS (1993–96), *Budget of the Central Government (Ministry of the Interior).*
  2. Taipei City Government (1993).

expenditure on women partly reveals the changing attitude of the government towards women's welfare (see Figure 6.3). Basically, the amount of welfare expenditure on women between 1991 and 1996 was based on the *Six-Year Administrative Plan of the Ministry of the Interior*, connected to the *'Six-Year National Development Plan* introduced by the former Premier, Po-chun Hao (Ministry of the Interior, 1990). Under the Six-Year National Development Plan, public spending on public construction as well as social welfare was greatly expanded.

Although money spent on women has increased from a very low base, the character of welfare provision was still deficient if analyzed by allocation. As shown in Table 6.7, women's welfare still focused on institutional services, such as setting up more welfare service centres for women and more emergency shelters for disadvantaged women, or lectures and entertainment. Of these services, only the establishment of welfare centres and services for disadvantaged women were new. By 1994, there were 18 welfare service centres for women, which provided counselling, legal support, parental education and information provision, and 20 shelters for disadvantaged women, which could house 249 people. The establishment of welfare centres and emergency shelters has led to service work for women becoming more organized. Moreover, the living allowance for disadvantaged women, evaluated by social workers, is the only allowance designed for women. This allowance is only offered in cases of emergency and the maximum

Figure 6.3   Welfare expenditure on women in Taiwan, 1985–95

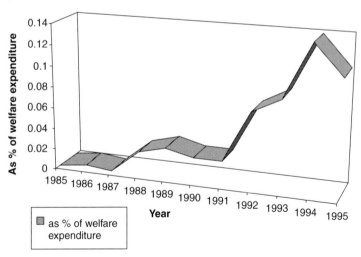

Source: Lee (1995: Table 2.2).

period was three months. In 1993, 1016 women received this kind of allowance in Taiwan Province, the total amount being 22 815 710 NT dollars (Taiwan Provincial Government, 1995b: Table 1.3).

If we analyze social services for women in different provincial governments, we find that the provision in the two major cities is superior to that in Taiwan Province (see Table 6.8). Help lines and help centres are provided for consultation and protecting women's rights. The content of lectures is not only limited to family topics but also concerned with women's careers. Moreover, the service is extended to lone parents and single women.

Summary

Social security in Taiwan is means-tested and based on employment achievement. Joining the labour market is the only way to obtain the best welfare. For instance, working women have statutory maternity leave and maternity pay provided by both social insurance and employers; civil servants are allowed to apply for parental and family leave. Nonetheless, working women cannot receive as many benefits from social insurance schemes as working men, since the schemes are designed to meet the needs of 'male' employment patterns, for the continuously employed. Linked to employment contributions, men are the primary beneficiaries in social insurance systems while women are

Table 6.8   Social services for women provided by local government

Item	Taiwan Province	Taipei City	Kaohsiung City
1. Lectures and activities for working on relationships	√	√	√
2. Mother's Classrooms	√		
3. Women's college			√
4. Shelters for disadvantaged women	√	√	√
5. Teams working for women protection			√
6. Help centre for women's rights		√	
7. Services for lone parents	+	√	√ ++
8. Help line for women		√	
9. Flats for single women		√	

Note: + Arrange for low-income and lone parent families to visit structures in Taiwan
        Province.
        ++ Including special loans for lone parents.
Source: Annual Administrative Report of the Taiwan Provincial Government (1995c),
        Taipei City Government (1995) and Kaohsiung City Government (1995).

in the peripheral sector of insurance, as upheld by the dual labour market theory.

The distribution of welfare resources has been severely unbalanced in Taiwan. The majority of welfare expenditure has been directed at particular occupations, such as military servicemen, government employees and teachers, positions mainly occupied by men. Welfare expenditure on women was very low though it has increased greatly since 1991, being mainly spent on building more service centres for women and shelters for disadvantaged women. Except emergency living allowances for disadvantaged women, social welfare for women is provided in kind, such as activities, lectures, and information provision; many of them show women how to be good mothers and housekeepers.

Promoting women's employment: employment policy

Historical review

From 1937 to 1949, the KMT government was busy resisting firstly Japan then the Communists. During this period, women were encouraged to devote themselves to the state. Due to the shortage of labour, women were encouraged to produce food and other essentials. In 1945, Japan surrendered, and the KMT controlled Taiwan. In 1949, the KMT retreated to Taiwan. The KMT government kept encouraging women in Taiwan to devote themselves to the state, for example sewing clothes for soldiers and pursuing social service (Chian, 1967: 14), and also encouraged women to participate in the production work as well as agriculture.

In the 1940s, employing women workers was encouraged to avoid the increase of wage requirement among men workers:

> Due to the labour shortage, the number of casual workers has increased and they have asked for high wages … To develop new source of labour, state companies should consider about employing women workers to some extent. (Taken from a scheme for maximising resources, increasing productivity, practising planned economy during wartime, 1941.)
> – The KMT (1976c: 197), Revolutionary Document

In the early stages, from the 1950s to 1960s, women were expected to participate in production work because of the special needs during wartime (see Table 6.9). Using the *Current Guidelines for the Women's*

Movement of the KMT in 1951, the KMT mobilized women for the purpose of accumulating capital for a possible future war. Women were described as 'the burden of society,' so they themselves should try to contribute to society instead of relying on men. Chian, who was the chairman of the KMT Central Women's Department, said:

> Half of the population in China is women. The reason why our country was weak before is that we did not utilize women's power. On the contrary, women depend on men to supply everything for life. The double burden on men eliminates our country's competitiveness ... Women should not only ask for equal rights. They should be under an obligation.
>
> – Chian (1968: 5)

Thus the state hoped that women would learn frugality and participate in production work in order to adapt them to war life. Under the 'Principle of People's Livelihood,' everyone should have the ability to produce.[8] From the time of the Eighth National Representative Meeting of the KMT in 1953, the concept of 'promoting employment opportunities for women' was included in the party constitution of the KMT. A full employment policy was necessary when the state wanted to accumulate capital fast. Women were encouraged to do family subsidiary work and to work in factories in order to accumulate production for the future war (Chian, 1967: 20).

From the 1960s to 1973, the economy in Taiwan was booming. The economic strategy in Taiwan switched from import-oriented to export-oriented after 1966. An export-oriented economic strategy needed a lot of cheap and flexible workers, and women workers met these demands. At that time, the majority of people in Taiwan were farmers. In order to utilize the surplus labour on farms comprehensively, to raise farmers' income, and to improve farmers' living standards, the state proposed several plans, such as the *Current Guidelines on Rural Economic Development* in 1970, the *Measures for Promoting Farm Construction* in 1972, the *Regulations for Agricultural Development* in 1973, and the *Raising Farmers' Income and Improving the Construction in Rural Areas* scheme in 1980. Through those schemes, on the one hand, the state encouraged businessmen to set up small factories in rural areas, mainly processing industries and light industry. It hoped that farm labourers could earn extra money when they finished their work in farming, and their young people would not need to leave home to find jobs. The development of agriculture, therefore, was able to harmonize with that of industry (*China Daily News*, 6/7/1980). On the other hand, the family in rural areas was also encouraged to do subsidiary work and make craftworks to earn extra money; some people could not leave home to work, such as housewives (*China Daily News*, 23/6/1980). At this stage the principal impediment to married women working was that they could not work far away from home, but the two strategies conquered the problem and attracted them to enter the labour market successfully.

Before the council of Labour Affairs was founded, employment policies were planned by the economic department and presented in economic projects. From the 1950s, the state in Taiwan executed a planned economy to lead national economic development. Within the first two phases of the *Four-Year Economic Plan* (1953–60), the state did not say a word about any labour force programme. The chief problem at that stage was the shortage of jobs, so the most important thing for the state to do was to create job opportunities for people instead of to cultivate manpower. The third phase of the *Four-year Economic Plan* (1961–64) began to refer to the education of technicians and the importance of education for the economy as a whole (CEPD, 1971). It was not until the fourth phase of the plan (1965–68) that the state realized the importance of employment policies for the national economy, and began to plan employment policies systematically, including education, vocational training and employment services. In the sixth phase of the plan (1973–76), population policies were introduced to control the quantity of future labour.

In the later economic plans, employment and welfare policies gradually played more important roles.[9] In the *Middle- and Long-term Plans for Manpower Department for the Economic Development (1986–2000)* introduced in 1986, training women was regarded as one of the middle-term objectives. It was first time that training the female labour force was mentioned in formal public documents. However, in the plan, women were regarded as disadvantaged individuals in the labour market, as were the disabled and the elderly, who needed extra assistance to find jobs. In the latest *Six-Year National Development Plan* (1991–96), the state also began to establish vocational training for women who wanted to return to the labour market. Again, those women returners were marked as disadvantaged individuals in the workplace.

From the mid-1980s, state policies concerning the female labour force changed. Official documentary data showed two directions of policies: creating vocational training for women and encouraging firms to provide part-time and flexible-time work for married women (see Table 6.9). Married women became the targets of state policies. Additionally, women's policies in the latest Constitution of the KMT were entirely different from previous versions. All this may mean that the ideas of the ruling party about the female labour force have changed. The KMT not only indicated its intention to increase employment opportunities for women, but also mentioned the development of women's potential and the training of a larger female elite.

Judging by these policies and the KMT's pronouncements, women in Taiwan have been regarded as a flexible labour force rather than as a regular one. In the years following 1945, the KMT government encouraged women to do craftwork to earn extra money (The KMT Central Women's Department, 1980: 65). Since the majority of people were farmers at that time, this was almost the only way for women in rural areas to earn extra money besides the income from agriculture. From the 1960s to 1970s, the 'Living rooms as factories' and 'Small Factories in Rural Areas' schemes urged women, especially housewives, to become flexible waged labour. This idea was prevalent until recently. In the 'Work Plan of Promoting Employment Services for Women in Taiwan Province' in 1989, encouraging housewives to do subsidiary, part-time and flexible-time work was still a main objective of the Taiwan Provincial government. Further, encouraging business to provide part-time and flexible-time work to married women has been a major objective of the Council of Labour Affairs in recent years. The Taiwan Provincial government also encouraged women to return to the labour market after they had finished their childcare responsibilities. Therefore, although the state still wished to utilize the surplus labour of housewives, it also wanted women to stay at home to take care of their families, and put their families in first place.

Foreign workers and their effect on the female labour force

Before 1986, the majority of foreign workers in Taiwan were skilled workers and professionals. After that, more lower skilled workers from other South-east Asian countries gradually began to work in Taiwan. There were two important forces, push and pull, which led to this phenomenon. On the one hand, since the economies in some South-east Asian countries have been in recession, job opportunities in their home countries declined. On the other hand, the economy in Taiwan has been booming, and the exchange rate between Taiwan NT dollars and US dollars has increased sharply. Therefore, the real wage in Taiwan has been higher than that in these workers' home countries.

152

Table 6.9 Important policies and pronouncements of the KMT for promoting women's employment

KMT-controlled China

Year	Reference	Contents
1945	*Guidelines of the Racial Protection Policy*	The government to promote industrialization in order to absorb surplus labour in agriculture. To create jobs that are suitable for women in order to increase national productivity.

KMT-controlled Taiwan only

Year	Reference	Contents
1947	*Work Guidelines of Farmers' Movement and the Economic Revolution Scheme*	1. The KMT to promote subsidiary work in rural areas in order to improve their living standard. 2. Small factories can set up in rural areas in order to absorb surplus labour.
1951	*Current Guideline of Women Movement of KMT*	1. The KMT to help women find jobs. 2. The party to promote frugal movement.
1953	*Revised KMT Constitution*	The party to protect women's rights, to increase employment opportunities for women and to expand their ability to serve society.
1957	*Revised KMT Constitution*	The party should maintain women's rights, protect their equal status, increase the employment opportunities for women and develop their ability to serve society during wartime.

Table 6.9 Important policies and pronouncements of the KMT for promoting women's employment   *(continued)*

KMT-controlled Taiwan Only

Year	Reference	Contents
1964	*Current Social Policies within the Principle of Livelihood*	The government to ... encourage the family to do subsidiary work ... in order to increase family well-being.
1968	*Work Guidelines for Community Development*	The government to encourage the family to do subsidiary work at home and teach women to do some craftwork to earn money.
1970	*Current Guideline of Rural Economic Development*	The government to set up farm nurseries,so that women living on farms can take on some farm work and subsidiary work.
1969 1976	*Revised KMT Constitution*	The party to maintain women's rights and increase employment opportunities for women.
1983 1986	*Measures for Solving the Present Unemployment Problem, Taiwan Province*	The government to assist unemployed women to do subsidiary work.
1986	*Middle-and Long-Term Plans for the Manpower Department for Economic Development (1986–2000)*	The government to promote vocational training for those people with low employment abilities, such as women, and encourage them to accept vocational training.

Table 6.9 Important policies and pronouncements of the KMT for promoting women's employment   (continued)

KMT-controlled Taiwan Only

Year	Reference	Contents
1989	*Revised KMT Constitution*	Article 78: Increasing development opportunities for women: in order to develop women's potential, the government to identify and train female elite, encourage women to contribute to national construction, provide equal opportunities for competition and promotion, and increase women's professional knowledge and working skills. Article 79: The government to investigate the possibility of creating flexible-time jobs for women with children and implementing paternity leave for fathers …
1989	*Plan for Promoting Employment Services for Women, Taiwan Province*	1. The government to publicize part-time/flexible-time employment pattern and encourage housewives to undertake this kind of work. 2. The government to encourage the family to do subsidiary work at home to utilize women who have to stay at home. 3. The government to encourage women to return to the labour market after they finish their childcare responsibilities. 4. The government to provide vocational training for women to improve their working skills. 5. Utilize women's welfare institutions to provide employment service for women. 6. The government to help disadvantaged women find jobs.

Table 6.9 Important policies and pronouncements of the KMT for promoting women's employment   *(continued)*

KMT-controlled Taiwan Only

Year	Reference	Contents
1989	***Measures for Solving the Labour Shortage***	Promote part-time and flexible-time work for women.
1991	***Third Phase of the Vocational Training Project (1991–97)***	Promote vocational training for women and disadvantaged individuals in the labour market. The government to plan and provide suitable training courses for women returners and for middle-aged women.
1992	***Employment Service Law***	Article 24: The government to assist five groups of disadvantaged individuals to find jobs, including female breadwinners, the elder, the disabled, the native peoples and low income families. Article 26: The government to provide vocational training for those women who have left the labour market due to pregnancy or bringing up children.
1994	***Measures for Promoting Women's Employment***	1. Enlarging vocational training for women. 2. Reducing the obstacles to women's employment. 3. Promoting employment services for women.

Table 6.9   Important policies and pronouncements of the KMT for promoting women's employment   *(continued)*

KMT-controlled Taiwan Only

Year	Reference	Contents
1994	*Guidelines of Social Welfare Policies*	Implementing equal opportunities for employment and forbidding employment discrimination. The government to provide vocational training and employment services to five groups of disadvantaged individuals.

Source: 1. Council of Economic Planning and Development (1986: 62, 76), *Middle and Long-term Plans for the Manpower Department for Economic Development.*
2. Commission on Population Policies (1995: 168–73), *Data on Population Policies.*
3. CLA (1988: 2–65, 398–435); (1994b: 1–15).
4. Ma (1992: 154–174, 290–3).
5. Chen (1993: 40–3).
6. Lin et al. (eds) (1996).

Foreigners working in Taiwan could earn money quickly than in their home countries.

Between 1986 and 1988, the labour department announced several times that the government had no plan to let foreign workers work in Taiwan legally, and the police also arrested some illegal foreign workers. However, in 1989, under pressure from a labour shortage, the government finally allowed 14 major government construction projects to import foreign workers, and they began to come to Taiwan in 1991. Since 1992, the government has allowed some hazardous industries which find it difficult to find workers, to employ limited numbers of foreign workers. By November 1996, there were 245 821 legal foreign workers in Taiwan, and another 47 988 with entry permits (see Table 6.10).

Although one of the conditions of employing foreign workers is that the business or the family concerned cannot find domestic workers, agencies have found ways of getting rid the rules. According to Chang's economic model (1995: 591), the import of foreign workers will let employers and highly skilled workers reap benefits, but it decreases the opportunities and wages of low skilled workers. Therefore, the entry of foreign workers could affect some women's working opportunities, but it is difficult to evaluate the effect. For instance, the import of foreign maids could affect the working opportunities and wages of domestic maids; in the manufacturing industry foreign workers may substitute for low skilled Taiwanese workers, who are mainly middle-aged married women. The other influence of foreign workers is their effect on state policies on women. Since the mid-1980s, especially after the entry of foreign workers, the labour government has tended to develop a potential labour force with some urgency in

Table 6.10   The number of foreign workers in Taiwan

unit: person

Year	Major governmental construction projects	Industry	Foreign nurses	Foreign maids	Total
1991	3 105	–	–	–	3 105
1992	6 691	9 091	317	378	16 477
1993	17 897	75 077	1 367	6 424	100 765
1994	29 238	113 966	4 300	9 526	157 030
1995	40 396	141 360	8 992	8 805	199 553
1996+	46 789	168 554	15 549	14 929	245 821

Source: Vocational Training Bureau (1996: 169–76).

order to reduce the need for foreign workers. I will discuss this issue further in the discussion section of this chapter.

Related policies of the opposition parties

Although the DPP is a left-wing party and its policies are usually radical, its ideas on gender are conservative. In comparison with other policies, its policy on women's employment is deficient, blurred and unprogressive (see Table 6.11). This is probably because the party is not concerned about women's policy. Like the KMT, it encourages married women to do informal work, such as half-day or part-time work. The policy of the New Party on women's employment is more distinct. Besides vocational training and employment opportunities, it also mentions the necessity of providing special funds for women to run their own business.

Important schemes for promoting women's employment

'Living rooms as factories' scheme

'Living rooms as factories' was the slogan for a set of government actions during the 1970s and 1980s which encouraged families to do subsidiary work. The scheme was the first concrete policy employed by the state in Taiwan tried to mobilize women. The government mainly promoted 'Living rooms as factories' schemes by way of the *Community Development Plan*, which was promoted by the UN and has been an important social policy in Taiwan since 1965. In 1968, the government introduced the *Work Guidelines of Community Development* in order to improve people's living standards. There were three thrusts of the plan: improving physical construction, promoting economic development and raising the moral development of communities. By 1993, 29 per cent of communities had already introduced craftwork and family subsidiary work to their residents (Ministry of the Interior, 1995: 23).

Several surveys were undertaken to measure the extent of surplus labour in different communities. The state found that there were many 'idle' housewives with productive ability. So, the 'Living rooms as factories scheme' was promoted. This scheme was designed to absorb the surplus labour of families into production work (Hsiung, 1996: 52). The chief aim of this scheme was to utilize fully manpower to solve the labour shortage problem (CEPD, 1978: 1–2). The scheme encouraged the family to do subsidiary work and housewives to devote themselves to production work. As part of a factory production line, the family might need to buy machines. The state provided special loans for this purpose. Consequently, those families, likes satellite factories, became production lines or departments of larger factories, (Hsiung, 1996).

Table 6.11 Important pronouncements of two main opposition parties for promoting women's employment

Party	Reference	Content
DPP	*The DPP Constitution (1986)*	4. Welfare Society: Article 4: ... For women with children, the government to create half-day or part-time work.
	The Action Plan of the DPP (1986)	Article 93: The government to help women to access employment actively ... Article 94: For women with children, the government to create half-day or part-time work.
New Party	*The New Party's Policy White Paper*	New Family, Women and Children Policy: The government to assist women to have necessary skills, funds and opportunities to access employment, to return to the labour market, or to run their own business, especially women returners.

Source: 1. Party constitution and constitution of the DPP (1995).
2. White paper on policies of the New Party (1995).

This kind of satellite factory system is still a phenomenon in Taiwanese society today.

The government also stressed that the 'Living rooms as factories' scheme benefited both the employer and the family. On the one hand, the family could improve its economy and the pressure of finding a 'breadwinner' would be relieved. On the other hand, the employer did not need to worry about either the labour shortage problem or the pressure of wage rises due to labour shortage. Employers were able to reduce expenditure on facilities and labourers' accommodation, and to avoid the trouble of personnel management. The government report even stated that this scheme could minimize the conflict between the capital and the labour. For employers, however, one of the most attractive advantages about family subsidiary work was its flexibility. They were able to utilize the surplus labour according to the number of trade orders (CEPD, 1978: 30–1).

The scheme encouraged women to be incorporated into production work. Not just housewives were exploited but also children and the elderly. Housewives became waged labour, and the family became a production line for capitalists. It was regarded as disguised proletarianization or partial proletarianization. In order to accumulate capital fast, the state encouraged businesses to set up small factories in rural areas, thus capitalists extended into farms, and the scheme let capitalism extend into the family.

'Mothers' Classrooms' scheme

This scheme was another system to teach women the required skills for family subsidiary work. It was basically an adult education programme, but it played an important role in carrying out the government's orders, including advertising family planning and social services, teaching production skills, improving the environment of communities and so on. By 1984, 4063 communities had implemented the Community Development Plan in Taiwan. About 90 per cent of them had Mothers' Classrooms (Chao, 1985). In 1993, there were still 42 per cent of Mothers' Classrooms provided vocational training for their members (Ministry of the Interior, 1995: 42). In addition, the KMT Women's Department also sponsored many training courses to teach women to make craft products.

Measures for promoting women's employment

Because the labour force participation rate has decreased gradually in recent years and the state has not wanted too many foreign workers in

Taiwan, it has tried to encourage the potential new labour force to enter the labour market. In 1993, 52 per cent of the potential labour force were housewives, and 39 per cent were students (DBAS, 1994b: 70). Since 99.6 per cent of the former were women, married women became the new targets.

After the passing of the Employment Service Law, the government began to think harder about training women. The law stipulates that the government must help female breadwinners to attend vocational training, and offer vocational retraining for women who have left the labour market through pregnancy or childcare. As a result, the *Measures for Promoting Women's Employment* were introduced in 1994 (see Table 6.9 for detailed contents).

There are some meaningful proposals in these measures for promoting women's employment. First, the government resolves to survey the demands of the female labour force, then design vocational training to meet the demands. It should also entrust private organizations with providing training courses for women, publicizing training opportunities and providing living allowances for female breadwinners during the training periods. Secondly, the government should provide employment service for women, collect and publicize employment information, and provide consultation and counseling for female job-seekers. Thirdly, with regard to increasing employment opportunities for women, these measures emphasize the importance of providing part-time, flexible-time and piece-work for women, since that kind of work will be convenient for women to reconcile work and family responsibilities.

These measures, by and large, are the first official document produced by the central government specifically directed at women's employment. Compared with other labour policies, the ideas in these measures are more distinct and advanced. However, the state still pushes women towards part-time jobs by regarding them as a flexible labour force.

Practical actions: vocational training

State policies on vocational training are usually associated with trends in national economic development. They are also a way of seeing how the state meets the needs of new employment forms and the needs of business. Until the 1990s, the Taiwanese state was not concerned about providing vocational training for women. It only provided training courses for special kinds of women, such as criminals, prostitutes and adoptees, and hoped they could find decent jobs thereafter.

In the early stages of economic development, the government promoted vocational training in order to meet new skill requirements
along with industrial change. Therefore the training courses offered at
public vocational training centres focused on developing skilled and
semi-skilled labour. The government also entrusted training to factories
and polytechnics. The courses were free of charge, and usually lasted
between several months and one year. Trainees had to attend courses
full-time and to live in the centres or factories. After the Bureau of
Vocational Training was founded in 1981, public vocational training
became more systematic. Further, because the global economic structure was changing, the service sector was expected to play an important role in the national economy. In 1986, the government decided to
add training courses for the service sector, so six public training centres
were established courses (according to the 1986 'Second Stage in
Promoting Vocational Training Schemes' and the 1988 'Promoting
Vocational Training for the Service Sector Programme'). In 1987, the
government also realized the importance of training people in second
specialism, which might be possible unemployment problems caused
by rapid change in the labour market. In fact, the major trainees in
second specialism have been women (see Table 6.12).

Because most of the public training courses were regarded as being in
traditionally 'male jobs,' the number of women trainees has been
much lower than that of men (see Figure 6.4). In the past, many

Figure 6.4:　Number of vocational training trainees by gender and type

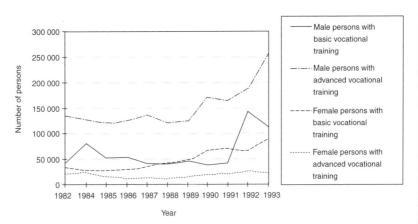

Source: Ministry of the Interior (1982–93), *Vocational Training in ROC*.

Table 6.12   Welfare expenditure and outcome of the policy of promoting employment for people with low employment abilities*

Unit: NT$ 1000

		7/92–6/93	7/93–6/94	7/94–6/95	7/95–6/96
Budget	For women	–	7921	9442	65 880
	as % of total budget	–	3.8	4.3	19.1
Second specialism training	Number of women	2249	2796	1573	–
	as % of total persons	83.1	64.6	85.7	–
Food allowance	Number of women	0	0	9	–
	as % of total persons	0.0	0.0	1.3	–
Living allowance	Number of women	–	14	15	–
	as % of total persons	–	3.4	1.1	–

* People with low employment ability include women, the elderly, the disabled, the native peoples, low income families and unemployed people.
Source: Lin (1996).

courses were limited to men only. Nowadays, in order to avoid public blame, educational attainment, rather than gender, is used as the criteria for attending training courses. Moreover, since the main target of public vocational training was young people, courses often had age restrictions.

In 1992, the government began to design some vocational training courses especially for women in order to give them second specialism to join the labour market. The courses included restaurant management, fashion designing and trading, advertisement design, modelling, household management, secretarial studies, etc, which either belonged to the service sector or were easy for women to run as their own small-size business. The training period was about two to four months, and the timetable suited housewives. Private organizations were also sponsored to hold activities and to give lectures on new employment opportunities for women.

It was difficult for the public vocational training centres to change their regular courses and to provide new courses since they had to buy new equipment. Thus, the government often entrusted private organizations or colleges with the new training courses. For instance, since 1987, the Taipei Social Welfare Bureau has sponsored a 'Taipei Women's Development Centre' to offer training courses on nursing care. The Centre, founded in 1983, is possibly the first and only women's group in Taiwan which concentrates on vocational training for women (Ms Chen, interviewee). The original principle of the centre was to help women whose families meet unexpected change and lost income. Nowadays, besides nursing care training course, the centre also provides courses on computer and business management and extends its service to low income women, indigenous young girls and ordinary women returners. It also has a 'women's manpower bank,' helping women understand their employment abilities and introducing job opportunities. The age limitation on public vocational training makes the services of the centre especially meaningful for middle-aged women.

Finally, since 1993, regulated by the Employment Service Law, the state has had to provide food allowances and/or living allowances to female breadwinners during their training period.[10] However, the outcome was not as good as expected. As shown in Table 6.12, only 29 women received this kind of living allowance and nine women received food allowances. Since eligibility is limited to who are the sole earners in their families, few women are qualified to apply. Moreover, even if a woman is qualified, how can she feed her whole family on only NT$ 6000 per month?[11]

The division between the state and capitalists

In the past, the state had strong powers to arrange the provision of the labour force for economic development, but it has gradually lost this power. In the 1960s and 1970s, as we mentioned before, the state encouraged the business sector to change their production methods and to extend their production lines into the family. Public officers advised the businesses on 'living rooms as factories' schemes, and also encouraged families to do subsidiary work (CEPD, 1978). Special loans were given to encourage small-size factories to set up in farm to absorb surplus labour (*China Daily News*, 6/7/1980). Girls in junior high schools were permitted to leave school earlier or to work during their school years in order to meet the labour shortage in factories. Social welfare has been focused on enhancing social capital, such as education and health, in order to provide a qualified labour force for capitalist development (Ku, 1995).

However, as young women workers have had more choice to work in the service sector, some companies, mainly in the industrial sector, offering low wages and tough working conditions, have had difficulty finding suitable, long-term workers. Highly paid labour forced some businesses to move their factories abroad; others which stayed in Taiwan began to ask the state to develop more cheap labour for them. From 1992, the state began to allow some industries to import foreign workers in response to requests from the business sector. However, for reasons of maintaining social order, the state hoped that business would utilize domestic labour instead of foreign labour since the latter could result in more social problems. Therefore, it also issued some employment policies to reduce the need for foreign workers: the development of the future potential labour force, the possibility of using prisoners, the automation of industry, and education training on employment issues (Chao, 1993). Policies for promoting female labour after the mid-1980s were mainly based on the need for a labour force (interviewee Mr Tung).

Nevertheless, the business sector would rather employ foreign workers than women when they face a labour shortage problem. The government is no longer seen to be in line with the capitalists. Sixty-seven per cent of businesses which currently employed foreign workers regarded the employment of foreign workers as the primary strategy for improving management in order to make profits rather than as a temporary expedient (Cheng, 1995: 40). We can also see the lack of willingness among businesses to utilize women from several official surveys. Fifty-two per cent were unwilling to employ women workers who were currently jobless (CLA, 1994a: Table 14).

Furthermore, businesses would not rely on women workers when they had labour shortage problems. As shown in Table 6.13, every industry had a different expectation of the state to solve this problem. For instance, commercial industry hoped that the state would help it become automated, so that they did not need to rely so much on human labour; the construction industry hoped the state would provide more employment services and vocational training. In a 1989 survey, more than 30 per cent of businesses thought that developing more potential labour was a good strategy for any labour shortage. However, in later surveys, fewer businesses approved of the state developing more women workers to solve their labour shortage problems. Half of manufacturing industry, which has the highest number of job vacancies, looked forward to importing more foreign workers.[12]

In order to absorb the potential labour force, especially married women, the promotion of part-time work has been one of the important policies of the Labour Department.[13] The labour department has encouraged businesses in the service sector to create more part-time jobs and has enacted a guideline for protecting the working rights of part-time workers in1992. Mr Chao, the Chairman of the Labour Department, stated: '*restaurant work is an important occupation in Taiwan and employs a great number of full-time workers ... We (the CLA) have thought: if restaurants could substitute part-time workers for full-time workers, then the labour shortage problem in the manufacturing and construction industries would be improved.*' However, the policies for promoting part-time work were also inefficient. Although the number of part-time workers that businesses wanted to employ has increased, the labour force participation rate of women has not increased and the need for foreign workers is still high (DBAS, 1990: 4; 1994d: 45; 1995e: Table 6, 11). The number of foreign workers required by the industrial sector within one year was 393 567, 13 per cent of all employed workers.

Summary

The state in Taiwan always wanted to utilize the female labour force. During wartime, women were encouraged to devote themselves to the state. They were described as the burden of society, and the state ordered that they should make themselves useful. It was not until the mid-1960s, when the economy in Taiwan was booming, that women had great opportunities to join the labour force. At that time, the state had strong power to determine economic development and labour supply. The state proposed several schemes to absorb surplus labour on

Table 6.13 Surveys of business: measures the government should take to solve the problem of labour shortage

unit: %

Method	Manufacture		Construction		Commerce	
	1989	1994	1989	1994	1989	1993
Allow more foreign workers to work	31	32	34	16	13	5
Teach youth correct employment ideas	43	22	49	19	59	39
Assist businesses to buy equipment for automation	24	17	17	9	15	30
Improve employment services	22	11	22	17	32	20
Provide more technical assistance for automation	20	7	12	6	11	37
Enhance vocational training	25	4	31	28	16	13
Encourage women and the elderly to work ++	31	3	43	1	29	7

Note: + The data from 1989 indicates that business approved the individual method. The data in 1991 and 1993 showed the first priority for the state to do.
++ This item in the 1989 survey was: 'to develop the potential labour force.'
Source: derived from DBAS (1990: 20); (1995b: Table 14); (1994d: Table 48).

farms for industrial development. Businesses were assisted to set up small factories in rural areas, and families were urged to do subsidiary work. Many women became waged workers, but most of them worked at home.

Public vocational training was originally directed at young men. From the mid-1980s, the government began to provide special vocational training for women. It also advocated that business should provide part-time or flexible-time work for women, and encouraged married women to return to the labour force after they finished child-care responsibilities.

Judging by this review of state policies in Taiwan, the leaders of the state value the importance of vocational training for women as a way of developing the female labour force. Providing vocational training is also regarded as a useful method of encouraging women who leave the labour market due to pregnancy or bringing up children to re-enter the labour market. Therefore, we conclude that these state policies on the female labour force are based on a belief in human capital theory. Once the state regards the reason why women are disadvantaged individuals in the labour market is due to their lack of skill, it believes that improving women's human capital is the best way to stimulate them to join the labour force (refer to Chapter 2). If the state tends to believe in human capital theory, it will make less effort to eliminate other obstacles which affect women's willingness to work, such as women's caring role in the family and gender discrimination in the workplace.

In the early stage of rapid economic development, the state had strong powers to arrange the provision of the labour force. Nowadays, the strategy of the state and the capital is divided in terms of developing new labour. Businessmen rely on foreign workers to solve the labour shortage problem; while the state wants them to use more home labour, such as married women. After the mid-1980s, the main purpose of state policies for promoting female participation in the labour force was based on the need for a labour force rather than an understanding of women's working rights.

Protection or equal treatment? Equal opportunities policy

Like many other countries, the Taiwanese state imposed protective legislation on women workers. In Western countries, egalitarian feminism, with its opposition to protective legislation, argued that women should be treated equally instead of being specially protected. As an alternative, it was argued that the protective legislation should be extended to men. Attitudes towards working women has shifted in some countries from difference to equality (Lewis and Davies, 1991). What is the situation in Taiwan? This section will historically review protective legislation and equal opportunities policies, and examine the implementation of protective legislation in Taiwan.

Historical review

From the time it governed mainland China, the KMT had been concerned with the protection of workers. Its fundamental labour policies were introduced at that stage, the Labour Movement Guideline in 1926 and the Guidelines of Labour Policy in 1945. Many current labour policies still follow the spirit of the latter policy. In addition, the KMT also enacted the first labour law in 1929, the Factory Law, which regulated basic working conditions of workers, including protective articles directed at women workers. Protecting workers and farmers was also included in the Constitution as a basic national policy. Basically, the previous labour policies of the KMT mainly followed the regulations of the International Labour Organization (hereafter ILO), as with the protective regulations for women workers.

The 1984 Labour Standards Law is the most important labour legislation in Taiwan at present. It inherits the spirit of the Factory Law but covers more occupations.[14] However, occupations in the service sector, with mostly women workers, are not regulated by the Labour Standards Law. So, half of all working women are outside these basic working regulations. Tsai (1989: 44–5) explains that the backgrounds to the Factory Law and the Labour Standards Law are different though their contents are similar. The former was drawn up in accordance with the needs of the economy and labour conditions at that time; the latter was based on the regulations of the ILO and labour legislation in developed countries. In other words, the enactment of the former was due to the needs of national environment, but the enactment of the later was affected by international regulations.

Before 1988, almost all the policies and pronouncements of the KMT government concerned the working hours and conditions of women workers and the protection of maternity rights. There were three main kinds of protective policies during this period. The first focused on protecting women and child workers as weak workers, with prohibitions on their working conditions. For instance, they were regarded as unsuitable to do some hazardous jobs, to work past midnight and take on overtime work over two hours a day and twenty-four hours per month. The second kind of policy emphasized protecting women as mothers, with promotion of maternity benefits and prohibition on women working with substances that might harm their reproductive abilities. Additionally, the legislation protected a woman's working rights during her maternity leave. All the legislation follows the stipulations of the Constitution. According to the Constitution, the basic ideology of the state on women is that 'women's rights to welfare are based on their roles as mothers.' The third kind of policy pronounced equal pay for equal work. It is interesting that the KMT government was already making pronouncements about equal pay in 1926. It was too advanced for the KMT to bring forward such an idea under the prevailing social and economic conditions. Perhaps the pronouncements were affected by the debate in Western countries at the time, or under the pressure of early women's activists (Tan, 1952: 33).[15]

It was not until the late 1980s that state policies gradually recognized the trend for the state to sustain an equal environment for working women. The KMT constitution, passed by the Thirteenth National Representative Convention in 1989, indicated that the state should eliminate impediments to equal employment and enact a law to maintain an equal environment for working women. Further, the concept of 'eliminating gender discrimination in the workplace' was mentioned in the Six-Year National Development Plan in 1991. This was the first time that the state had admitted the existence of gender discrimination in the labour market. In 1994, 'eliminating gender discrimination' was included in the Revised Constitution as a basic national policy. President Lee even took pride in the highly evolved revision of the Constitution on women's rights (Government Information Office, 1994: 238).

In recent years, the Council of Labour Affairs has also subsidized private organizations to publicize the concept of gender equality in the workplace. These policies reveal that the ideas of the KMT government on the position of working women have changed. Women workers should not only be protected, but also need equal opportunities to participate in the labour market. The changing policies of the government on working women were much affected by the women's movement which emerged in Taiwan during the late 1980s. Around the time of the lifting of Martial Law in 1987, social movements were booming and social systems transferred to democracy. Women's groups asked the state to protect their equal rights in the labour market. These events forced the KMT government to announce its intention to eliminate gender discrimination in the labour market. A case study in the debate on equal opportunity between genders from the late-1980s in Taiwan will be discussed in Chapter 7.

Table 6.14 Important policies and pronouncements of the KMT on protection and equal opportunity for women workers

KMT-controlled mainland China

Year	Reference	Contents
1926	*Women's Movement: Guideline of KMT*	The government to draw up a woman workers law, based on the principle of equal pay, to protect women and child workers.
1926	*Labour Movement: Guideline of KMT*	The government to protect child and women workers. Women workers should be offered 60 days' maternity leave and be paid wages at the regular rate during leave.
1926	*KMT Latest Constitution*	Women workers should be offered two months' maternity leave and be paid wages at the regular rate during the leave.
1929	*Factory Law*	Article 7: No child or women worker to be permitted to do any dangerous work. Article 13: No women workers to be permitted to work between ten o'clock in the evening and six o'clock the following morning. Article 24: Men and women workers performing the same type of work with equal efficiency should be paid wages at the same rate. Article 37: Women workers should be given leave before and after childbirth up to a total of eight weeks. Such leave of absence should be paid for at the regular wage rate if the worker has been employed in the factory for more than six months, or at half rate if they have been employed in the factory for less than six months.

Table 6.14 Important policies and pronouncements of the KMT on protection and equal opportunity for women workers *(continued)*

KMT-controlled mainland China

Year	Reference	Contents
1929	*Enforcement Rules for the Factory Law*	<u>Article 23</u>: A female worker who suffers a miscarriage after being pregnant for three months or over to be given 4 weeks' leave. <u>Article 24</u>: The factory should have breastfeeding rooms and, if possible, also provide nurseries.
1931	*Regulation Government Constitution*	The state to protect women and child workers according to their age and health status.
1945	*Guidelines of Labour Policy of KMT*	Child and women workers should not be employed in hazardous work and nightwork. Women workers should be offered leave and medical benefit before and after childbirth.
1948	*Constitution*	Article 15: The state should protect the domestic, employment, work and property rights of all people. Article 152: The state should provide appropriate job opportunities to people with working ability. Article 153: … The state should protect women and child workers according to their age and health status. Article 156: In order to develop our nation, the state should protect maternity right and implement welfare policies for women and children.

KMT-controlled Taiwan Only

Year	Reference	Contents
1974	*Health and Safety at Work Law*	Article 21: No employer may employ a woman worker to do any of the following types of hazardous and harmful work …

Table 6.14 Important policies and pronouncements of the KMT on protection and equal opportunity for women x workers (*continued*)

KMT-controlled Taiwan Only

Year	Reference	Contents
1975	**Factory Law Revision**	Article 22: No employer may employ a woman worker who is pregnant or has given birth within the previous year to do any of the following types of hazardous and harmful work ... Article 13: Women workers should not be employed to do work between ten o'clock in the evening and six o'clock in the morning. However this should not apply for any factory that provides requisite facilities (three working shifts, safety precautions, sanitation, accommodation and transportation) by agreement with the trade union or the worker and upon approval of the authority-in-charge.
1984	**Labour Standards Law**	Article 13: An employer to not terminate a contract with a worker who is taking maternity leave or who is receiving medical treatment, unless she cannot continue business by reason of force, catastrophe or other acts of God, and prior approval has been obtained from the authority-in-charge. Article 25: the same as Article 24 in the Factory Law. Article 32: An employer may extend working hours with the prior consent of the labour union or the workers, and approval from the local authority-in-charge. For a male worker, the total amount of overtime to not exceed 3 hours/day and 46 hours/month; for a woman worker, 2 hours/day and 24 hours/month. Article 49: the same as Article 13 in the Factory Law. (There are six exceptions.) However, these exceptions to not be applied to women workers during pregnancy or babyfeeding ... Article 50: The same as Article 37 in the Factory Law and Article 23 in the Enforcement Rules of the Factory Law. Article 51: A pregnant woman worker may apply for transfer to easier work. The employer should neither reject the application nor reduce wages.

Table 6.14 Important policies and pronouncements of the KMT on protection and equal opportunity for women workers *(continued)*

KMT-controlled Taiwan Only

Year	Reference	Contents
		Article 52: Where a woman worker is required to breastfeed her baby of less than one year of age, the employer should permit her to do so twice a day, each time for thirty minutes. The breastfeeding time referred to in the preceding sentence should be deemed outside work time.
1987	*Current Guidelines of Labour Policy of KMT*	The party to implement the Labour Standards Law thoroughly, especially the protection of women and child workers.
1989	*Revised KMT Constitution*	Article 63: In order to protect labourers and to promote every field of national development, the party to revise the Labour Standards Law, enlarge its coverage, and implement the protection of women and child workers. Article 78: The party to … provide equal opportunity of competition and promotion for women … eliminate the restrictions on women's employment, and draw up legislation to promote equal pay and equal environment for women.
1989	*Work Plan for Promoting the Women's Employment Service, Taiwan Province*	1. The employer should provide nurseries, welfare facilities and transportation for working women. 2. Publicising equal pay for equal work.
1992	*Employment Service Law*	Article 5: In order to protect the equal opportunities in civil employment, an employer should not discriminate job seekers due to their … gender.…
1992	*Enforcement Rules for the Employment Service Law*	Article 5: Every local government should set up a commission on employment discrimination, to include official departments, labour groups, representatives of employers and scholars, in order to judge discrimination cases in the workplace.

175

Table 6.14   Important policies and pronouncements of the KMT on protection and equal opportunity for women workers   *(continued)*

KMT-controlled Taiwan Only

Year	Reference	Contents
1994	*Measures For Promoting Women's Employment*	Implementing labour legislation to protect the employment rights of women.
1994	*Constitution Revision*	Article 9: The state should ... eliminate gender discrimination, and promote real gender equality.
1996	*Labour Standards Law Revision*	Article 30–1: The following working hours can be adjusted by prior consent of the labour union or of half the workforce ... Article 30–4: Nightwork by women workers does not need to be limited by Article 49, but the employer has to provide excellent safety and sanitation equipment. Article 84–1: The following workers do not need to be limited by Articles 30, 32, 36, 37, and 49 (nightwork ban for women workers): the workers have responsibility for supervision, monitoring or intermittent jobs, and special work.

Source: as Table 6.9.

Related policies in the opposition parties

Neither the DPP nor the New Party mentioned anything about protective legislation (see Table 6.15). They did not express an opinion as to whether protective legislation should be retained or abolished. On the contrary, they concentrated on equal opportunities policies. They both highlighted their view that the state should eliminate gender discrimination in the workplace, especially discrimination against women's marriage, pregnancy and childbirth, which was the most serious obstacle to women's employment in Taiwanese society. The New Party's White Paper also showed their support for the GEEB. However, their policies only focused on the popular debate of gender discrimination, without a long-term and clear stand on gender contracts in the workplace.

Practical actions

Official inspection of working conditions

The government implements an annual inspection of working conditions. This inspection is concerned with three kinds of protection of

Table 6.15   Important pronouncements of two main opposition parties on equal opportunities policies

Party	Reference	Contents
DPP	*Guidelines of the DPP (1986)*	Article 84: The government should respect women's status and rights, and remove all kinds of obstacles for women to access the public sphere. Article 93: The government should actively help women to access employment, protect women's working rights, and avoid any discrimination due to gender, marriage, pregnancy or childbirth. Article 94: Equal value, equal pay ...
New Party	*The New Party's White Paper (1995)*	New Family, Women and Children Policy; Labour Policy: 1. The government should eliminate the existing gender discrimination in examination, promotion and training opportunities in government departments. 2. The government should enact the 'GEEB'. 3. The government should enlarge the coverage of the Labour Standards Law, especially for women workers in the service sector.

Source: as Table 6.11.

women workers – hazardous work, nightwork and maternity leave. As shown in Figure 6.5, few firms were against these regulations, but there were still many firms which let female employees work at night. Moreover, 'equal pay for equal work' was not included in this inspection. Although the notion of 'equal pay' was approved by the KMT from a very early stage, and became law in 1929, the government has never implemented it seriously.

Single article inspection and publicizing gender equal employment

Marriage and pregnancy discrimination has been a serious problem in Taiwan. A series of disputes took place between 1993 and 1995. Many women workers in co-operative banks were forced to quit their job after marriage, so they filed petitions with government departments to protect their working rights and got support from women's groups and unmarried couples in these banks (refer to Chapter 7). Under pressure from women's groups, the Council of Labour Affairs implemented a special inspection in March 1995, called the *'Single Article (marriage discrimination) Inspection,'* according to the anti-discrimination regulation in the Employment Service Law. Thanks to this inspection and the attention of the media, marriage discrimination in co-operative banks has improved (CLA, 1995c).

Figure 6.5   The result of inspection of working conditions for women workers, 1978–95

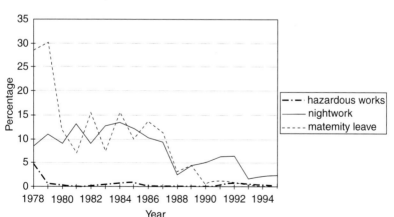

Source: CLA, *Annual Report of Inspection on Working Conditions*, 1979–95.

Besides, the Council of Labour Affairs enforced every local authority to set up an 'Evaluative Commission on Employment Discrimination' as soon as possible to deal with dispute over gender discrimination.[16] It has also sponsored private organizations to publicize moves towards gender equal employment, and prepared brochures and data for organizations such as the Ministry of National Defence, who want to educate their members about equal employment between genders (interviewee Mr Tung).

Protective legislation: protects women or men?

As in other countries, the original purpose of protective legislation in Taiwan was to protect motherhood on the one hand and comparatively physically weak women workers on the other. However, the law became a way to limit women's careers and to enforce their responsibilities in the family. Some feminists oppose protective legislation as a device that can only undermine women's competitive positions in the labour market and reinforce their dependence. Some feminists argue that it only enhances gender divisions in the workplace. Men workers can exclude women from particular occupations and positions, and maintain their superiority in the labour market (Lewis and Davies, 1991: 13–14). Consequently, as proposed by the dual labour market theory, employers may exclude a woman from the supervisory position on account of the nightwork ban and the restriction on working hours. Women can only stay in occupations which legislators (most of whom are men) think women are capable of or suited to.

The protective legislation was sometimes used by employers as a weapon to reject women workers. There was a particular case in Taiwan in May 1996. Six Chinese female translators for South Africa Airlines complained to their company about inappropriate overtime, which was against the Labour Standards Law. Consequently, the company dismissed all of them using the excuse of the nightwork ban on women under the Labour Standards Law.

Nevertheless, protective legislation never became a popular issue in Taiwan. Women's groups and women workers have never questioned or discussed the implication of protective legislation on women. On the contrary, the labour authority-in-charge wanted to loosen the limitations of the law in respect of women's work. In relation to the original version of the Revised Labour Standards Law, drafted by the Council of Labour Affairs, there were two major changes. First, the limit on overtime was relaxed, and women could undertake nightshift work once employers the permission from individual workers. In contrast with the original law (refer to Table 6.4), employers no longer needed the permission of trade unions, and did not need to provide as many facilities for women to do nightwork. Secondly, new mothers could return to work earlier with medical certificates, but at least four weeks had to be taken after the birth. Although the final result did not match the original plan of the Labour department (refer to Table 6.4), there were three issues of note in terms of the action.

First, the state wants to loosen the limitation of labour legislation on women probably for economic reasons rather than for women's benefit. The original aim of the Labour Standards Law was to regulate basic working conditions for workers to avoid capitalists controlling the conditions of labour reproduction (Wang, 1993: 114). If the state relaxed the rules on basic working conditions, workers would have to negotiate or fight with their employers for basic rights. Also, whether workers could get their rights of labour reproduction would depend on supply and demand in the labour market. Businesses have asked the government to abolish the nightwork ban on women for a long time since many (such on the media) employed women and had to operate at night. Although the Council of Labour Affairs stressed that the amendment was in the interests of women, it also mentioned that the withdrawal of some restrictions on working conditions would enhance employers' freedom and flexibility to cope with the changing market. Wang (1993: 114) pointed out that the state in Taiwan began to amend labour legislation in 1988 as a compromise with capitalists. If the state's action was for women's benefit, it should have deregulated all the restrictions on women workers. There are still a lot of unreasonable restrictions in the legislation; for instance, women workers are prohibited from working as much overtime as men (Article 32 in the Labour Standards Law), and are forbidden to do some types of so-called 'hazardous work' or to handle weights (Article 21 in the Health and Safety at Work Law). These restrictions could limit women's opportunities for promotion to supervisory roles, to earn extra money or to work in particular occupations. In other words, these restrictions could guarantee men's working opportunities in these occupations, and could increase men's opportunities to be promoted as they were more 'flexible'.

In the 1970s, socialists and feminists in Britain argued neither for abolition nor for retention, but for the extension of protective legislation to men (Meehan, 1985: 50). If some working conditions could harm workers' health and safety, protective legislation should extend equally to men. If the legislation were directed at maternity protection, the restriction should not include large numbers of women who were not of 'reproductive capacity.' In the report of the Equal Opportunities Commission in Britain in 1979, it was recommended that restrictions on women's hours should be lifted rather than extended to men (due to economic and administrative difficulties), but that the health and safety legislation should be extended to apply equally (Lewis and Davies, 1991: 20).

Secondly, the state tried to weaken the power of trade unions and regarded individual workers as free agents. In the original draft of the Revised Labour Standards Law, the trade union no longer had the right to approve when an employer wanted to adjust working hours or wanted women workers to do night-shift work. This idea perhaps came from employers. However, it met with strong opposition from a social movement, the *Workers' Action Commission on Labour Legislation*. It was ironic that the labour group was only concerned about whether trade unions still had the power of approval in terms of women working at night, but did not insist on the provision of adequate facilities for women's safety to do nightwork. Consequently, trade unions kept their right to decide on the adjustment of working hours and approval of nightwork for women workers, but the requirement that employers should supply women's safety facilities was eliminated. Under the Revised law, an employer only needed to provide good safety equipment and sanitation for women workers to work at night.[17] Women who were pregnant or breastfeeding were not prohibited to do night shift work.[18]

The point is not how many facilities an employer should provide for women working at night, but whether a woman worker is able to choose for herself to work at night, and not be penalized if she chooses not to. It seems that women are the victims of a power struggle between trade unions and capitalists – both are dominated by men. They only want to have the power to control the female labour force.

Finally, the state has withdrawn from its role from protecting maternity rights. Protective legislation was debatable, but the spirit of labour legislation for protecting maternity was seldom questioned; on the contrary, it was even expected to be enforced. However, the state in Taiwan only considered business freedom and flexibility, without considering the most positive purpose of protective legislation – protecting maternity. Statutory maternity leave in Taiwan shorter than the minimum maternity leave regulated by the ILO, while the state still tended to allow new mothers to return to work earlier. Although this has not been approved by Legislators, the state's sincerity about protecting maternity is doubtful.

Lewis and Davies (1991: 20) said that protective legislation fell uneasily between employment policy and anti-discrimination policy. In employment policy terms the government was highly pro-active, in anti-discrimination policy it was exceedingly reactive. Some see protection as restrictive, others see it as natural due to women's needs as workers and as mothers. The abolition of some protective legislation could be seen as a step towards equality. However, the state in Taiwan still needs to learn how to survive between the threat of business and the threat of women.

Summary

Until 1989, the state in Taiwan has treated women as a 'different' group of workers rather than an 'equal' group to male workers. Under patriarchal ideology, the state puts forward a view of protecting women workers and sets special conditions for working women in order to keep them away from exploitation by capitalists. In the workplace, women workers were traditionally regarded as child workers, who were weak and needed special protection. This notion has been changing since 1989. The state has admitted that gender discrimination does exist in the labour market. The outcry from women's groups signalled a new social force which demanded that the state modified market order and protected women's rights in the workplace. The state has had to do something in response to women's needs as working women have gradually become aware of their inferior status in the labour market.

The recent Labour Standards Law revision demonstrates that state policies favour business. Today the abolition of protective law is regarded as a step towards gender equality since the law often restricts women's opportunities in employment. However, the state in Taiwan wants to loosen the law for business flexibility rather than women's benefits. Judging by debates on the protective law, one can say that none of the political actors – the state, labour unions, and capitalists – are concern about women's needs. Both employers and labour unions want to own the power to control the female labour force; they neglect women's safety and their autonomy to choose nightwork.

Reconciling work and care: care policy

Many married working women faced caring duties, which were the main reason why they quit their jobs or could not join the labour force, as discussed in Chapter 4. Usually, a state will provide more support for carers if it wants the female labour force to be released. By way of reviewing caring policies, one can understand how far the state offers mothers sufficient flexibility to choose between entering the labour market and caring for their family members by themselves. Much research concerned with this issue has only discussed state child-care policies. However, due to cultural factors, many Taiwanese women could not join the labour force due to their responsibilities for caring for the elderly and the disabled in their families. In this section, there-fore, I would like to discuss caring policies related to children and other dependants.

Historical review

There are several means of enabling working parents to cope with childcare problems, but the state in Taiwan seems to be only con-cerned about the supply of nurseries. Before 1945, the KMT govern-ment stressed that the state should set up nurseries for labourers (see Table 6.16). The childcare business was historically run by private charity organizations, while the state was seldom involved in it (Shiu, 1992: 42–7). The policies of the KMT before 1945 show that the state would have liked to intervene in childcare provision. The KMT govern-ment also ruled that every factory and mine should set up a nursery for employees (Chang, 1988: 147).

After the KMT government retreated to Taiwan, it did not pay much attention to childcare. During the period 1963–74, many neighbour-hood nurseries, which were regarded as quasi-public, were set up through the support of the UN. At the time, the UN provided grants for Third World countries to improve facilities for children's welfare and for community development. The Child Welfare Law, was the first welfare law in Taiwan, and at this stage, the state strongly intervened in the provision of childcare.

However, after the 1980s, state policies tended to emphasize the responsibilities of firms to set up nurseries for their employees. In other words, the government hoped that the childcare problem could be solved by employment welfare since this problem occurred due to the utilization of the female labour force by business. In fact, as early as 1940, the KMT government enacted a measure to supervise and reward private nurseries, but it never implemented this measure once it retreated to Taiwan (Chang, 1988). A clear and positive scheme to reward nurseries was issued in 1991 (refer to Table 6.16).

Present state policies in terms of childcare focus on two areas: assist-ing every local authority to set up at least one 'showpiece nursery,' and

Table 6.16 Important policies and pronouncements of the KMT on caring

KMT-controlled mainland China

Year	Reference	Contents
1924	*Home Policy*	The state to ... provide caring assistance for the elderly, children, disabled and an educational system for labourers.
1926	*Women's Movement: Guideline of the KMT*	The state to set up nurseries.
1945	*Guidelines of Labour Policy*	The state to set up nurseries and related facilities to protect child and women workers.

KMT-controlled Taiwan only

Year	Reference	Contents
1964	*Current Social Policies of the Principle of People's Livelihood*	The local government to set up more nurseries and child welfare centres in urban, rural, industrial and mining areas, and encourage public and private institutions to provide more facilities for childcare.
1970	*Current Guidelines for Rural Economic Development*	The government to increasingly set up farm nurseries, so that women on farms can do some farm work or subsidiary work.
1973	*Child Welfare Law*	Article 13: The local government to subsidize any family which finds it difficult to raise children under 14 years old. Article 15: The local government to set up or subsidize private institutions to set up the following facilities for children: nurseries, play

Table 6.16 Important policies and pronouncements of the KMT on caring   *(continued)*

KMT-controlled Taiwan only

Year	Reference	Contents
1980	*Disabled Welfare Law*	Article 8: The local government to set up or subsidize private institutions to set up welfare organizations for the disabled. Article 14: The local government to assist the disabled to be housed according to their need … Article 15, 16: provide medical treatment, rehabilitation, support facilities to subsidize the disabled from low income families.
1980	*Elderly Welfare Law*	Article 7: The local government to set up or subsidize private institutions to set up welfare organizations for the elderly.
1989	*Revised KMT Constitution*	Article 79: … The government to implement … paternity leave for fathers. The government to also set up more welfare organizations for the elderly and for children, and consulting centres to relieve the pressure on women
1989	*Work Plan for Promoting Female Employment Service, Taiwan Province*	The government to encourage businesses to provide nurseries, welfare facilities and transportation for working women.
1989 1991	*Measure for Solving the Shortage of Labour*	The government and private institutions to set up nurseries and kindergartens. The government to also encourage businesses to provide childcare services, transportation and other welfare facilities for their employees, so that more women can join the labour market.

Table 6.16 Important policies and pronouncements of the KMT on caring (continued)

KMT-controlled Taiwan only

Year	Reference	Contents
1990	*Revised Disabled Welfare Law*	<u>Article 8</u>: The local government to set up or subsidize private institutions to set up welfare organizations for the disabled … These organizations can charge fees for using their service and facilities. <u>Article 12</u>: The local government to assist the disabled to be housed … If there is no suitable organization, the government to provide assistance to the disabled from low income families, in cash or by other methods, before the establishment of welfare organizations. <u>Article 13</u>: Any family with the disabled member is entitled to apply for tax relief and special tax deduction according to its economic situation and the level of the disabled. Allowances and benefits from the government are tax exempt. <u>Articles 14, 16</u>: In respect of medical treatment, rehabilitation, housing, livelihood, education and support facilities, the local government to give the disabled economic support according to the economic situation of their families and the level of the disabled. <u>Article 15</u>: The government should pay insurance fees for the disabled according to the economic situation of their families and the level of the disabled.
1991 1994	*Work Points for Promoting Childcare Services for Labourers*	In order to solve the problem of childcare and increase their productivity, (the CLA to) reward business, commissions of employee welfare funds, all levels of workers' unions and labourers' co-operative societies to provide more childcare services.
1992	*Employment Service Law*	<u>Article 43</u>: Foreign workers are allowed to do the following occupations, … maids, nurses …

186

Table 6.16 Important policies and pronouncements of the KMT on caring   *(continued)*

KMT-controlled Taiwan only

Year	Reference	Contents
1992	*Temporary Measures for the Families with Disabled Members*	1. The government to train qualified nurses to help families with seriously disabled people and the welfare organizations for the disabled. 2. Encouraging people to do nursing work. 3. In a case where a family with a seriously disabled member cannot find a home nurse, they are entitled to apply for a foreign nurse.
1994	*Measure for Promoting Women's Employment*	1. The government to provide in-service training for teachers in nurseries and kindergartens, childminders, and nurses in hospitals or day care centres. 2. The government to provide more day care service, home care services and living allowances for the elderly and the disabled. 3. The government to reward businesses which provide parental leave or which provide day care for their employees. 4. The government to encourage women to do volunteer work to care for children and the elderly.

Source: as Table 6.9.

rewarding private organizations to set up more nurseries (Taiwan Provincial Government, 1992: 16). The government would rather subsidize corporation, business units, workers' welfare commissions, trade unions and labour co-operative societies to set up nurseries for working parents than provide more public nurseries. In addition to provision in the workplace, the government is also concerned about provision by the market. It supports the training of staff and monitors the quality of facilities in private nurseries. Since 1988, it has entrusted private organizations to train and qualify childminders. Therefore, public nurseries will not be the main providers in the future. In terms of childcare, the state will be a regulator rather than a provider.

Compared with childcare, the government seldom announced its policies for supporting care of other family dependants. As shown in Table 6.16, the earliest one was the *Home Policy*, announced at the First National Representative Meeting of the KMT in 1924, then in the Revised Constitution of the KMT in 1989. The latest one was in the *Measure for Promoting Women Employment* in 1994. The government recognized women's tasks in caring for the elderly and the disabled as it wanted the female labour force to be released.

Since the 1990s, state policies towards caring have become more varied. Female staff in the Executive Yuan and Taipei City Government and female teachers in public junior high schools, primary schools and kindergartens are entitled to apply for parental leave. A working couple with young children and old parents are eligible to apply for a foreign maid, and since 1992 families with a seriously disabled member are also entitled to apply for a foreign nurse. Nevertheless, since the 1980s in some cities, more social services have been offered to relieve the caring burden on families, such as day care and home care services for people with serious disabilities. We will discuss the provision of social services in the next section.

With regard to recent tendency in state policies towards caring, the state in Taiwan would like to regularize and assist the market to supply qualified and varied services for the family instead of providing services itself. Although women's groups in Taiwan claim that childcare is not a woman's responsibility but the responsibility of society and the state, the state prefers the family, the market and firms to find the solution.

Related policies of the opposition parties

Unlike the KMT's policies, the two main opposition parties in Taiwan have stressed that the state should be actively involved in the childcare business and set up more public nurseries, as shown in Table 6.17. The

Table 6.17   **Important policies and pronouncements of two main opposition parties on caring**

Party	Reference	Contents
DPP	*Guidelines of the DPP (1986)*	<u>Article 80</u>: The party to promote caring system for the elderly, raise their pensions, and set up nursing homes. <u>Article 85</u>: The party to set up public nurseries widely for the benefit of working women and to ensure children's safety.
New Party	*The New Party'sPolicy White Paper (1995)*	<u>Social Welfare Policy</u> 1. To take care of the elderly and to show filial obedience are the responsibilities of children. This traditional system could reduce the financial burden on the state. However, it is the responsibility of the government to house the elderly who are without children or whose children cannot take care of them. 2. The government should provide free pre-school education and set up nurseries and kindergartens to reduce the burden on the family. The government should also subsidize private nurseries and kindergartens, and monitor their quality. <u>New Family, Women and Children Policy</u> 1. The government should enact a law to encourage people to take care of their parents and elder relatives. 2. The government should subsidize childcare costs for working women.

Source: as Table 6.11.

New Party also claimed that the state should provide free pre-school education and subsidize childcare costs, based on a belief that childcare was not only the responsibility of the family but also that of the state.

By contrast, the New Party emphasized that the elderly were the responsibilities of their children. If every old person could be cared for by his/her offspring, the financial burden on the state would be relieved. This party also suggested that the state should enact a law to force the family to support the elderly.

Practical actions: social welfare for caring

Childcare

State welfare has been directed at children in low-income families in Taiwan. Educational allowances, living allowances and travel allowances have been generously offered to children in low-income families in order to help them escape from poverty in the future (Commission on Population Policies, 1995: 179). Free daycare and after-school care for children have also been offered so that the adults in the low-income family can take on paid works; some children's homes have accepted children from single-parent families for the same reason. In comparison with other welfare care provision, allowances and childcare services for children in low-income families started early (see Table 6.18).

In recent years, childcare allowances and service have begun to be offered to children not from low-income families. Since 1984, the Kaohsiung City Government has provided 'after-school care.' Since 1988, some local governments began to train and qualify childminders. In 1998, The Taipei City Government announced universal childcare and medical allowances to children under six. This policy has been criticized by many Ministers in the central government as an action with political purpose. They argued that social welfare should only be offered to these people who really needed help (*Central Daily News*, 13/8/97).

The state has provided more generous assistance to civil servants, teachers in public schools and military servicemen in terms of caring. Education subsidies and food stamps have been provided to their children and parents.[19] Since 1990, some of them have been entitled to apply for parental leave. In 1996, the Kaohsiung City Government announced the offer of flat-rate daycare allowances to its female staff. These benefits, however, were treated as employment instead of state benefits as they were offered to government employees only.

Other dependants' care

In Taiwan, the family was the main institution shouldering the burden on caring for dependants, and female family members were the main carers. In 1994, 67 per cent of elderly people over 65 years old lived with their children or next door (76 per cent wanted to). Of those elderly people who were unable to take care of themselves, 84 per cent were cared for by their families, only 8 per cent lived in nursing homes or hospitals (DBAS, 1995f: 15). Women were the main carers; 68 per cent of old men were looked after by their wives, daughters or daughters-in-law; 51 per cent of women were looked after by their daughters-in-law (Hu, 1995: 59). In relation to the disabled, 63 per cent were cared for by their families, only 13 per cent lived in welfare institutions (DBAS, 1994e: 14).

Table 6.18   Social welfare for caring in Taiwan area, 1955–98 +

Time	Taiwan Province	Taipei City	Kaohsiung City
Before the 1980s ++	Farm nursery-free daycare (1955) Private nursery-reduced fees (1955) Living allowances for children under 15y (1959)	Living allowances for children and students Travel allowances Free milk and vitamins for babies and new mothers Scholarship (1969) Student Loan (1976)	Education allowances (1967) Living allowances for children (1976) Free daycare for children
1982	Provision of daycare for those with severe learning difficulties		
1983	Providing daycare for the elderly	Home care services for elderly people who are alone or ill +++	Home care service for elderly people who are alone or ill +++
1984			After-school care for 6–7 year old
1985	Home care service for elderly people who are alone or ill +++	Daycare for the disabled children Subsidy to the disabled ++	Home care service for the immobile elderly people ++ Free milk and vitamins for babies and new mothers ++
1987		Extending subsidy to all the seriously disabled over 15y	
1988	Children's Homes (orphanage) accept children in single families	Training qualified childminders	

Table 6.18 Social welfare for caring in Taiwan area, 1955–98 +   (continued)

Time	Taiwan Province	Taipei City	Kaohsiung City
1989		Daycare for the elderly	Daycare for the elderly Extending after school care Training qualified childminders
1991	Living allowances for the seriously disabled ++		
1992	Living allowances for young people ++		
1993	Home care and teaching service for the seriously disabled	Respite care for the seriously disabled	
1994	Living allowances for the elderly ++	Subsiding home care service for elderly people who are alone or ill ++	Daycare for the disabled
1996			Childcare allowances for female civil servants to support their children staying in nurseries
1998		Childcare allowances for all children under 6y (inc. edu., medicine, daycare)	

Note: +   The data have been corrected by senior officers in the Taiwan Provincial Government and the Taipei City Government.
++ The data indicate that welfare provision is only for low-income families.
+++ There are some conditions for application.

In the past, the state only provided very few old people's homes or nursing homes for those in low income families. Since 1982, the Taiwanese state has provided more service for the elderly and disabled (see Table 6.18). Three main kinds of service were developed. First, the state began to provide home care service to the seriously disabled and to elderly people who are alone or poor. The main reason for providing the service was the shortage of institutional care and welfare budget. Besides, for cultural reasons, old people felt ashamed to live in nursing homes since it meant that their offspring had abandoned them.

Secondly, since 1985 the disabled have been entitled to receive a small living allowance from the Taipei City Government. Later, the allowance was extended to other cities and to all the seriously disabled over fifteen years of age. Moreover, since 1994 the elderly in low-income families have been entitled to apply for living allowances.

Lastly, day-care services have been offered to people with severe learning difficulties (s.l.d.), the elderly and the disabled. Unlike the other two benefits mentioned above, these services have been provided for relieving pressure on carers. Free services have been offered to people in low-income families, average families can pay for using the services.

In spite of the increasing social service provisions in recent years, insufficient staff and organizations mean in reality that very few people receive public service support. For instance, only 17 disabled people used the home care and teaching service and 1 604 people with s.l.d. used daycare services in 1994 (the total number of the disabled was 257 936). In 1993, 2 675 old people used home care service and 1 249 used daycare services (there were 1 265 265 old people in 1994) (Taiwan Provincial Government, 1995a: Table 1.4, 1.6). Moreover, although the government began to provide some allowances to help families take care of dependants, the level of allowances was far too low for the family to buy substitute services from the market. For example, living allowances for the seriously disabled from low-income families were 4800 NT dollars per month. However, employing a non-professional nurse needed NT 2000 dollars per day and a special nurse 6 000 NT dollars per day. The responsibility for caring is still on the family.

Tax benefits

Tax relief is also offered to relieve the burden of care on the family. There are three kinds of tax relief. First, families are allowed to deduct taxable income of 60 000 NT dollars per year for every dependant, including children, parents, grandparents, great-grandparents and siblings. Secondly, every disabled person in the family has an extra tax allowance of 45 000 NT dollars per year. Thirdly, the cost of life insurance for a couple and their direct line dependants, which does not exceed 24 000 NT dollars per year, can be set against tax. Expenses spent on childcare and dependant's care are not liable for tax deductions (*United Daily News*, 22/3/1990).

Foreign maids and foreign nurses

Since 1992, foreign maids and nurses have been allowed to work in Taiwan. In order to legalize foreign maids, some women's groups put Legislators under a lot of pressure, and many professional women also petitioned the government to let their illegal foreign maids stay (*United Daily News*, 9/5/1992). In 1992, the passing of the Employment Service Law made the employment of foreign maids legal. Although the government was reluctant to 'import' foreign maids, it had no choice but to follow the law. Not only the government but also some women's groups opposed this policy. They thought it would affect employment opportunities for some middle-aged women because foreign maids would be cheaper and more flexible than domestic maids. Besides, the law was not in the interests of women. The state should publicize notions of sharing domestic chores, develop part-time and flexitime jobs, and train some qualified nurses.

According to the government, the aim of importing foreign maids was to promote women's employment, encourage three generations to live together and to support single elderly people. In order to avoid people becoming lazy or avoid foreign maids becoming a symbol of riches, only the elderly over 70 who lived alone and working couples with children under 12 or elders over 70 were entitled to apply for one. However, since single parents also needed manpower supplement, this policy has since been extended to single parents. The quota of import foreign maids was limited. According to the Council of Labour Affairs, the government would allow more foreign maids to work in Taiwan, providing the unemployment rate stayed low and the labour force participation rate of women increased (*United Evening News*, 20/3/1995; *Free Times*, 5/1/1997). In other words, importing foreign maids is a strategy to relieve the female labour force. When the market needs more labour, more foreign maids will be provided; when it is in recession, support for caring will be limited. The foreign maid policy is based on the need of the market instead of the relief of the caring burden on certain Taiwanese women.

Unlike foreign maids, the import of foreign nurses did not meet any obstacles. Both the government and the people agreed that nursing was hard work and it was very difficult to find a home nurse. Not only the family but welfare institutions and mental hospitals needed nurses. For good moral reason, the import of foreign nurses has never been an issue and the quota of them was unlimited.

By November 1996, there were 17 714 foreign maids and 21 973 foreign nurses with work permits. Their country of origin was limited to four by the government: the Philippines, Thailand, Indonesia and Malaysia; 42 per cent of them worked in Taipei City. Their average wage was 13 812 NT dollars, the basic wage was 13 350 NT dollars in 1995.[20] They are regulated by the Labour Standards Law and can join the labour insurance scheme, provided that their employers apply for them. In 1994, 94 per cent of foreign maids joined the labour insurance. As regards their tasks, 91 per cent had household duty, 62 per cent had to take care of children, and only 15 per cent had to take care of the elderly (CLA, 1995d: 16, 21–2). The maximum period for them to stay was three years.

Undoubtedly, this policy largely benefited high income families, as shown in Table 6.19. The caring problems of low-income or middle class families remained unsolved. However, this policy at least gave some women more alternatives to deal with their caring problems. Although the original aim of this policy was promoting women's employment, the majority of women employers already had jobs before employing foreign maids. Therefore, the chief effect of this policy was helping working parents to balance their careers and families, especially those women in top position.

Summary

Before 1945, the policies showed that the state would like to supply childcare facilities for working parents. Between 1963 and 1974, through the support of the UN, the state was involved in the provision of childcare. Recent policies have shown that public provision of caring facilities will not be mainstream in the future. The state would like to assist the development of the caring market and to regulate the quality of service in the market. Employers are also expected to provide support schemes for their employees to relieve their caring responsibilities.

In Taiwanese society, caring is traditionally regarded as the responsibility of the family; the family shoulders the majority of the burden. Although the state offers tax relief to relieve the burden of care on the

Table 6.19 Backgrounds of employers of foreign maids in Taiwan

	Number of persons	Percentage share	Percentage of all women workers
Income of the family/month			
lower than NT$ 40 000	475	3.6	
NT$ 40 000–59 999	2 340	17.6	
NT$ 60 000–79 999	3 525	19.6	
NT$ 80 000–99 999	2 603	26.5	
higher than NT$ 100 000	4 344	32.7	
The employment situation of the housewife			
had a job before hiring foreign maids	11 171	86.7	38.4+
had a job after hiring foreign maids	1 457	11.3	
no job	261	2.0	61.6
The occupation of the housewife			
professional, technician	2 322	18.4	21.7
administrator, manager	4 818	38.2	1.7
clerks	817	6.5	18.0
service workers and sales people	4 193	33.2	22.0
agricultural workers and machine operators	477	3.8	36.7
The average wage of the housewife/month			
lower than NT$ 20 000	1 146	9.1	30.0
NT$ 20 000–29 999	3 170	25.1	35.2
NT$ 30 000–39 999	3 325	26.3	13.5
NT$ 40 000–49 999	2 537	20.1	4.7
higher than NT$ 50 000	2 450	19.4	2.7

Note: + the data are for all women over 15 years old.
Source: CLA (1995d: 117, 142); DBAS (1994b: Table 13); DBAS (1995f: Tables 7, 134).

Table 6.20   **Caring policies for different kinds of families**

	Childcare	Other dependants' care
Low-income families	1. children's home 2. providing free day care in public nurseries 3. subsidising day care in private nurseries 4. education, living and travel allowances for children	1. institutional care 2. home care service 3. living allowances for the seriously disabled and the elderly
Average families	1. regulating nurseries and setting up showpiece nurseries 3. training qualified childminders 2. allowing foreign maids 4. after-class care for school children (Kaohsiung City)	1. daycare service 2. allowing foreign nurses
Special benefits for the family with members in a government department	1. childcare allowances (Kaohsiung City) 2. parental leave 3. education subsidy 4. food stamps for children	food stamps for parents

family, the amount of deductions is far from enough and caring fees do not benefit from tax deductions. The market for caring is not too active because people feel guilty and ashamed of buying supplementary services from this sector. Social welfare for caring has mainly been provided for low-income families in order to help children escape from poverty and to let the adults go to work. Means-testing is the principal method of deciding who can claim state benefits. Besides, civil servants have been offered more assistance for caring, either in cash or in kind (see Table 6.20). For the average family, the government has allowed them to employ foreign nurses to solve the long-term caring problems of the seriously disabled and the elderly. Training qualified childminders and importing foreign maids were two important schemes promoted by the state for solving the childcare problems of working parents. However, the former aimed to utilize the 'surplus labour in the family,' and was regarded as a great employment opportunity for housewives to work at home. The latter was regarded as a means of relieving the Taiwanese female labour force. The supply of foreign maids would be limited as the labour market is in recession. Therefore, the two policies were used by the state as tools for capital accumulation rather than for women's benefit. Since the provision of childcare is controlled by the state, working women do not have the right to purchase service from the market as they need.

Social policies in transition

From the review of social welfare and state policy, one can see how strong the state uses several schemes to urge women to join economic activities. The state in Taiwan has professed full employment as an aspiration from the wartime days when quasi-public nurseries were provided to assist mothers to work. But the state created a two-tier employment pattern for men and women. It encouraged women both to join economic activities and at the same time to take care of their family. Social insurance and other occupational welfare schemes were established to provide a semblance of the male breadwinner model, and benefited those who followed male employment patterns. Labour legislation focused on protecting women workers as mothers and weaklings, and placing them in a different section of the labour market.

After the mid-1980s, the state still wanted to develop the female labour force but it began to invest in it. Social investment welfare has been emphasized, such as vocational training and short-term living allowances for trainees. However, the state no longer expanded public childcare facilities but assisted the family to buy service from the market. Protective legislation for women was deregulated on the demand of employers instead of at the request of women. On the other hand, however, the state was also forced to introduce another kind of 'protective' legislation under pressure from the women's movement – equal opportunity legislation (see Table 6.21).

To sum up, these are some characteristics of state policies before the mid-1980s:

1. State policies were based on national needs instead of human needs or citizenship.
2. Married women were encouraged to work and to take care of their families at the same time, but always to put their families first. The female labour force was the secondary labour force.
3. The state was involved in the provision of childcare.

Table 6.21 Changes in state policies on women's employment

	Women's welfare	Employment policies	Equal opportunities policies	Caring policies
Before the mid-1980s	vocational rehabilitation and Mothers' Classroom	encourage women to do craftworks or subsidiary work	protect women workers as mothers or weaklings	develop quasi-public nurseries
After the mid-1980s	diversity * welfare centre * assistance to disadvantaged women	encourage married women to return to the labour market * vocational training * part-time work * living allowances for female bread-winners during vocational training	announce equal opportunity between genders and protect women's working rights	support childcare market and encourage occupational welfare * train qualified childminders * import foreign maids * reward private welfare organizations * parental leave * daycare and home care services

The characteristics of state policies since the mid-1980s were as follows:

1. The state has had to consider human needs to maintain its legitimacy.
2. Married women were encouraged to work and to take care of their families at the same time, or to return to work after child-raising, but always to put their families first.
3. The family and the market to solve the childcare problem. The state prefers to help the market were left to supply qualified and varied services for the family instead of providing services itself.
4. The state valued the importance of improving women's human capital instead of building an equal environment for women to work in.

7
The Emergence of the Gender Equal Employment Bill

In Taiwan, increasing numbers of women workers wanted to continue working after marriage or childbirth but many were forced to quit jobs due to company policies. Many firms believed that women workers with family responsibilities were troublesome and had less aspiration to work hard, so they forced their female employees to quit once they were married or pregnant. Although the Constitution and the Labour Standards Law have established women's equal rights to work and the latter has also ruled that firms must follow the principle of 'equal pay for equal work,' current legislation in Taiwan is still insufficient to protect women's employment rights.[1] The social circumstances and market orders have changed over time. As equal rights between men and women in the workplace have become a complicated issue in industrial society, they cannot be regulated by only two or three articles whose main purposes are not to eliminate gender discrimination in the workplace. Therefore, women's groups have looked forward to having a comprehensive law to protect women's equal rights in the labour market.

In 1990, a women's group, the *Awakening Foundation*, introduced the GEEB, which led to a great debate, still ongoing, in Taiwanese society. The bill was presented in the Legislative Yuan by 39 legislators who belonged to either the KMT or the DPP. This was the first time that the members of these two main parties presented a bill together. Moreover, this bill was the first that the people themselves, through their Legislators, were able to send to the Legislative Yuan. Previously, in Taiwan, all legislation was introduced by government departments. The documentation was always treated as secret, so the public hardly knew the contents of a bill before it was sent to the Legislative Yuan. People found it difficult to express their opinions about any legislation before it was passed since they did not know what kind of legislation the government was enacting or reviewing. The drafters of the GEEB insisted that this bill should be discussed publicly by different interest groups during its draft stage. If those interest groups could reach a consensus, then the bill would be accepted by the majority of the public after it became law (interviewee Solicitor Yu).

The bill not only tried to eliminate gender discrimination in the workplace but also to give support to working parents. From the 1960s onwards, and in view of the increase in female labour force participation, more working parents needed support to deal with their family responsibilities. The bill introduced many childcare schemes such as paternity leave, parental leave, childcare leave, reduction of work hours for new mothers and assistance for women who sought re-employment opportunities after finishing childcare responsibilities, to eliminate women's disadvantages in the labour market due to their reproductive roles. Reproduction is not the business of Taiwanese employers. Under the terms of the bill, employers will be forced to share the cost of reproduction with the family.

This chapter is a case study. I will use newspapers, legislative documents and interviews to present the development of the GEEB in Taiwan. The legislative process of the bill is closely related to the discussion and viewpoints between the state, business and women. The discussion of this case will aid understanding of the interaction between the state, capital, and women in the political arena. I will first review the development of the bill in the political arena and then discuss the different opinions towards its enactment. The introduction of the bill has raised controversial issues reflecting the varied ideologies on working women and/or social welfare in Taiwanese society. This case can also lead to further discussion of existing theories from a gender-critical perspective.

The development of the Gender Equal Employment Bill – a historical review

Political and social background

As mentioned in Chapter 5, social movements were booming in the mid-1980s in Taiwan. The power of people began to emerge and put pressure on the state to establish a reasonable social and legal system. At first, people used strikes, marches or demonstrations to express their discontent towards social systems. Once the passion had passed, some social movement groups realized that the underdeveloped legal system was the major barrier to equality in Taiwan. The people had tried many methods to express their requests. At last, they found that legal reform

202 Working Women and State Policies in Taiwan

was the most effective way. The groups have, therefore, gradually transferred their arena to the political system, to enacting legislation or affecting public policies. Their efforts changed public perception, but the bills proposed by them were often watered down by the government. The government would enact similar but more conservative legislation, so that the final contents of the legislation seldom came up to their expectations. The process of enacting the Sex Discrimination Bill in Britain was a similar story (Meehan, 1985).

The legislature has also changed greatly since the mid-1980s. The Legislators who were elected in 1947 in mainland China had never before needed to seek re-election. In 1986, the KMT agreed that all Legislators should be re-elected every three years, as a result of public criticism. The new Legislature had some new characteristics. First, each group wanted to get their representative on to the Legislature in order to influence the bill related to their specific interest. The Legislative Yuan became a new arena for interest groups. Secondly, more young, well-educated, and non-KMT politicians entered the Legislature. They were more able to accept advanced ideas and bills, and were passionate for reform. Thirdly, the KMT government no longer controlled the operation of the Legislative Yuan so it had to take more account of people's interests in order to keep its government status. It sometimes had to follow people's demands for social reforms. Fourthly, in order to be re-elected, Legislators had to respect people's opinions and get their names known. They began to reflect social issues promptly, to introduce their own bills, and to support bills which were drafted by social movement groups. In this way, Taiwanese people could, for the first time, introduce their own bills into the Legislative Yuan and had opportunities to create new legal devices.

The introduction of the Gender Equal Employment Bill

As presented in Chapter 4, marriage and pregnancy discrimination has been a serious problem in Taiwan. In 1987, 57 women workers in the Dr Sun Yat-sen Memorial decided to sue their institutions as they were forced to resign if pregnant or over thirty years old. The head of the Memorial said that it was the most important educational centre in Taiwan, so needed dignified female employees (interviewee, solicitor Yu). He also observed: '*There are many guests, from home and abroad, visiting our exhibition hall every day. Pregnant women with big bellies are too ugly to serve those guests. Besides, since women over thirty-year-old are physically and mentally slower than young women, they are not suitable to serve guests*' (Lee, 1987). During the case of the Dr Sun Yat-sen Memorial, a group of solicitors in the Awakening Foundation wanted to aid the women workers to sue the Memorial but found that no suitable law in Taiwan could help working women suffering through employment discrimination (see Table 7.1). Besides, the group of solicitors found that many countries had had anti-discrimination law for many years following the UN's demand that its members review their legislation for eliminating gender discrimination in the period 1975–84. Since Taiwan was not a member of the UN, she had not reviewed this legislation during the decade (interviewee, solicitor Lu).[2] Although women's groups asked the state to enact a law to protect women's working rights after the event of the Dr Sun Yat-sen Memorial, the state was reluctant to do so. The example of the Consumer Protection Act encouraged the group of solicitors to enact an equal employment law by themselves. Because consumer protection groups were not satisfied with the Consumer Protection Act introduced by the government, a major group introduced another bill expressing their opinions and sent it to the Legislative Yuan. Two versions of the law for the same purpose were discussed together by the Legislative Yuan. Finally, some of the ideas put forward by social groups were approved in the law.

From 1987 the solicitors' group in the Awakening Foundation began to research the anti-sexual discrimination legislation in a variety of countries (see Table 7.1 for the development of the GEEB). In 1989 and 1990, the Foundation held two public hearings to let the public discuss the draft. In 1990, the first draft of the GEEB was released and introduced into the Legislative Yuan by Legislator Chao Shao-kang. On 19 October 1991, the bill gained a first discussion in the Legislature's Legal and Interior Ministry Commission (refer to Figure 7.1 for the legislative process in Taiwan). The Legislators concluded that they

Figure 7.1   The legislation process in Taiwan

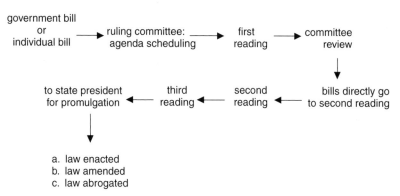

204

Table 7.1   Gender discrimination events and the development of the GEEB in Taiwan

The development of the bill and the actions of women's groups	Actions of the government and business groups
1. Gender discrimination events in early stage 08.1987 Dr Sun Yat-sen Memorial ruled the female employees over 30 years old who were married or pregnant should quit. Some women's groups made a stand against this event. 31.08.1987 Female employees of the Dr Sun Yat-sen Memorial and female employees of the National Historical Museum and Kaohsiung City Culture Hall petitioned the government to amend this policy and organized an 'Association of women workers in social educational institutes.'	The Memorial abolished the policy.
2. The development of the GEEB 1987 The Awakening Foundation began to research the enactment of the GEEB. 03.03.1989 The Awakening Foundation drafted the GEEB. 13.03.1990 Legislator Wu drafted another version of the same bill. 04.1990 The GEEB, drafted by women's groups, was supported by 39 legislators and sent to the Legislative Yuan. 19.10.1991; 11.01.1992; 10.06.1993 The Interior and Judicial United Commission in the Legislative Yuan discussed the bill drafted by women's Awakening Foundation. 1995.02.17 The GEEB drafted by Legislator Lee was included in the schedule of the Interior and Judicial United Commission.	11.1991 The Business Research Association, a business group, published a report: "Ten bad acts affecting the economic development in Taiwan,' which included the bill. 25.10.1991 The KMT asked Legislators to block the enactment of the bill, under pressure from businesses. 22.09.1993 The KMT negotiated with the DPP to slow down the processing of the bill, but the DPP did not agree with it. 13.05.1994 The National Industry Association and the National Commerce Association petitioned the Legislative Yuan to stop the enactment of the bill, and opposed the implementation of paternity leave. 05.1994 The CLA finished the first draft of the GEEB.

Table 7.1 Gender discrimination events and the development of the GEEB in Taiwan *(continued)*

The development of the bill and the actions of women's groups	Actions of the government and business groups
	16.02.1995 The draft proposed by the CLA was turned down by the Premier due to opposition by economic departments. 10.04.1996 The departments reached an agreement about the bill.
3. The 'Single Article (Marriage Discrimination)' Events 04.05.1993 Female employees of the Kaohsiung First Co-operative Bank and women's groups petitioned Legislators to force their banks to abolish the policy on marriage discrimination. 13.10.1994; 14.01.1995; 25.02.1995 Women's groups petitioned the government to take notice of marriage discrimination within firms being operated under the table. 12.11.1994 Women's groups marched in support of passing the GEEB, and demanded that the service sector should be regulated by the Labour Standards Law. 12.01.1995 Some social movement groups made a stand in front of the TYMC Bank to force it to abolish the policy of marriage discrimination. 14.01.1995 Women's groups published a list of the co-operative banks which still implemented the policy of marriage discrimination. 07.03.1995 Women's groups marched in support of the abolition of marriage and pregnancy discrimination.	04.07.1994 The CLA wrote an official letter to all co-operative banks to ask them to abolish the policy of marriage discrimination. 06.02.1995 Based on the policy of the Employment Service Law, the government asked local authorities to set up an Evaluative Commission on Employment Discrimination as soon as possible. 03.1995 The CLA finished a special inspection of marriage discrimination in co-operative banks. 13.03.1995 The TYMC Bank agreed to abolish the policy of marriage discrimination. 29.04.1995 The TYMC Bank became the first bank to be fined for marriage discrimination. 02.06.1996 The appeal by the bank was turned down by the Administrative Court.

Source: 1. Awakening (1995: 4–8).
      2. Newspapers, from 1991 to 1996.

should listen to the opinions of every interest group. Then they invited scholars, business groups and women's groups to discuss the bill for the second time on 12 January 1992. After the first discussion, the KMT informed its convenor in the Interior Commission, Legislator Lin Chih-chia, to block the bill due to strong opposition from business. Later, Legislator Lin expressed that the KMT would not let the bill pass before the revision of the Labour Standards Law (*United Daily News*, 26/10/91; *United Evening News*, 31/10/91).

On 10 June 1993, the bill gained a third discussion, especially the detailed articles. During the meeting, some legislators criticized the government for not presenting a parallel bill, and insisted on discussing the bill until the arrival of the government version. The meeting, however, was filibustered by some members of the KMT party. Finally, only the first article, the name of the bill, was approved.

After June 1993, the Legislative Yuan stopped discussing the bill and women's groups also slowed their steps. On the one hand, women's groups realized that it was impossible for the bill to be passed within a short period due to interference by business. On the other hand, the economy in Taiwan was in decline at that time, and it was not suitable to raise this issue during the recession. The Foundation, therefore, transferred their attentions to reviewing the Family Chapter of the Civil Code, and did not monitor the progress of the Gender Equal Employment Law as intensively. Solicitor Yu explained that they would continue the cultural work until the majority of people could accept the ideas put forward in the bill.

After the women's group proposed the bill, the labour department began to research the legislation, though it was reluctant to introduce a new law at that time. In 1994, the Executive Yuan ordered the Council of Labour Affairs to present the government bill as soon as possible since the bill was regarded as the first objective of legislation by women's groups for that year. When the labour department submitted his draft to the meeting of the Cabinet in February 1995, the bill was blocked by the economic departments for its possible negative effect on economic development. The draft was finally turned down by the Premier (*China Times*, 17/2/95). This event was criticized by civil women's groups as a proof of the innately patriarchal and capitalist nature of the Cabinet.

On 10 April 1996, those government departments associated with the bill finally reached a consensus under the aegis of the Council of Economic Planning and Development. The government bill was therefore sent to the Executive Yuan, to await discussion by the Cabinet.[3]

Officer Tung in the Bureau of Labour Conditions, which took charge of the draft, blamed women's groups for not keeping up the pressure on government and legislators so the draft was lodged in the Cabinet archives for many years (interviewee Tung).

On 4 March 1999, under no apparent pressure from women's groups, the Cabinet suddenly passed the government bill as a gift for Women's Day, regarding it as one of the key objectives of legislation in that season of legislative meetings. Nevertheless, the government's action was not approved by women activists. The ruling party published its *White Paper on Women* before the last presidential election in 1996, but to date very few of its promises have been fulfilled. As a result, feminist scholars and women activists criticized the bill as being a publicity stunt for the presidential election in 2000 rather than a positive move towards promoting women's benefits.[4]

Single article events

By 1994, the Council of Labour Affairs had received many reports of marriage discrimination (see Table 7.1 for the development of the Single Article Events). Although working contracts related to marriage discrimination were declared illegal by the Ministry of Interior in 1986 and by the Ministry of Justice in 1989, many women still lost their jobs after marriage. Employment discrimination towards married women was called the 'single article' (*Tan Cheng Tiao Kuan*) in Taiwan. In December 1994, Credit Cooperative of Yangming Mountain dismissed nine married women workers. This event drew much attention from the public, the government and social groups. Many women's groups and workers' groups made a stand in front of the bank in order to force it to abolish the policy of marriage discrimination (*United Daily News*, 12/1/1995; 13/3/1995). These groups also petitioned the labour department to protect women's working rights (refer to the documents in the Bureau of Labour Inspection). Since the chief of the executive board in the bank was the assemblyman of the DPP, the party also suffered severe criticism over this event. In January 1995, some workers' groups went to the office of the DPP to complain against their policy on women. The labour department also demanded that the Ministry of Finance should negotiate with the bank.

The action of the women's groups was finally supported by the Chief of the Bureau of Labour Inspection. Although the current legislation was sufficient to protect women's working rights, the Chief suggested citing the fifth article of the Employment Service Law to punish the banks for marriage discrimination, and promised that his department would deal with and punish those who applied the single article.[5] In February 1995, the Council asked local authorities to set up an *Evaluative Commission for Employment Discrimination* based on the regulation of the Employment Service Law. In March 1995, the Bureau of Labour Inspection launched a special inspection for examining cases of marriage discrimination in co-operative banks.[6] This was probably the first inspection of marriage discrimination in the world, the Chief of the Bureau of Labour Inspection said. 'It is a great opportunity to extinguish the single article; there is much media concern about this issue and the public support our action. If we do not do it now, we will not get a second chance' (*China Times*, 8/3/1995). The Chief added that the department would announce the names of firms without exception if they received any evidence of marriage discrimination.

Under great pressure from the public and the government, the TYMC bank still insisted on keeping its policy under wraps, like other banks, using provisional personnel ratings as an excuse. In May 1995, the bank held a recruitment examination but only single women were allowed to take it. Finally, the bank was fined by the labour department in Taipei City. The judicial system was also against the practice of marriage discrimination. In November 1995, the Superior Court explained that working contracts related to marriage discrimination were illegal (*Min Sheng News*, 6/11/1995). In June 1996, an appeal by the TYMC Bank regarding punishment of marriage discrimination was turned down by the Administrative Court (*Min Sheng News*, 3/6/1996).

Contents of the bill

The GEEB introduced by the Awakening Foundation mainly consists of two parts: equal employment and schemes for helping workers achieve a healthy balance between work and family roles. The first section aims to maintain an equal working environment, and to forbid any kind of gender discrimination in the workplace in respect of wages, recruitment, tasks, evaluation of performance, promotion, vocational training, welfare and retirement. The second section tries to help employees cope with the conflicts between childcare and work and to eliminate the disadvantages experienced by women workers due to their roles as mothers. It advocates maternity leave, paternity leave, one-year parental leave, family care leave, reduction of working hours for nursing mother, and re-employment measures. Male workers are also entitled to claim both parental leave and family care leave.

Since the introduction of the first draft, the solicitors' group of the Awakening Foundation has amended the bill several times. Based on public opinion, many articles have been amended to make them more reasonable. In the first draft, many articles were applicable to women workers only, whilst in the latest version all workers are covered.[7] Articles concerning sexual harassment in the workplace have been included, and maternity leave has been extended to twelve weeks based on the regulation of the ILO. Parental leave was no long compulsory for all firms since small business might have problems arranging cover. The latest version also mentions income support during parental leave. Workers should have the right to continue claiming all kinds of social insurance during their leave, and the state should share the insurance costs with them.

The contents of the government version have also been changed several times.[8] Originally, the strategy of the government was to introduce a bill which encouraged non-compulsory articles. Until society can accept the ideas introduced in the bill, the government will consider amending the bill with compulsory articles (*China Times Express*, 26/5/92). At first, the government version only contained items on equal employment, maternity leave and non-compulsory parental leave (*China Times Express*, 6/6/92). In October 1992, the government department decided to include articles on sexual harassment (*United Evening News*, 8/10/92). In October 1993, non-compulsory paternity leave was added to the government version, with leave pay left to be solved by collective agreement (*China Times*, 26/10/93). In March 1994, the Premier instructed that the government version of the GEEB should not be too conservative, otherwise the government would be blamed by the public. After that, the Council of Labour Affairs amended its policy for enactment (*United Daily News*, 24/3/94). On 12 May 1994, the Council of Labour Affairs at last presented a first draft containing articles on equal employment, sexual harassment (with penal provision), paternity leave (two days without pay), parental leave (up to one year without pay) and childcare leave (up to seven days without pay – regarded as absence). Firms with fewer than 50 workers would be exempt from implementing parental and childcare leave (*China Times*, 13/5/94). By April 1996, the seven-day childcare leave had been changed to family care leave for family emergencies (*China Times*, 11/4/96). In the final version revised in 1999, exemption from applying parental leave law has been extended to firms with fewer than 100 workers (*China Times*, 5/3/99).

Table 7.2   The important contents of the GEEB

	The version of the women's group		The government version
	First draft (1990)	Sixth draft (1999)	(1999)
Day off for menses	1 day/m with half pay	1 day/m with half pay	–
Maternity leave +	8 weeks with pay	12 weeks with pay	8 weeks with pay
Paternity leave +	14 days with pay	5 days with pay	2 days without pay
Parental leave for both male and women workers	up to 1 year without pay	same ++	same, can apply twice +++
Insurance costs during parental leave	–	shared by employees and the state	paid by employees themselves
Coverage of parental leave	all kinds of workers (inc. civil servants)	firms with more than 10 workers	Firms with more than 100 workers
Reduction of work hours	1 hr/day for up to two years, no pay	same	–
Articles for anti-sexual harassment	–	yes	yes (pertaining to employers' behaviour, nor workers' or clients')
Childcare leave/family care leave	up to 10 days with pay for caring for sick children under six	up to 10 days without pay for caring for sick families	Up to 7 days without pay for caring for sick family members ++++
Nurseries in the workplace	–	firms with more than 250 workers should have nurseries	The competent authority should subsidize firms to set up nurseries

Table 7.2 The important contents of the GEEB (*continued*)

	The version of the women's group		The government version
	First draft (1990)	Sixth draft (1999)	(1999)
Assistance for re-employment	yes	yes	yes
Transfer of burden of proof	on the employer or business entity	same	same
Penalties	applied to those who denied equal employment, maternity, paternity and childcare leave	same + sexual harassment, set up nurseries, family care leave, job security for workers in litigation	same + sexual harassment and family care leave
Initiative inspection	yes	yes – the authority should publicize the name of firms which are fined	–
Effective date	childcare leave should be implemented 2 years after the bill becomes law	parental leave, family care leave, nurseries should be implemented 1 year after the bill becomes law	date of the bill becoming law

Note: +   Employees who work in firms less than six months should be paid half-wages.
++   The state should offer childcare allowance to workers during parental leave according to the financial situation of the family. This allowance should be regulated in other related legislation.
+++   Employees who work in their firms less than one year should be excluded.
++++   Firms with fewer than *50 workers* were exempt from implementing the regulations.

212 Working Women and State Policies in Taiwan

Through the co-ordination of the Council of Economic Planning and Development, the related government departments finally reached agreement about the contents of the bill. Judging by the final government version, the gap between the version prepared by the women's group and that of the government was diminishing. As shown in Table 7.2. Despite shorter periods being granted, the government version contained all kinds of leave demanded by women's groups. For some of the regulations, the government version offered even more generous benefits than the original version drafted by women's groups. Parental leave and family care leave became compulsory (with penalties) although only 42 per cent of employees (0.8 per cent of firms) were qualified to apply for parental leave and 50 per cent to apply for family care leave. Interestingly, civil servants were excluded from the government bill. So, even though the attitude of the government appeared more generous, private companies were still having to pay for the benefits (*Min Sheng News*, 5/3/99).

In this new political and social environment, women's groups took action to introduce their own bill for equal employment between genders. The progress of legislation was not without problems; the bill met strong opposition from business, the government and some legislators. Although the bill has not yet been passed, the government has been forced to draft a parallel bill and the notions of the public have changed after the 'Single Article Events' of 1995. In the past, both employers and employees thought that the marriage and pregnancy discrimination was normal, while companies began to cover up such policy for fear of public criticism. In the Single Article Events, one can see how the attitude of the government has changed, beginning to intervene in company employment rights. Institutional inspections and administrative measures to stop employment discrimination have been in operation, even before the GEEB became law.

In recent years, workers' groups have marched on special days for labour rights and women's groups have also marched for women's rights on Women's Day. The enactment of the bill has become one of the major themes of the marches, for example, those held on 12 November 1994 and on 30 April 1995. As solicitor Yu said, they have not given up the GEEB, they have just extended the battle. Time will tell. After ten years of debate on the issue of gender equality, women's groups and the government are drawing closer in terms of resolving the contents of the bill. The government would like to provide administrative assistance but not provide any financial support and benefits to working parents.

Opposition opinions and public responses towards the bill

Obstruction by businesses

After the GEEB had been set in the schedule of the Legislature's Legal and Interior Ministry Commission, business groups began to express their disagreement as well as put pressure on the KMT government. Mr Kuo, the assistant secretary in the National Industry Association, said: 'We are in a very nervous state. We have held an emergency meeting to discuss how to deal with the bill and to demand the Legislators who belong to business groups slow down the progress of the bill' (*United Evening News*, 22/10/1991).

Employers stress the difficulty of implementing the bill if it was passed. First, it would be difficult for them to arrange cover during employees' leave, especially in the manufacturing sector. Secondly, any legislation which aims to protect particular sections of the labour force would lead to contrary results. Since the cost of employing a women worker would increase after the passing of the bill, employers would probably substitute other cheaper labour, such as foreign workers. Thirdly, the passing of the bill would lower the competitive abilities of businesses in international markets. Some businesses may lose interest in domestic investment, and move their capital and factories to other countries (refer to Table 7.3).

Most of the negative opinions from employers towards the bill have focused on all kinds of family leave. Few businesses have commented on the main section of the bill, on equal pay and equal opportunity. They have argued that the current legislation has enforced equal employment so there is no need for a new law to protect women's working rights. The Labour Standards Law has, for instance, regulated equal pay for equal work, and the Employment Service Law has forbidden employment discrimination. If women felt dissatisfied, they should demand a review of the Labour Standards Law (interviewee Mr Kuo). However, when some Legislators tried to enlarge the coverage of the Labour Standards Law, business groups still blocked it (*Business Daily News*, 23/10/1996; 25/10/1996). The opposition of businesses to the family leave was regarded as a means of impeding the whole bill by both solicitor Yu and officer Tung.

Employers also complained that the current statutory holidays and leave for employees were generous enough for employees to arrange their family care. All assistance for childcare should come under the auspices of welfare or belong to the responsibility of the family. They refused to undertake any of the cost. Leave for childcare may, if necessary, be applied to women workers only because childcare is a 'natural obligation' of women. Nevertheless, it was intolerable that male workers could also take parental or childcare leave. Mr Kuo said: 'Men do not go to work and stay at home to care for children? What a joke!' Moreover, they argued that the family would not need grandparents' labour and refused to live with them if parents could apply for parental leave. The passage of the bill would result in the disintegration of the traditional family system and the waste of the labour force.

Finally, businessmen suggested that laws should be the product of social custom. The enactment of legislation had to consider the domestic social situation instead of duplicating foreign legal systems. Only developed countries were qualified to implement this legislation, but Taiwan, with a low GNP, was not. Besides, working conditions should be negotiated through collective bargaining instead of being regulated by legislation since the situation of each industry was different. Most firms were concerned about their employees and would like to offer as much flexibility to their employees to cope with family responsibilities as they can. Workfare is one means for employers to keep their employees. The state should not intervene in the provision of workfare (*United Evening News*, 10/6/93).

Essentially, the provision of family leave and maternity leave is related to the reproduction of the labour force. Since the cost of reproducing labour used to be paid by women, they were unable to have equal opportunities with men in the labour market. Through the bill, part of the cost would be transferred to men and employers. Therefore, businesses have opposed the bill with all their strength.

The state and the opposition party

The bill met with opposition not only from business but also from most departments of the state. Initially, the Chairman of the Council of Labour Affairs, as the authority-in-charge, stressed that the current labour legislation was good enough to protect women's working rights so there was no need for a new law. The business community would be upset if such a strict bill was passed. The economic departments were critical of the bill, saying that it would affect businesses' willingness to invest. The Ministry of Personnel, which deals with the business of civil servants, refused to apply the bill to civil servants because it worried about the negative influence of the bill on the efficiency of these workers (refer to Table 6.3). Former Premier Lien also stressed that the state should positively encourage women to join the labour market instead of passively protecting women's working rights. He said:

> The labour force participation rate of female in Taiwan was lower than that in other main Asian countries. But we should investigate whether it is the result of low pay, short periods of maternity leave, lack of parental leave or other reasons before we enact the GEEB.
>
> — *Independent Daily News, 17/2/95*

Although the Council of Labour Affairs refused to draft the bill, it now regarded the enactment of the bill as one of its important working objectives. During the Cabinet meeting, the Labour Minister even spoke in defence of it. Officer Tung explained that the reason why the government enacted the bill was force of pressure from women's groups. In this case, the government amended its policy to take account of the needs of the people. The Council has also recently debated its policy for enacting the bill. It exclaimed:

> The bill aims to build a reasonable and equal society. A society which respects equality should try to maintain sexual equality because the rest of the world is moving in this direction. The bill is not for protecting women only. Male workers can also benefit from the bill. It is very unfair for businesses to exclude women workers due to the enactment of the bill.
>
> — *People Daily News, 12/4/96*

> The enactment of the bill will raise the labour force participation rate in our country, solving the current problem of labour shortage. Besides, the possible negative effects of the bill on businesses will be insignificant (newsletters for the GEEB).
>
> — *Min Sheng News, 5/3/99*

It was not only the attitude of the Council of Labour Affairs towards the enactment of the bill which changed but also their policies on promoting gender equality. As mentioned in Chapter 6, the council began to subsidize private organizations to publicize ideas about gender equality, and to support the organizations which wanted to educate their employees. They also considered adding 'complaints procedures for sexual harassment' as one indicator in their annual evaluation of enterprises.

Although the Labour Department supports the bill, the attitude of the Cabinet as a whole towards it remains uncertain. In contrast, the bill was fully supported by the DPP. Since the DPP was historically close to social movements, it usually supported their actions. The party knew that it should keep close to social issues when planning ahead (interviewee Liu). The DPP legislators have played an important role in furthering the progress of the bill, although some DPP members, who were also businessmen, did not support the bill even though they would not dare to advertise this in public.

Legislators

In 1993, the Awakening Foundation investigated the attitudes of Legislators towards the GEEB. Seventy-two Legislators expressed their opinions, while 88 refused to answer. Seventy of their sponsors supported the bill (41 to the DPP; 21 to the KMT), 58 supported the proposal to offer male workers 14 days paternity leave, and 43 supported the idea that both men and women could apply for one-year parental leave (*China Times Express*, 9/10/93; *Independent News*, 10/10/93).

Legislator Hung observed that whether employers or employees, legislators had to consider every level of society affected by a bill. Generally speaking, Legislators were worried about two negative influences of the bill. First, the passing of the bill might reduce the willingness of employers to hire women workers. Secondly, the bill may affect the investment willingness and competitive abilities of enterprises. Besides, some Legislators thought that it would be problematic to implement parental leave because employers would not only have the problem of arranging cover but also need to re-train returning staff (refer to Table 7.3).

Many Legislators were also employers and owned firms. In order to defend their interests, they might impede the passing of the bill or water it down. In fact, many Legislators supported the bill following the call for reform from the public. Few Legislators really understood the nature and content of the bill. Legislator Hung thought that all the female legislators would definitely support the bill no matter which party they belonged to. It was *gender identity*. Female Legislators would support women's issues but none wished to be associated only with women's issues. Most male legislators, however, were still very conservative, and could not accept some of the ideas in the bill. Since the majority of Legislators were male, the bill could be watered down in the future (interviewee Legislator Hung).

Table 7.3 Opinions against the legislation

Opposes	Reasons for opposition
1. Government departments	
P.K. Chiang, Minister of Economic Affairs	Opposes all types of family leave. Protecting women too much will reduce companies' willingness of investment (*China Times*, 17/2/95).
L.T. Hsu, Chairman of the Council of Economic Planning and Development	The period of maternity leave is too long (*Independent Daily News*, 17/2/95).
S.P. Chao, Chairman of Labour Affairs	The government would like to amend the Labour Standard Law and related legislation instead of enacting a new bill (*United Daily News*, 26/10/91).
Ministry of Personnel	Against the bill being applied to civil servants because it will affect their efficiency (*Central Daily News*, 6/4/92).
2. Legislators	
Y.T. Ts'ai and H.C. Chen	The enterprise will avoid hiring women workers if the bill is passed (*Independent Daily News*, 11/6/93).
H.C. Chen; C.I. Huang; S.S. Lin	1. Difficult for companies to implement parental and paternity leave. 2. The government should amend the Labour Standards Law instead of enacting this legislation (*Independent Daily News*, 11/6/93).
3. The business sector	
Y.H. Kuo, assistant secretary of the National Industry Association; Business Research Association	1. The bill will make companies struggle to survive and force them to move abroad (*United Daily News*, 29/9/93). 2. The issue should be solved by collective agreement instead of by legislation. 3. Employee leave mentioned in the bill should belong to the sphere of social welfare so that the costs could be paid by insurance or by the state, instead of by business (*Independent Daily News*, 11/6/93). 4. The number of statutory holidays in Taiwan is already the highest in the world. We should not offer workers any more leave (*United Daily News*, 4/5/93).

Table 7.3 Opinions against the legislation *(continued)*

Opposes	Reasons for opposition
A resolution made by the board of directors of the National Industry Association	The association opposes the enactment of this legislation. The government should amend the Labour Standards Law and the Employment Service Law instead of enacting a new law (*Taiwan Daily News*, 12/1/92; *Economy Daily News*, 23/9/93).
Wu, the convener of legal subdivision of the Business Research Association	Childcare leave should belong to the area of Child Welfare Law (*Taiwan Daily News*, 12/1/92).
Wong, head of the executive board of the National Commerce Association	Doubts whether Taiwan would still want to develop economy if such bill is passed (*United Daily News*, 29/9/93).
Business Research Association	1. The bill will make companies struggle to survive and force them to move abroad (*China Times*, 13/6/93) 2. The aim of the bill is about equality of labour conditions. If we enact a law to protect women workers from the perspective of social welfare, it will be against the spirit of employment equality in the labour market (*United Daily News*, 29/9/93).
N.T. Huang, executive of a private company S.C. Wu, president of a private company	1. It is reasonable for women to have the right to apply for maternity and family leave, but it would be unbearable if men were also entitled to have such leave. 2. Family leave will make the problem of labour shortage worse (*United Daily News*, 5/5/93). Grandparents cannot have the pleasure of raising their grandchildren if parents have parental leave. Not only will social productivity decrease, but the investment of

Table 7.3 Opinions against the legislation *(continued)*

Opposes	Reasons for opposition
C.M. Liu, bank manager	Parental leave is contradictory to the 'three generations living together' tradition, and will result in increasing nuclear family size since the family will no longer need help from grandparents (*Business Times*, 93).
K.N. Chang, president of Eva Airline and Shipping; Hong Kong Business Association	1. The bill will increase the cost of production and reduce the competitive abilities of business. 2. Taiwan is not qualified in such legislation because it is only a developing country (*Free Times*, 11/6/93).
Mr Hung, chairman of the Business Research Association	1. The government should consult business opinions before it enacts the bill. 2. The period of paternity leave (fourteen days) is too long. 3. Employers cannot cope with parental leave if applied to male workers (*United Evening News*, 22/10/91).
Electronics Industries Association and Textile Industries Association	It is difficult for companies to arrange cover during employees' parental leave because most firms in Taiwan are small or medium-sized (*United Evening News*, 22/10/91).

Public responses

Since the Awakening Foundation introduced the GEEB, equal employment between men and women has become the single most important issue for those concerned with improving women's employment in Taiwan, whether or not they are in the labour force (DBAS, 1994a: Table 64). Additionally, based on a private survey in 1995, 'enacting a law for protecting equal employment' and 'physical safety' were the two top social issues with which women were concerned (Twenty-first Century Foundation, 1995). Thus, without a doubt, the enactment of the GEEB was widely supported by women.

A survey taken by the Council of Labour Affairs also showed 30 to 40 per cent of the 500 largest firms in Taiwan supported some parts of the bill, such as parental leave, family care leave and reduced working hours for nursing mothers. In practice, however, almost none of them have implemented those policies (*Economic Daily News*, 29/7/96; *Min Sheng Pao*, 29/7/96). 'A sense of morality' was the possible reason for the great gap between the attitude and the practice of these companies. As public opinion approved these policies, some businesses would not display their opposition. Research into the legislative process of the Labour Standards Law in Taiwan also showed that business avoided expressing an opinion in public when the public overwhelmingly approved the enactment of the law (Chu and Hsieh, 1989: 81). Moreover, all of these companies agreed that leave for caring for family members could only be applied to women workers; while 54 per cent agreed with parental leave. Although 89 per cent did not think that the bill would affect their domestic investments, 32 per cent admitted that they would reduce recruitment of women workers if the bill was passed (*United Daily News*, 29/7/96).

To sum up, women gradually became aware of their unequal status in the workplace, and became more concerned about the development of the GEEB, even if they were not in the labour market. The bill was suspended because both the state and employers convinced themselves of its negative effect on economic development. To be specific, employers worried about the burden of payments and the problems of job cover during employees' leave periods. Businesses contended that the provision of welfare should be consistent with economic growth. Under the threat of capital flowing out of the country, the state did not respond positively to women's demands. Some legislators spoke in favour of the bill but most did so for the purpose of bolstering their political kudos. However, as a result of public pressure, the enactment of the bill has been included in the manifesto of the three main political parties in Taiwan.

Controversial issues

The introduction of the GEEB has raised various debates in Taiwan. From 1990 to 1996, public discussion focused on the provision of family leave, and exploring cases of unequal treatment between men and women. Many ideas in the bill were regarded as too 'advanced' when they were introduced to the public. After seven years, debate more people, including some government officers, have accepted some of ideas in the bill. The government has also announced its intention to eliminate gender discrimination in the labour market.

In this section, I will analyze the different viewpoints of groups on some controversial issues. Key people representing six groups have been interviewed in order to ascertain the different viewpoints. The six groups include women's groups, the government, business groups, Legislators, the opposition party, and labour groups. The representatives of women's groups and the government are the main drafters of the two parallel bills; others usually express the viewpoints of the groups they represent. In this event, trade unions have not been involved in promoting the bill at all, so I have chosen an active 'external system' labour group as the representative of labour.[9] The name, title and representative group of each interviewee are listed in Appendix 3. The guidelines of interviews will be presented in Appendix 4.

Childcare responsibilities

Based on my interviews with representatives of women's groups and the government, there was a clear assertion that childcare responsibilities should be shared by the whole 'society' instead of by women or the family. In the current plan of the solicitors' groups of the Awakening Foundation, the majority of the costs of family leave is to be paid by employers. Employers needed to take responsibility for income support during employees' leave, except one-year parental leave. To be in line with the regulation of the Labour Standards Law, solicitor Yu explained, employers were expected to pay fully wages to employees during maternity leave. Since the periods of childcare leave and paternity leave were short, the women's group hoped that employees would be full paid during these periods. Compared with businesses, the responsibilities shared by the state were far less, since the women's group was generally worried about the financial ability of the state. The state was expected to share the insurance costs with employees during their parental leave, to provide employment assistance to women who wanted to re-enter the labour market, and to reward firms whose performance was excellent in terms of providing childcare facilities. The only new burden to the state was the share in insurance costs; the others, which were regulated by other legislation, had already been implemented by the state. However, the representative of women's groups, solicitor Yu, also suggested that income support during family leave should be paid by the national insurance systems in the future. In other words, employers, employees and the state should share the cost of childcare.

Although the labour department worried about the executive abilities of business, it placed an emphasis on their social responsibilities:

> Most employers think that childcare is none of their business. However, the cost of childcare should be shared by the whole of society. Business of course should share childcare responsibilities once women are working for them.
>
> – Interviewee Mr Tung

According to the design of the government, the state only needed to take over the responsibilities of administration. The state would be a supervisor instead of a provider. Firms should provide flexible jobs for employees with children. The cost of child-raising was the responsibilities of the family, but income support during leave was expected to be solved by collective agreements. The state seemed to regard all workfare for workers as the employers' business. On the contrary, employers could not and cannot accept the idea of sharing childcare responsibilities. The views of Mr Kuo on employers' responsibilities of childcare are very typical:

> Parents should consider whether they have the ability to bring up a child before they decide to have one. If they cannot afford the cost of bringing up a child, they can choose not to have one ... Alternatively, the state should undertake responsibilities for childcare, depending on its population policy. If the state is worried about the decline in the population, it can offer allowances to families with children. But it is by no means one of the social responsibilities of capitalists ... I do not understand. If working parents feel it is difficult to take care of children, for the children's sake, why can't women sacrifice their careers?
>
> – Interviewee Kuo

For employers in Taiwan, any company scheme to assist employee to reconcile family and work roles is a kind of 'favour' rather than a 'responsibility.' These family friendly schemes should not be regulated by labour legislation as a basic working condition. They are a means by which employers can stabilize their employees and a way of showing kindness. Because the state wants to show that it is a 'benevolent agency,' it intends to enact a law to please the labour.

Legislator Hung also emphasizes the family's responsibility for childcare. Neither the state nor employers should be involved in providing welfare to working parents. She said:

> I approve the spirit of promoting family leave for working parents, so that they can take care of children by themselves. However, I believe that the family should take the majority of childcare responsibilities ... I do not think that the state should provide childcare allowance to aid the family with children. The state can assist the family by way of providing education and benefits to low-income families.

> – Interviewee Legislator Hung

Most of the KMT Legislators may have the same views as Legislator Hung, but the DPP Legislators think in a different way. In accordance with its thinking on other welfare policies, the DPP stresses the state's responsibilities for childcare. In 1993 the election of county chiefs and city mayors, the DPP put forward the issue of childcare. The party asserted that the state was responsible for the provision of childcare. It was an advanced idea at that time, and no one had manifested such a political view before. Ms Liu, the Vice Chairman of the Women's Development and Action Committee of the DPP, confirmed the DPP's emphasis on childcare issues in terms of family policy because 'it was a fundamental problem and the most common problem faced by the family.' In August 1997, the Taipei City Government, led by DPP members, announced its policy on childcare, including universal childcare allowance, nursery subsidy, and medical subsidy for children under six (refer to Chapter 6). Those actions support Ms Liu's description of the political ideology of the DPP on childcare policy: the state is the body which should take the greatest responsibility for childcare.

Both women's groups and workers' groups stress that employers should pay for childcare because children are the future labour force. The representative of workers' groups, Ms Chou, particularly emphasizes the responsibilities of capitalists. She insists that all regulations in the bill are basic working conditions and that workers have the right to take days off for family responsibilities. The enactment of the bill is essential so that workers do not need to beg for days off for childcare or childbirth. Employers ought to offer their workers family leave with full pay because they reap the benefits of exploiting their workers. With regard to the state's role, Ms Chou said that the state can assist working parents to deal with childcare problems in other ways, such as providing public nurseries stuffed by qualified people.

It is clear that the views of different groups on this issue are extremely varied. In fact, it was this difference of opinion which resulted in the failure of the bill. Women's groups and labour organizations insisted the burden of childcare had led to women's inferior status in the labour market. Businessmen and some legislators thought that it was ridiculous to mix childcare issue with issues of gender equality in the labour market. Children were historically regarded as the property of the family in Taiwanese society so the family naturally bore all the costs of childcare. It was not ease to change these traditional views.

Promoting gender equality

Employers completely deny any gender inequality in the workplace; therefore, they think it is unnecessary to enact a law on employment discrimination, and no one should intervene in the mechanisms of a free market. They do not think that companies discriminate when they consider who should be taken on, promoted or trained (memos in the Legislative Yuan). For them, in keeping with the presupposition of human capital theory, any decision regarding employment arrangements are the consequence of rational choice. Since the characteristics of men and women are distinct, they are naturally suitable to do different kinds of jobs. Mr Kuo said:

> Where there is a policy, there is a countermeasure. Any legislation which tries to protect the employment opportunities of a particular section of the labour force will end in an opposite result. The Disabled Welfare Law is an example. Companies were fined rather than take on more disabled workers. The passing of the law did not increase the working opportunities for disabled people, but simply raised the amount of savings in the Disabled Welfare Fund for doing nothing.
>
> — Interviewee Kuo

Except for the representative of the business group, every interviewee highlighted the importance of enacting the GEEB. Each believed that a law could drive the actions of employers in relation to equal employment and family friendly schemes, and educate the public and employers to have a more positive attitudes towards gender order. According to her experiences working with women workers, Ms Chou pointed out the importance of legal protection. She said:

> Women workers in Taiwan usually dare not get into conflict with their employers when they suffer unequal treatment. Sometimes, we encourage them to take action but they feel that the law does not allow them to do so. They do not think that the legal systems are wrong and fail to protect them. Therefore, without the legal promise, we can hardly educate women workers to strive for their working rights and benefits.

From their point of view companies considered themselves to be the conduits for implementation of equal employment and should provide the necessary administrative support. Trade unions and labour unions should educate their members on their rights and obligations, be arbitrators in disputes between the members and their employers, and strive for an in improvement in the welfare of their members. However, the function of trade unions in promoting opportunities for women in the field of employment is underestimated by the interviewees from women's and workers' groups. One reason is that the running of trade and labour unions is dominated by men. Without a doubt, they do not care about gender discrimination in the workplace as they are the advantaged group. 'The weakness of trade unions is the major problem of the current labour–capital conflict,' solicitor Yu said. Without collective power, it is difficult for disadvantaged labour to negotiate with their employers.

The representative of the DPP highlighted the role of the state in providing an equal environment for women. Ms Liu said:

> The state should not let women workers negotiate on their own with their employers when they suffer gender discrimination. The state should act on their behalf. In other words, the state should strongly intervene in gender discrimination cases. The state should set up Equal Opportunity Commissions both in central and local government. Since workers seldom understand their rights and legal

systems, it is necessary for the state to set up an institution to aid workers. Moreover, the state should compel employers to set up an equal employment office in firms, where employees would be able to seek justice for unfair treatment.

The representative of workers' groups also relies on the labour department to represent workers to counteract the economic departments in terms of the enactment of legislation. Ms Chou said:

> As the highest authority of dealing with labour affairs, the Council of Labour Affairs should consider workers' welfare. It should not assume that their draft can overcome opposition from the economic departments, then itself propose a weak bill with few effective articles.

In sum, every interviewee, except business, approved the importance of state's intervention in the promotion of equal employment. They may criticize the attitude and efficiency of the state, but still emphasize the responsibility of the state.

The route to equality

Both the bills of the women's groups and the government include remedies and inspection procedures for promoting equal opportunities in employment. I will distinguish six aspects of implementation. First, the central government should establish an 'Equal Opportunities Commission,' and each local government should have an equal employment subagency, both being responsible for supervising, investigating and implementing matters relating to the enforcement of the bill. In the government bill, the functions of the equal employment agencies are examining, consulting and promoting related matters. Secondly, the executive authority should have the power to send its personnel to make inspections at any time. In the government bill, an inspection would be made by the executive authority and the labour inspectorate. Thirdly, workers or job seekers can file a complaint with the executive authority or local authority, if they discover that employers fail to implement the bill. Alternatively, in the government bill, workers can complain about employers to the labour inspectorate. Fourthly, employers will be fined if they are in violation of some of articles in the bill (refer to Table 7.2). Fifth, employers or business entities are liable to pay compensation to workers or job seekers who suffer discrimination. Lastly, the executive authority would publicize the details of employers or business entities who are penalized under the bill and punished. The executive authority would give administrative support until the situation in those firms improved. The last two devices are not included in the government bill.

As regards the route to equality, although individual litigation offers workers a way to strive for their working rights, none of the interviewees approves of this method. The process of litigation may take many years. Applicants have to deal with victimization in their search for justice. Few can get through the procedure of litigation since they are short of money and legal knowledge. Besides, there is no subsidy for applicants to have a solicitor in Taiwan. In the light of experience in Britain, although litigation provides individuals with a way to justice, the judicial system does not fully support them (Gregory, 1987). Moreover, the process of litigation involves applicants breaking their relationship with their employers and losing their reputations. In Taiwanese society, people who appeal to the judiciary are seen as trouble makers and may be put on a black list by other employers. They will then find difficulty in getting another job and may suffer a long period of unemployment.

Therefore, Legislator Hung prefers trade unions to act as arbitrator between employees and employers if a union member considers the actions of the employer are in violation of the provision of the GEEB. If arbitration fails, then individuals go to court. Legislator Hung asserts that the state should not act as arbitrator or sue on behalf of a worker. The representative of workers' groups, Ms Chou, also highlights the role of trade unions but suggests that the government bill offers trade unions power to monitor the implementation of the law by business. 'Theoretically, any dispute between employees and employers should be solved by collective agreement, provided that the trade union is effective,' she thinks, 'however, in Taiwan this is not the case.'

Solicitor Yu preferred the administrative route to equality. Trade unions should provide legal representation for their members if litigation is necessary, especially in the case of systematic discrimination, which affects an entire class or group. The representative of the DPP thought that punishment by the state is the most efficient way for challenging gender discrimination in the field of employment. The state is expected to play a much more active role in inspecting and punishing firms which do not follow the regulations of the bill. Individual workers can complain to either the equal employment official authority or their trade unions. After the investigation by the authority, the government directly amends the behaviour of firms by way of further penalties.

In conclusion, women's groups claim that the state and employers should share the responsibility for childcare, including service provision and financial support. The state favours capitalists and the family solving the problems together, but capitalists stress that either the family or the state should pay the costs of childcare. Employers insist that any scheme for relieving employees' family responsibilities is a kind of 'favour' instead of a 'responsibility.' For employers, welfare is the state's business and the state should not try to modify the market order. Legislator Hung agrees with the necessity of enacting a law to eliminate unreasonable treatment of women workers, but does not wish to put too much responsibility onto the state. In her account, families, workers and trade unions should take up the major responsibilities for childcare and challenging unfair employment practices. Women's groups and labour groups place emphasis on the responsibilities of employers since the latter benefit from exploiting women workers, while the DPP expects the state to play a more active role. Since the power of trade unions is historically weak, Taiwanese society relies heavily on the state to deal with disputes between employees and employers. As far as the route to equality is concerned, none of the interviewees approves the method of individual litigation. Administrative intervention by the state is regarded as the most effective way at this time, while trade unions should learn how to be proper arbitrators between labour and capital.

Discussion

Women have historically been excluded from citizenship as they are marginal in the arenas which confer and define citizenship. Research on the legislative process of sex discrimination Acts indicates that the law was either introduced or passed as a new government searched for social reform, such as the case in Australia (Ronalds, 1990) and in the United Kingdom (Meehan, 1985; Callender, 1979). In Taiwan's case, democratization provided a space for women to ask for their social rights. The pressure from international institutions, such as the 'International Women's Decade' promoted by the UN, was also a crucial factor in the widespread enactment of legislation at international level. The influence of global citizenship, according to Lister, challenged national citizenship (Lister, 1997: 196). Even if Taiwan was excluded by international society, it was still affected by policy diffusion.

When we focus on the analysis of policies related to working women, it is doubtful whether 'politics really makes a difference'

(Pierson, 1991: 33). In this case study, political parties did not play a key role in the introduction of equal employment policy though there were some legislators, from both right- and left-wing political parties, who supported the enactment of the bill. The three main political parties all included the passing of the bill as one of their important policies, yet none of them put it into action. It is also doubtful whether more women participating in politics enhances social reforms and women's welfare. Women politicians are more interested in popular, mainstream issues rather than limiting themselves to the sphere of women's issues. Once women enter the political arena, they play the boys' games. Even the pioneer of the civil women's movement in Taiwan became a legislator, and was not involved in promoting any legislative reform for women – though women's groups had high hopes of her. The issue of gender equal employment was mainly raised by women victims. However, the state did not take any action to improve gender discrimination in employment until women's groups introduced the bill and the issue came to public attention. In Taiwan, as Skocpol (1992: 30) maintains, women's modes of politics are not prevalent throughout political parties, elections, trade unions and official bureaucracies (refer to Chapter 5). They promote policies for themselves by petitioning the government and going to the public, using demonstrations and the media.

Many interviewees in this study think that the reason why the bill failed to pass is that women did not show enough power – even the representative of the government said as much. Burstein's research (1991) on the American situation has contended that collective action is directly associated with court case victories over employment discrimination. In the Taiwanese case, Ku (1995) also found a high correlation between collective movements and the development of social welfare. Strong collective action may lead to the victory of legislation and appropriate measures, but it does not automatically mean equal rights in employment, especially in the case of Taiwan where the government executes social policy inefficiently.

Those approaches which recognize the contribution of working-class movement within welfare capitalism, including the power resource model, incorrectly speak of the formation of 'women's policy,' as if women or indeed women workers should not be regarded as a class. It is hard to say whether women have any class consciousness or class solidarity. On the other hand, their opinions about how to transform their status are usually divided, and many of them agree with the original male-dominated culture. Moreover, these approaches ignore the importance of the role of elites in policy-making. Women's collective action is largely created by women elites who raise issues of welfare reform for women. The majority of women keep silent. Especially in Taiwan, the cries of women's groups seem loud, but the number of active participants is small. Therefore, women's struggle with capital should not be analyzed as typical class conflict.

As far as the state's role in this event is concerned, two phenomena are found. First, state policies have been swayed by both business needs and pressure from women. However, the original purpose of introducing the government bill was to water down women's collective action. By introducing an ineffective law, the state tried to release the pressure from collective actions which posed a threat to its authority. Furthermore, although the labour department has taken more positive action to maintain women's equal employment in recent years, they still view the introduction of the bill from an economic perspective, looking at the needs of national development and capital accumulation instead of human rights. The chairman of the Council of Labour Affairs stated: 'The aim of the bill is to develop the female labour force, to eliminate the barriers for women's employment, and to enable more women to participate in the labour market' (*Free Times*, 5/5/93). Officer Tung also said: 'The aims of many recent labour policies related to women are to explore potential female labour in order to overcome the current labour shortage.' If the raising of the gender equal employment issue was regarded as the result of the emergence of social citizenship, state officials were seemingly incapable of catching up.

The other phenomenon is functional differentiation within the state. When discussing the nature of the state, we tend to treat the state as a whole. Judging by the emergence of the GEEB, the views of the government departments vary. According to their functional divisions, government departments are more concerned with the interests of relevant groups and as such have begun even to represent them. As a consequence, however, the relationship between capital and labour in the real world is reflected in the fact that economic departments are usually the prevalent actors in the Cabinet, and their viewpoints dominate the objectives of state policies. Many policies which might have a negative effect on business profits have often been thrown out or watered down by economic departments. Moreover, the analysis of the state as a whole also ignores the personnel which constitute it; state officials more or less have administrative autonomy. They may be unable to affect the policy of the Cabinet, but they could, using their administrative authority, promote small-scale measures and services to

fulfil equal opportunities. The expansion of education and global information affects not only women but also certain male officials who
would like to promote gender equal policies. Under male-dominated
politics, women's groups in Taiwan had to employ methods both
inside and outside the sphere of formal politics.

Judging by the case study, we can see how strong the power of
capital has become. Businesses tried to use their structural power to
stop the enactment of the bill. They threatened that companies would
move abroad and Taiwan's economy would decline if such a bill was
passed. The majority of ordinary people would not stop supporting a
law just because of company threats. In recession, however, people
could be affected by such 'ideological control,' including the state and
women's groups. Since 1993, for instance, the discussion of the bill has
been suspended as the economy in Taiwan has been in decline.
Women's groups also thought that it was not a good time to discuss
labour legislation, and did not continue pushing for the passing of the
bill. Economic power spoke for capital. Additionally, business shows its
privilege in the labour market by threatening not to take on many
women workers if the bill is passed. Simultaneously, women's groups
also tried to use their structural power by winning public support. They
publicized their ideas regarding gender equal employment, and many
of these ideas have been approved by the public. For instance, nine
years ago, no one had ever heard of 'childcare being the responsibility
of society.' Today this idea is often discussed in public. Therefore,
women's power usually comes from public support. Women's groups
acknowledge that ideological reform is as important as legal reform.

Will the Gender Equal Employment Legislation open a door for
women to access employment on an equal basis to men? Experiences
in other countries have shown less positive results than one would
hope. Comparatively few women have been to court to seek justice.
Even though they have won cases, compensation has amounted to
only small sum of money (Gregory, 1987). The legislation has not
achieved equal treatment between men and women on childcare
either. Fewer male workers have used their right to parental leave and
child sick leave than women workers, which results in the disadvantaged status of women in the workplace. Career breaks or frequent
absence are likely to damage women's careers and decrease the value of
women workers. Women are still the principal bearers of the costs of
childcare (Forbes, 1989; Widerberg, 1991; Lewis and Astrom, 1992).
Moreover, the advocacy of 'family friendly schemes' could enhance
inequities between women workers in different workplaces. Compared

with women with professional skills, women in low-level work, who need more legal protection, could lose their working opportunities since the cost of hiring women is believed to be higher and they are easily replaced by other cheap labour. The GEEB was introduced by the female, usually professional, elite. They cared about market order related to their own benefits, such as equal opportunities in promotion and training. However, most women work in the secondary labour market with low wages and no promotion prospects or work at home as unpaid family workers or home workers. They do not get as much benefit as professional women.

Forcing employers to provide family friendly policies is regarded as being in the sphere of social policy. Social welfare cannot solve the problem of economic inequality between men and women caused by unequal opportunities in the workplace. However, unequal opportunity in the workplace will result in unequal opportunity in welfare. The function of this proposal legislation cannot be replaced by any other welfare scheme.

8
Conclusion: Towards a Theoretical Historical Account of Gender Inequality in Taiwan

This study has concentrated on exploring the changing relationship between the state and working women in Taiwan by incorporating social, economic, political and ideological factors in the historical analysis. We have been interested in analyzing how women's employment has been treated by the state in Taiwan and how the state deals with the conflict between capitalist development and the maintenance of the traditional family system. This section will analyze the influence of three forces – patriarchy, capitalism and women's collective power – on the state's performance in different historical periods. Figure 8.1 shows the interaction between these factors and the state. State structure and state policies can be affected by patriarchy, capitalism and women's power; state policies are also affected by state structure. Lastly, state policies create different opportunities for men and women, which impact on women's choices between the family and work. Conversely, patriarchy, capitalism, and women's power can also be transformed by state policies. This reverse influence is especially significant as state autonomy is strong

The power of each force has emerged at different times and so state policies have been under different influences at every stage. Regarding women's employment, the beginnings of industrialization in the 1960s made the factor of capitalist development more meaningful. Since the mid-1980s, the women's movement has became a new force acting on state policies, asking for more women-centred policies to improve women's inferior status, both in the public and in the private spheres. Moreover, our research shows that the state is not simply swayed by each of the different interest groups, but has its own considerations. Table 8.1 shows the changes of these factors and state autonomy at different stages.

Figure 8.1   **Concepts of this study**

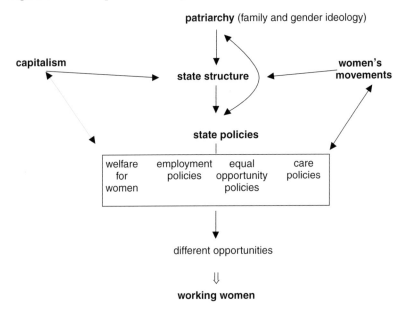

Table 8.1   **The factors affecting state policies in Taiwan, from 1945 to the present day**

	First stage 1945 to mid-1960s	Second stage mid-1960s to mid-1980s	Third stage mid-1980s onwards
Patriarchy	partly relaxed	reinforced	search for a new gender regime
Capitalism	slow development, lack of job opportunities	rapid development needs a lot of cheap and flexible female labour	utilize female labour force fully/look for new cheap labour, affect state policies
Women's power	controlled by the state, urges women to devote themselves to the state and the army	maintain traditional gender regime; the emergence of the civil women's movement	women's groups intervene in formal systems to ask for gender equality and human rights
State autonomy and structure	strong, single party	strong, single party	slight weakening, multiple parties

The first stage: from 1945 to the mid-1960s

Patriarchal ideology is a cultural factor instilled in the family system and gender regime, and influences the state as well as capitalists and women themselves. Before the mid-1960s, when the influence of other factors was still weak, it dominated the relationship between the state and women. As a revolutionary party and under pressure from feminists and liberals in mainland China, the KMT government aimed to reform all social inequality, including gender relations. In a new political environment, the KMT tried to reform the imperial system as well as patriarchy. The KMT trained women organizers, set up women's groups, educated local women about the meaning of the revolution, and service in the army. In 1949, after the KMT retreated to Taiwan, many new social and political systems were also applied to Taiwanese women without pressure from the local women's movement, such as the right of inheritance, owning property, choosing their marriage partner and suffrage. Although the KMT government began to revive traditional gender division in the 1930s, Diamond's emphasis on the KMT as a patriarchal state is not without problem (Diamond, 1979).

At this first stage, policies concerning women mainly followed 'state needs.' Without a stable political position, the state motivated labour for its own survival. Women were encouraged to play more active roles outside the family and, in particular, to devote their labour to the state. Many women's organizations led by Madame Chiang Kai-shek mobilized women for the war effort. As residents in a colony, however, the lives of women in Taiwan were hardly changed by the inspiration of nationalism. They were not only under the original oppression of patriarchy but also under the oppression of colonists. Additionally, lack of job opportunities was another important obstacle to women joining the labour force. Although modern schooling allowed women to attend formal education, the purpose of women's education was to cultivate good mothers. Women's entitlement to welfare was through their roles as mothers.

The second stage: from the mid-1960s to mid-1980s

As a capitalist state isolated from the international community and attempting to survive the threat of mainland China, national resources in Taiwan mainly flow to capital accumulation. Before the mid-1980s, state autonomy was strong under severe social controls (Ku, 1995: 413). Thus the state was able to guide the direction of economic development and managed the supply of cheap labour for capital accumulation. During the mid-1960s to mid-1980s, women were an important source of cheap and flexible labour in a labour-intensive export-oriented economy. Girls in junior high schools were permitted to leave school earlier or to work during their school years in order to meet the labour shortage in factories. Married women were encouraged to do subsidiary work at home as part of the production line in factories. To maintain a favourable investment climate, the state in Taiwan had to mute women's consciousness. In Gallin's account, two strategies were used to achieve this. First, through the educational system and the mass media, the state tended to sustain a traditional patriarchal ideology and to teach women to put the family as their first priority. Secondly, the state pursued restrictive policies towards trade unions to ensure political stability (Gallin, 1990). Since collective movements were prohibited under Martial Law and non-government organizations were restricted before 1986, people found it difficult to express their thoughts and to demand their rights.

During the mid-1960s to mid-1980s, the state had to face the conflict between capitalist interest and patriarchal interest. On the one hand, economic development needed the female labour force. On the other, the Cultural Revolution riots of 1967 in mainland China prompted the KMT government in Taiwan to reinforce traditional family ideology. Two important economic strategies of the state in the 1960s, small factories in rural areas and family subsidiary work, successfully absorbed surplus female labour, especially married women. Those two working patterns diminished the possibility that capital accumulation would destroy the patriarchal family system. Many of those family-type factories offered married women as much flexibility as they could. Women were allowed to bring their children to the workplace, and thus avoided childcare problems. They could leave factories temporarily during the working day to fulfil family responsibilities, such as cooking lunch, whenever they needed to. Therefore, Cheng and Hsiung argue that the state in Taiwan plays an active role in allowing capitalist development and the patriarchal family system to exist harmoniously. I would argue that these strategies were a compromise with the pre-existing system during early capitalist development. Once married women have become waged workers, employers have flexible full-time workers, while families only have part-time housewives and carers. Thus, the state restructured a new gender regime for women – a good woman should stay at home after marriage and do subsidiary work at home to relieve the burden on the family economy. Women's groups and educational organizations also publicized traditional values and morals to maintain social harmony. The new gender regime and related employment policies assisted capitalism to extend into the family and to reduce the influence (disturbance) of the traditional family by capitalist development.

In this second period, the state encouraged women to work based on 'family benefits' instead of 'state needs.' The state emphasized that the family economy would be improved if women did subsidiary work at home. Even though the state intended to maintain the family system, it was involved in the provision of childcare to release more of the female labour force. Although the state began to provide nurseries, its role in childcare remained unimportant. Most children were cared for by their mothers. Additionally, equal access to modern schooling gave women opportunities to improve their human capital and to learn to question their inferior status in the public and private sphere. The state can be said to have led to Taiwan's economic development and economic development has offered women the power to transform the state.

The third stage: from the mid-1980s to today

Block (1977) argues that state autonomy is especially strong when the nation is in danger, such as in wartime. During such a period, any threat from capitalism is ineffective. The state will not enact any policy to damage labour welfare. However, once the risk is past, the influence of capitalists towards the state will be recovered. Before the civil war, the state heavily intervened in regulating the conditions of labour reproduction. By the 1980s and 1990s, however, the government failed to enact gender equal opportunity legislation as a basic working right although the leaders of the state were aware that there was serious gender discrimination in the workplace.

State autonomy in Taiwan declined due to the rise of democracy and social movements in the mid-1980s. Women's groups started to express their needs and to put pressure on the state to establish a reasonable social and legal system with gender equality. Since the mid-1980s, the state has been enmeshed in the contradictions of two antagonistic forces in terms of policies on women. On the one hand, capitalists ask the state to deregulate labour legislation, which can enhance their flexibility to utilize labour to cope with the changing economic environment. The state has to loosen labour legislation to sustain accumulation and to avoid investment flowing abroad. The deregulation of the Revised Labour Standards Law in 1997 is a good example of this. On the other hand, women require the state to protect their working rights and to enhance their welfare. They stress that the state should avoid capitalists over-exploiting female labour and that capitalists have a responsibility to pay for labour reproduction. For its legitimacy, the state has to enact more labour legislation, such as the GEEB, to regulate capitalists' behaviour. The case of Taiwan echoes the work of Gough (1979; 1987: 279): the welfare state is the outcome of two sets of forces. One is the ability of the state to respond to the changing requirements of capital; the other is the pressure from the working class and civil society to adjust the market order to improve the level of welfare

However, the influence of the two forces cannot fully explain the state's contradictions on utilization of the female labour force. The state also has to consider '*internal social order and stability,*' including the family system and national security, as it aids capital accumulation. The Taiwanese state regards the family as the most important mechanism in maintaining social order. It is clear that the state in Taiwan does not want the original family system to be changed. First, the state does not provide many schemes or qualified childcare services to avoid working women quitting their jobs to take up childcare responsibilities. Instead, it encourages women to re-enter the labour market after they have finished childcare responsibilities. Besides, although there is a home care service for the elderly, only single and infirm older people without any children, or abandoned by their children, are entitled to apply for the service. The family itself is expected to deal with the burden of dependency. Lastly, through the educational system and the 'Mothers' Classroom scheme,' the state stresses that women's primary roles are as wives and mothers in the family.

On the other hand, the state by no means follows capitalists' requirements all the time. During the recent economic development, the state's employment policies have sometimes conflicted with capitalists' willingness to consider national security. To capitalists, foreign workers are the cheapest way to solve the labour shortage. In spite of its failure to provide efficient schemes, the state would rather develop a greater female labour force than import more foreign workers since the latter can result in social problems.

In this third stage, state policies towards working women are based on 'economic efficiency' for the purpose of accumulation. Any policy for equal opportunity or childcare is evaluated to see whether it will increase the labour force participation rate of women. However, the state has had to face more serious conflict between capitalist interests, patriarchal interests and women's interests. Women began to be aware that they have a 'right' to work rather than this being simply dictated by the needs of the labour market. They asked the state and the employer to share their burden of childcare. However, employers are reluctant or find it difficult to share the responsibilities of childcare with the family; they would rather if necessary find substitutes for women workers. Moreover, the state has failed to intervene in the original welfare functions of the family. The maintenance of traditional Familism means that the state could keep its welfare budget at a minimum. Finally, people find solutions by themselves. Grandmothers take care of children for working mothers. Their power in the family is not as high as in the past. Sometimes, they have to show that they are useful labour in the family if they want to live with their married children. On the other hand, the provision of childcare by the market has increased. Childminding has become a new occupation for housewives who leave the labour force for childcare, and foreign maids are another new solution.

From the first stage to the third, we found that women were encouraged to combine work and family but the form of this encouragement has changed. At the first stage, the state tried to define a new gender regime to mobilize women for its own purpose. At the second stage, the state needed to face the conflict between capitalism and patriarchy. Women were encouraged to work at home for the purpose of capital accumulation. At the third stage, the state hoped that women could work after they had brought up children to avoid the waste of labour. However, women began to ask the state to work for them; they wanted to define a new gender regime for themselves. Nowadays, the state needs to consider how to reach a balance between capital's needs, women's requests, and internal social order and stability.

Further implications for theoretical debate

From the discussion of the interaction of each force at different stages of Taiwan's history, one can gain a clearer idea about the changing relationship between the state and working women. However, there is also the *'longue durée'* in history, aspects of culture and institution which change much more slowly than policies and strategies. In this section, I would like to point out some issues which echo or differ from the existing theories discussed in Chapter 2.

Generational contract and civil contract

As far as women's employment is concerned, it is also important to discuss the family-centred Taiwanese welfare state. In Taiwan, the family is the main welfare provider. Scholars have therefore regarded the Taiwanese welfare system as 'Familism.' Protection of the family is so strong and comprehensive that the role of state welfare can remain relatively minor. In Taiwan, there is a strong contract between generations. Parents often pool their resources with their children, for example they support their children to finish their studies, and provide accommodation and financial support to the young couple. In the three-generation living arrangement, women are the main care providers. The older generations of women take care of the children of the younger generations, and, sometimes, do the cleaning work. Simultaneously, the younger generations live with and financially support their elderly parents. For women, a generational contract only exists in their marital family; they have no obligation to their original family after marriage. Thus the generational contract between children and parents is not completely based on a belief of 'reciprocal debts' or affection, but on a feeling of obligation.

The state usually enforces the boundaries of family and state roles through the reproduction of 'good' patterns of family life and 'good' mothers. Unlike the corporative welfare regime of Europe, in Taiwan, state action for maintaining the traditional family system is mainly through the educational system rather than cash transfer. The state's role in creating the gender regime at the ideological level should also not be ignored. During wartime, the state maintained that a 'good' mother should encourage male family members to serve in the army, and she should join production work to accumulate capital for a possible future war. During the mid-1960s to mid-1980s, a 'good' mother would work and take care of her families at the same time. A 'good' woman should fulfil filial piety towards parents-in-law and manage the household well. Since the mid-1980s, a 'good' mother should return to the labour force after bringing up her children, to avoid eroding the labour force.

Generally speaking, the Taiwanese state has been reluctant to intervene in the family. Although in the late 1960s the state began to provide quasi-public nurseries for the purpose of rapid capitalist development, the quantity of childcare provision was limited and society could not accept women with young children working outside the family. However, childcare responsibility did not transfer from the family to the state. In recent years, the belief that 'childcare is the responsibility of mothers' has partly receded. Taiwanese society can accept that mothers with young children work outside the family. The state also assists in childcare provision by training childminders and importing foreign maids. Weighed down by the considerations of capital accumulation and some Taiwanese women's needs, there is not much room for discussion of the moral dimension of broader women's rights. Also, we will not discuss this issue in this book. However, state policies keep away from intervening in the family responsibility towards the aged. Old people's homes and home helps are mainly for older people without children. A working couple with elderly relatives over 70 or a family with a seriously disabled person can apply for one foreign maid or nurse. No part of state policy assists the aged to live independently.

Taiwan has been under the control of empires and authoritarian governments for a long period. Under Confucian teaching, obedience apart, there is no contract between the state and the people. The non-intervention of the state in the family also results from the lack of a civil contract. Although people's rights are written down and protected by the Constitution, in practice this is meaningless since the current meaning of citizenship in the Constitution is duplicated from the experience of Western countries. Both the state and the people are confused about their mutual obligations. In the family-centred Taiwan welfare system, there is a clear and strong generational contract, and a blurred and weak civil contract.

State policies reinforce the dual labour market between genders

Although the labour demands of capitalists result in gender segregation in the labour market, state policies in Taiwan also enforce a dual labour market between genders. Extending from family roles, both capitalists and the state exhibit a strong gender division of labour. In the educational system, textbooks teach girls and boys to have different expectations of their future occupations. In the past, in the public vocational training system, many courses were single-sex; women were not accepted for courses related to male-dominated occupations. In public departments and state enterprises, women were excluded from many job opportunities which were regarded as conflicting with their family responsibilities. When the labour market failed, men were offered special loans to run small businesses, becoming part of capitalism; women were encouraged to do subsidiary work at home. Additionally, subsidiary work, part-time work and childminding have been directed at women. Official women's organizations and 'Mothers' Classrooms' provided another kind of vocational training for women which led them to do craftwork or subsidiary work. Therefore, we argue that state policies play an important role in encouraging women to choose so-called 'women's jobs' and 'women's careers,' and to confine women to separate areas. Gender division in the labour market is not a simple issue as maintained by human capital theory – it is not only down to women's choice.

The state in Taiwan regards women as a flexible labour force rather than as a regular labour force. Both the early policy of subsidiary work and the recent policy of part-time work position women as secondary labour. In this study, although we found that state policies resulted in different forms of unequal treatment between genders, such as vocational training and social security, it is inappropriate to conclude that these policies attempt to maintain men's benefits. 'Gender inequality' may be the result of these policies but it should not be explained as their purposes.

In some Western countries, after the Second World War, women were encouraged to concentrate their attention on the household once the labour market no longer needed them, while childcare services were offered when the market required more labour. In contrast, women in Taiwan were always encouraged to join the labour force *and* to take care of their family at the same time.

Control of childcare for the purpose of accumulation

For feminists, childcare responsibility should be shared by the public as women have the right to seek economic independence and personal development through their labour force participation. However, the provision of childcare is seldom for the reason of citizenship but, in many cases, for economic profits. In the Netherlands, for instance, the notion that expansion of childcare is immoral has been replaced by a notion of daycare as a means of avoiding the waste of the female labour force (Bussemaker, 1998). According to the experience of the United States, Frohmann (1978) concludes that childcare programmes are discouraged by the government during a period of high unemployment, since they do not want more women flowing into the labour market. Social policies on childcare are based on the economic need for increasing the labour force.

In Taiwan's case, my evidence indicates that the state controls childcare provision for the purpose of accumulation. The provision of daycare was regarded as an instrument of labour market policy and as a means of developing the female labour force. The foundation of neighbourhood nurseries was a means of releasing the female labour force on farms. The promotion of childminders was intended to increase female labour force participation. The state emphasizes that the childminder system can benefit both the new mother, who can continue working, and the childminder, usually a housewife, who can have a new job opportunity. Actually, the new mother's real income is diminished, and the childminder works as low-waged labour without the protection of social security.

The foreign maid policy further demonstrates that the state controls childcare provision for the purpose of accumulation. The increase in female labour force participation is the main reason for importing more foreign maids. The government refused to permit more foreign maids into the country due to the small increase in women's employment after this policy was implemented. The rationale of economic needs seems more important than that of Taiwanese women's needs. Even the latest policy on gender equal employment is for economic reasons. The labour department also stresses that the recent policies on working women are based on the development of the potential labour force. The argument of women's groups, for a release from childcare responsibility and the right of women to work, has been partly implemented by the state in recent years. However, the policies are carried out under different dialogue between the state and women's groups – that is women activists regard it as women's rights but the state considers it from an economic perspective.

The foreign maid policy is an arguable issue as it results in the exploitation of other women from Third World countries. In this study, we do not attempt to discuss this moral issue, but argue that any solution of women's caring burden should not be controlled by the dominant party for its own purposes. Women should have greater autonomy in their choice of whether to be carers or workers. In Taiwan, however, 'state's needs' or/and 'economic needs' instead of 'women's needs' or 'human needs' are always the main justifications of policies and welfare schemes.[1]

Making the state work for women: women's influence and functional differentiation within the state

In this study, we argue that research on women in the policy process should not be bound by the classic analysis of power resources, such as political parties, elections and trade unions. These mechanisms are historically dominated by men, leaving limited space for reform. In Taiwan's case, we find that women's issues are wholly ignored by trade unions and political parties. For a more comprehensive understanding, it is vital to explore women's methods of affecting policy not only through traditional loci of power but also through individual officials, politicians, social movements and the media. In Taiwan, women's

244 Working Women and State Policies in Taiwan

movements are seldom in coalition with particular political parties. Activists in women's groups seldom stand for election to enter the representative institutions. They do not attempt to develop a long-term relationship with public officials. They are not invited by any political party to be consultants or to discuss party policies on women. Many women do not show their power through the ballot box to push politicians on women's rights. However, in recent years, to some extent women's groups have achieved legal and social reform towards gender equality. They have raised the issues via the media and social movements to get public support. They have also co-operated with individual Legislators to create legal reform. The emergence of the GEEB in Taiwan is a concrete example of the direct impact of the women's movement at the policy level. Women's groups introduced their own bill to the legislature to push the government to enact its equal opportunity policy. Lovenduski is sceptical about the direct relationship between the women's movement and policy outcomes, and argues that labour shortage is an important factor in the promotion of women's rights in employment. Our report does not support her conclusions. In Taiwan, policies for women's rights in employment are raised by the women's movement. Businessmen and the government did not support the bill even though many industries faced a labour shortage at that time.

Although this study finds that the women's movement is a touchstone to urge the state to change its women's policy, the power of reform inside the state is also important. Liberal politicians and state officials, many of them male, support gender equal policies. The labour department also supports having more comprehensive gender equal policies. They can cooperate with women's groups to reform the legal system and policies within their administrative authority. Therefore, the perception of the state as one unified entity must be broken down when we discuss the relationship between women and the state. It does not mean that the state is composed of interest groups, but different departments are concerned about the opinions of different interest groups. We should look at conflicting interests within the state and the functional differentiation within the state.

The East Asian model – a distinct welfare regime?

As discussed in Chapter 2, it remains debatable whether East Asian societies are a distinct welfare regime. It is not appropriate to generalize the finding of this study to other East Asian experiences. However, we may, using Taiwan as a case, discuss its distinct features in comparison with 'Western' welfare regimes, and its contribution to a debate on the East Asian model.

Can Taiwan be classified as one of the three existing regimes upheld by Esping-Andersen or as a combination of these regimes? As we discussed in Chapter 6, in Taiwan, welfare provided by the state is limited, and welfare expenditures remain low. State welfare and service is means-tested, but the market is reluctant to provide service or social security, and tax concessions are too low for most people to buy service from the market. The state is committed to full employment in the Constitution, but in practice married women are not included in this commitment. The state encourages women to join the labour market, but provides a very low level of public responsibility for social care of children, the disabled and the aged, and fails to reduce barriers to employment for women. The family is the most important social institution in Taiwanese society, and the state attempts to maintain the traditional family system. However, cash transfers are not offered by the state to cover the income needs of the male-breadwinner family system. It may be a noticeable phenomenon that the government is incapable of implementing its policies; therefore the state does not have an important role in terms of welfare provision. The community and corporate sectors are not important in terms of welfare provision. Therefore, family support becomes the central trait of 'Taiwanese welfare,' which is based on mutual help between generations as we discussed above. Other informal social resources, such as relatives and friends, also play important roles in term of financial support, employment assistance and caring

As a study focused on women's employment, we are interested in the implications of the Taiwanese welfare model for women's employment. Confucianism had been perceived as a positive historical force which led to economic success in the region. However, it has a negative influence on the position of women. Influenced by strong gender divisions under Confucian teaching, employers and the state reinforce the dual labour market between genders. The heavy reliance on the welfare role of the family under Confucian values keeps women in the private sphere as carers. The female labour force participation rate is still comparatively low despite a dynamic economic environment. Many women join the labour force for a short period before their first or second children are born and never return to work afterwards. The lack of any policies to support maternal employment, such as statutory parental leave, qualified nurseries and after-school services, absent mothers from the labour market. Companies do not offer enough flexibility to working parents either, such as flexible working hours and child care facilities. The unfriendly market offers working mothers fewer alternatives. As transient passengers in the labour market, Taiwanese women usually cannot receive any old age benefit, so that they all too easily depend financially on their children in old age. Taiwanese family-centred welfare is different from the Familism of the corporative welfare regime. The state of the latter supports maternity and children, while the state in Taiwan emphasizes familial responsibility.

Turning to scholars who work on the East Asian welfare model, Taiwan's case supports part of the analysis. Family-central welfare is an undoubted feature. State's intervention is minimal. Economic development is the overwhelming national mission, so that state policies are often justified in terms of accumulation. The social insurance system is status-segmented and residual. Only health insurance is well developed, other protections are either absent or too low to meet people's needs. After democratization, the state has been under pressure to be more involved in welfare provision.

However, we find some features of the East Asian model which do not fit Taiwan's case, or have different implications. First, the private market does not play an important role in welfare provision; neither does the voluntary sector, the community and the firm. The family (in Taiwanese terms, it should include relatives) shoulders the major part of welfare provision. Informal social resources are also important alternatives. In recent years, although the state in Taiwan has tried to promote community service and corporate occupational welfare as another welfare alternative, the result has been insignificant. Secondly, except for maternity payments, there are no welfare schemes compensating for absence from work, such as sick payment or parental payment, and they are unlikely to be introduced in the near future. More legislated job protection has been provided or is being discussing in Taiwanese society, but social insurance systems or the government will not cover employees' income maintenance. Lastly, social services and the market have been promoted to reduce the social care responsibilities of women. However, only those policies which were expected to both develop the female labour force *and* maintain the 'three generations living together' family system have been introduced.

Therefore, although Familism has been perceived as the most important trait of the East Asian model, countries may adopt various aspects of welfare into their own systems. For instance, in Japan, occupational welfare provides considerable protection to employees. In South Korea, the service market is active; many professional service companies provide the middle-class family with another choice. In Taiwan, individual service is developing. More childminders, foreign maids and foreign nurses are taking over the responsibility of social care of working women. However, it is unlikely that these countries will follow a Western welfare trajectory, as some scholars argue. Even if expectations concerning the state's role in welfare provision are increasing, the development of future welfare policies is unlikely to conflict with two basic principles: economic development and the maintenance of the traditional family systems

As a final conclusion, we argue that Taiwanese society is still in the process of transition since every system has been changing rapidly. Every actor in the political arena tries to make a new contract with the state. The state is enmeshed in the contradictions of forces, but it also has to consider the maintenance of internal social order and stability. The development of capitalism provides women with a wider range of opportunities and choices. Women in Taiwan are still bound by many traditional values and role expectations, but they have, in recent years, begun to ask the state to work for them. Their struggle with capitalists has transferred from the industrial arena into the political arena, and they expect the state to be a neutral instrument in modifying social and market orders. The intervention of women in state policies and their efforts to change social notions could make a society of equal opportunities possible.

Appendices

Appendix 1

A general summary of social surveys collected by the government, cited at length in this study

1. Yearbook of Manpower Survey Statistics in the Taiwan Area

Objective: The purpose of this survey is to gain an insight into the supply of civilian manpower, to know the employment status of the labour force, and to perceive the developing trends of manpower.

History: from 1978 to present (once a year).

Survey method: The sampled households are surveyed by well-trained interviewers selected and assigned by local governments. Conducted once a month in the week immediately after the reference week, this survey records events occurring in the reference week which covered the 15th day of the month. People who have died or have moved out of the sampled households during the reference week are excluded. Meanwhile, those who resided in the sampled households during the reference week but died or moved out of there later are still included.

Sampling: Most samples are drawn through sampling method as proposed above but firms in the electricity, gas and water industries all directly provide survey results, without sampling. A two-stage sampling scheme was used to draw off households for this survey: sample units drawn in the first stage of sampling were Tsun's or Li's, while those drawn in the second stage were households. Approximately 515 Tsun's or Li's were drawn in the first stage of sampling and about 19 600 households were sampled in the second stage. In these sampled households, about 60 000 persons aged 15 or above were surveyed.

2. Report on Fertility and Employment of Married Women

Objective: The survey is to understand women's marriage, fertility, family and employment in the Taiwan Area.

History: from 1981 to present (once a year before 1990; once every three years after that).

Survey method: Data is obtained by face-to-face interview. The sampled households are surveyed by well-trained statistical professionals who work in local government.

Sampling: A two-stage sampling scheme was used to sample households for this survey: sample units drawn in the first stage of sampling were Tsun's or Li's, while those drawn in the second stage were households. Approximately 510 Tsun's or Li's were drawn in the first stage of sampling and about 19 600 households were sampled in the second stage. In these sampled households, women aged 15 or above were surveyed.

3.   Yearbook of Earnings and Productivity Statistics

Objective: The survey is to provide information on number of employees, earnings, working hours, and turnover in various industries in the Taiwan area for the preparation of economic plans, planning or business operations, formulation of manpower policies and compilation of statistics on national income.
History: from 1990 to present (once a year).
Survey method: By face-to-face interview, mailshot, or a combination of both, with different methods for different industries. Concerning the reference period, the number of employees on the payroll at the end of a month is collected, while earnings, working hours and turnover of employees for the month are recorded.
Sampling: State enterprises and large-scale private companies use the method of the complete survey. For medium and small private companies, stratified random sampling is adopted.

Appendix 2

Historical events in Taiwan

	Politics	Social and Economy	Policies
	Ching Dynasty		
1895	Japan colonization	the beginning of capitalist development	
1912	the KMT attained political power in China		
1929			Factory Law (maternity leave and pay)
1930		industrialization	
1931			the passing of the Civil Code
1934			The New Life Movement
1938		the establishment of official women's organizations	
1943	the issue of the Wartime Non-governmental Organization Law		the beginning of social insurance (old-aged payment and compensation for government employees)
1945	KMT began to rule Taiwan		the issue of the Constitution
1948	1. the issue of Martial Law		

Appendix 2

Historical events in Taiwan   *(continued)*

	Politics	Social and Economy	Policies
	2. the reserved-seats for women representatives in elections		
1949	KMT retreated to Taiwan		women were encouraged to devote themselves to the state
1950		the establishment of business groups and trade unions	labour insurance military servicemen's insurance
1952		import-substituted economy	
1958			government employee's insurance
1966		labour-intensive export-oriented economy	women were encouraged to work in factories or to do subsidiary job at home
1967			the Chinese Culture Revival Movement
1968			1. 9-year compulsory education 2. Mothers' Classrooms
1970s		the emergency of the civil women's movement	
1984			the passing of the Labour Standards Law
1985			1. the Family Chapter revision 2. welfare expenditure on women is listed separately
1986	1. the lifting of the Wartime Non-government Organization Law 2. the foundation of the DPP		
1987	1. democratization 2. the lifting of Martial Law	the establishment of civil women's groups	

Appendix 2

Historical events in Taiwan *(continued)*

	Politics	Social and Economy	Policies
1990		the introduction of the Gender Equal Employment Bill by women's groups	
1992		the Family Chapter revision introduced by women's groups	1. the passing of the Employment Service Law 2. foreign maids and nurses are allowed to work in Taiwan
1994		'Single Article' events	the Constitution revision added an article for promoting gender equality
1995			1. the establishment of the Evaluative Commission on Employment Discrimination. 2. National Health Insurance
1996	first presidential election	cross-straits relations in dangerous point	the Family Chapter revision
1997		25% of party nominees in public elections should be women (DPP)	
1998	the abolition of Taiwan Province Government	Asia's financial storm	1. Unemployment insurance 2. Enlarging the coverage of the Labour Standards Law
1999	the setting of the Promoting Women's Benefit Foundation by the KMT government		
2000	The DPP won the presidential election		1. The new government promised to launch national pension, and nursery voucher 2. over 1/4 of cabinet numbers are female

Appendix 3

List of interviewees

Name and title	Representation	Note
1. Solicitor Yu Mei-Nu	Women's groups	She was the convener of the drafters of the GEEB. She used to represent women's groups to explain the spirit of the bill.
2. Officer Tun Tai-Chi	The government	He was the head of the Bureau of Labour Conditions in the Council of Labour Affairs. The Bureau was in charge of drafting the government version of the bill.
3. Mr Kuo Yung-Hsing	Capitalists' groups	He was the assistant secretary of the National Industry Association He usually represents the Association to express capitalists' views on state policies.
4. Legislator Hung Hsiu-Chu	Legislators	As a legislator for nine years, she was the co-signatory of the bill proposed by the women's group, and also the Vice-chair of the Women's Department in the KMT.
5. Ms. Liu Hui-Chun	The opposition party	Ms Liu was the Vice-chair of the Women's Development and Action Committee in the DPP. The Chairperson of the Committee was temporarily absent.
6. Ms. Chou Chia-Chun	Workers' groups	Ms Chou was the head of the Pink-collar Union, the so-called 'external system' labour union. The Union belongs to a private organization and focuses on welfare reform for female labour in the service sector.

Appendix 4

Guidelines for interview

(Guidelines are varied for each interviewee. W = women's group, G = government, B = business groups, L = Legislator, O = opposition party, R = workers' groups)

1. What was the background and motivation of the *Awakening* for introducing the GEEB? (WG)

2. What were the reasons for the *Awakening* becoming the first women's group in Taiwan to change its work direction to focus on policy-making and legal reform? (W)

3. How did you begin to co-operate with Legislators when you planned to introduce the bill into the legislature? Why were they willing to promote the bill? (W)

4. What were the strategies for and progress of lobbying? (W)

5. During the promotion of the bill, what were the roles of other women's groups and trade unions? (W)

6. After the introduction of the bill, did you meet with any opposition from the public, business or the government? Why did they disapprove of the bill? How did they use their power to obstruct the passing of the bill? Which part of the bill was most contentious? (WGL)

7. It is already eight years since the *Awakening* introduced the bill. According to your observation, has the attitude of the government, public and business sector towards the bill changed? (W) Reason? (B)

8. Regarding the promotion of gender equal opportunity in employment, what kind of action should be taken by the government, employers and trade unions respectively? (WGBLOR)

9. There are two main themes in the bill: equal opportunity in employment and childcare schemes. Why did the *Awakening* include childcare schemes in the bill? Who should take the responsibility for childcare – women, family, employer or the state? (WGBLOR)

10. Do you think there are any problems for employers in Taiwan in implementing parental leave? (WGBLOR)

11. Is it necessary to include 'sexual harassment' articles in the bill? (WGO)

12. Currently, what is the main obstruction to the passing of the bill? Do you think the bill will be passed? (WGO)

13. Does the *Awakening* have any plan for pushing the passing of the bill? (WOR) against (B)

14. Has the government ever investigated public opinion towards the bill? (O)

15. What are your personal opinions towards the GEEB? How about the National Industry Association? (BLOR)

16. Do you think there is any gender discrimination in the labour market in Taiwan, such as wage differentials, unequal opportunity for promotion, welfare and training? If yes, in your opinion, which reasons account for gender discrimination in the labour market? (B)

17. Do you think that we need a new law to avoid gender discrimination in the labour market? (B)

18. How did the National Industry Association express its disagreement on this bill to the government? (B)

19. When the GEEB was discussed in the Legislative Yuan, what were the main arguments for and against the bill? (L)

20. If the bill is passed, will it affect the willingness of employers to take on new women workers. (LORB)

21. Do you think the bill will be passed? If the Legislative Yuan begins to discuss it again, will you support the passing of the bill, or will this depend on your party's policy? (L)

22. If the bill is passed, is it reasonable for male employees to also apply for parental leave and childcare leave? (BL)

(other questions for the opposition party)

1. What is the women's policy of the DPP? Do women's issues attract attention in the DPP?
2. As far as promoting working women's welfare is concerned, based on the DPP's policy, what kind of role should the state play?
3. What is the DPP's policy for promoting the bill?
4. What are your personal opinions towards the GEEB? Do you think that we need a new law to avoid gender discrimination in the labour market? What is the DPP's policy on this bill?

(other questions for the workers' group)
About the organization

1. The background, the principle of establishment, working objectives and achievements of the group.
2. The members of the group.
3. The method of action.
4. The way to contact or to co-operate with trade unions and working women.
5. The situations of women's groups that were set up specifically for women workers in Taiwan.

Notes

1 Introduction

1. According to Morrow and Brown (1994: 250), intensive research designs employ small numbers of cases; on the contrary, extensive research designs define the objects of research in a distinctive way, requiring a large number of cases.

3 Family and gender ideology

1. The Shang Dynasty was founded in about 1766 BC. The Song Dynasty was established in about AD 960.
2. The Republic of China was founded by the KMT in 1912 in mainland China. From 1949, mainland China was ruled by communists, leaving the KMT to retreat to Taiwan.
3. This is a Chinese proverb. The 'three rules of obedience' is an important guide to women's behaviour.
4. Although the Chinese prefer the extended family type, this has not always been the norm (Lee, 1982). Scholars still argue about which family type dominates and whether the nuclearization of Taiwanese family happened as a result of modernization. In the 1994 national social survey, 58 per cent were nuclear families, and 18 per cent were stem families.
5. Kao and Yi (1986) found that education achievement levels and mothers' employment type correlated with women's sex-role attitudes.
6. In the past, only husbands could divorce their wives.

4 Capitalist development and the female labour force

1. Income recipients mean those who are main income earners in the family or who are paid more than NT$ 87 000 per year (£ 1 = NT$ 52).
2. Taiwan, Hong Kong, The Republic of Korea and Singapore are called the 'four little dragons,' which means that these four countries have fast economic growth and have more potential to play an important role in the world economy, in comparison with other Asian countries.
3. In this public statistical report, part-time workers were those who had paid jobs and worked less than 40 hours per week.
4. It is difficult to see that any occupation is dominated by women. However, the classification of occupation in this study is broad. If the classification is more detailed, one may find some occupations are female-dominated.
5. According to the research of Lai and Chang (1993), skilled work is still dominated by male workers, and women usually work as machine operators.
6. The working positions in government departments are classified into fourteen degrees. The higher the rank, the higher the working position. Public

officials of 'rank ten' are high level officials in every department. Officials with a rank of under six are non-commissioned officials.
7. This policy was abolished in 1987.
8. In Taiwan, the Business Promotion Association, National Industry Association and National Commerce Association are called the three 'primary' business groups; Business Research Association, Medium and Small-size Company Association, Young Enterprise Association are called the three 'secondary' business groups. The former groups are mainly controlled by big business enterprise, while the latter are composed of young or middle and small-sized business enterprises.

5   Women's movements and women in the policy-making system

1. After petitioning from women groups, 10 women's representatives were allowed to sit-in at the meeting.
2. She is at present a member of the DPP and the Mayor of Tao-Yuan City.
3. Since 1987, the *Awakening* Publisher was registered as the 'Awakening Foundation.'
4. Although the Constitution declares that representative elections should reserve a certain percentage of positions for women, the percentage is regulated by individual regulations. Some of the regulations omit this ruling, so not all elections have representative systems for women.
5   According to the Vice-chairman of the Women's Department and Action Committee of the DPP, this action is for the development of the party rather than for promoting female politicians.

6   Social welfare and state policies

1. In 1997, the number of the KMT Legislators is just over half the total number of Legislators in the Legislative Yuan.
2. 1941 documentary data is able to help us understand its historical background.

   Due to the labour shortage, the number of casual workers has increased and they have asked for higher wages. Workers in factories, who have fixed wages, often quit their original jobs and would rather become casual workers. Moreover, new factories often offer high wages to attract skilled workers. Therefore, many workers change their jobs frequently ... We should ensure reasonable rates of pay and working hours, and increase welfare for workers in public departments and state companies to limit the number changing their jobs. (Taken from a scheme for maximising resources, increasing productivity, practising planned economy during wartime, 1941.)

   – The KMT (1976c: 197), Revolutionary Document

3. However, in 1957, the Taiwan Provincial Government refused women workers in the mining industry to join labour insurance (Taiwan Provincial Government, 1966: 58).

4. Military Servicemen's Insurance was excluded from the comparison since very few women workers have been covered by the insurance system and the related data has been regarded as confidential.
5. The period of statutory maternity leave in Taiwan is shorter than that in European countries and shorter than the regulation of the ILO. However, only seven countries in Europe offered 100 per cent of earnings for maternity leave.
6. Since 1998, some occupations in the service sector have been gradually included in the Labour Standards Law.
7. By 'adopted daughters,' it means women who have been adopted by another families as the future daughters-in-law of the families.
8. 'Three Principles of the People,' which was written by the national father of the Republic of China, is the basic national policy of the state in Taiwan. It is composed of the principle of nation, the principle of civil rights, and the principle of people's livelihood.
9. It includes the Six-Year Economic Plan (1976–81), the New Four-Year Economic Plan (1982–85), the long-term plan, the Ten-Year Economic Plan (1980–89), and the Six-Year National Development Plan (1991–96).
10. The food benefit is NT$ 1980 per month, and the living allowance is NT$ 6 000 per month. The maximum support period is six months.
11. According to 1999 data, the living allowance for female breadwinners during training periods has been raised to NT$ 10 000, and the number of cases has also increased.
12. According the survey in 1991, manufacturing industry had 139 000 job vacancies, the commerce industry had 67 000, and the construction industry had 10 000.
13. According to a government survey, 79 per cent of jobless persons who in future would want to work part-time, were female (CLA, 1994c: 38).
14. The Labour Standards Law originally covered the following business:
    1) Agriculture, forestry, fishery, pasturage
    2) Mining and quarrying
    3) Manufacturing
    4) Construction
    5) Water, electricity, gas
    6) Transportation, warehousing, and telecommunications
    7) Mass communications
    8) Other businesses as designated by the central authority-in-charge.
15. According to Tan's record, 'equal work, equal pay' was one of main target of women's groups.
16. The effect of the commission on employment discrimination is doubtful. According to two reports by commissioners in Tauyuan and Kaohsiung, only one or two out of ten represent trade unions and only one comes from a women's organization. Besides, both trade unions and the women's organization are usually controlled by the KMT.
17. In the original version of the Labour Standards Law, the employer had to provide three working shifts, safety equipment, sanitation, accommodation and travel arrangements.
18. Legislators added a note in the legislation about restrictions on women in pregnancy or breastfeeding to work at night since this failure to protect women violated international regulations (*Central Daily News*, 2/5/98).

19. Food stamps were paid in cash in recent years, but have now been abolished.
20. Ninety-four per cent of employers imported foreign maids and nurses though agencies. An employer needs to pay about NT$ 20 000 service fee to the agency. The employer has to pay NT$ 2 000 Employment Security Fee monthly to the competent authority; an employer of a foreign nurse pays NT$ 600.

7   The emergence of the Gender Equal Employment Bill

1. The Constitution cannot be directly applied to legal relations between citizens as relations belong to private law. Moreover, since a lot of industries are not regulated by the Labour Standards Law, many workers have not been protected by the law.
2. Taiwan was forced to withdraw from the UN in 1972 because the UN accepted mainland China as a member.
3. A government bill is usually drafted by a section of the department in authority. The draft of a bill should be approved by the meeting of the department, then by the meeting of the Cabinet. After that, it can be sent to the Legislative Yuan.
4. The KMT lost the presidency in the 2000 election. The new ruling government, DPP, is concerned about welfare and equal opportunity issues. Taiwanese people also expect the new government to built a society with equal rights. However, too many social problems await the new government and the GEEB may not receive immediate attention recently.
5. The fifth article of the Employment Service Law forbids any discrimination in the field of employment. During the Single Article Events, women's groups and women workers petitioned many government departments but all maintained that it was not their domain.
6. Co-operative banks are limited to local areas, and are often operated by local factions. They can do specific business, such as mortgage and business loans, but they are under the supervision of local government and the Ministry of Interior, not the Ministry of Finance.
7. Solicitor Yu explained that since the bill was drafted by a women's group, the first draft only covered women workers in order to stress the aim of protecting this group.
8. The CLA listed all documents relating to the bill as confidential and forbade the staff from revealing the process of enactment since the bill was very controversial. Thus, almost all data in connection with the contents of the bill come from newspaper reports.
9. As discussed in Chapter 5, trade unions in Taiwan have been controlled by the KMT, and have little or no power. When I contacted the National Trade Union, they said that they did not have any information about women workers. It showed the neglect of the organization of the benefits of this group. As only one trade union or labour union has been allowed to establish itself in each industry and company, some labour groups have been established informally after democratization; these were called 'external system' labour organizations.

8   Conclusion

1. 'Women's need,' in this thesis, means only the need of Taiwanese women.

Bibliography

Acker, Joan; Barry, Kate and Esseveld, Johanna (1991). 'Objectivity and Truth: Problems in Doing Feminist Research' in Fonow, Mary M. and Cook, Judith A. (eds), *Beyond Methodology: Feminist Scholarship as Lived Research*. Indianapolis: Indiana University Press.

Adult Education Association (1995). *Women's Education*. Taipei: Shih-ta (in Chinese).

Arrigo, Linda Gail (1980). 'The Industrial Work Force of Young Women in Taiwan', *The Bulletin of Concerned Asian Scholars*, 12 (2), April–June, pp. 25–37.

Averitt, Robert T. (1968). *The Dual Economy: The Dynamics of American Industry Structure*. New York: W.W. Norton.

Awakening (1995). 'Legal Reform Has not Succeeded, Sisters still Need to Work Hard', *Awakening*, September, pp. 26–7 (in Chinese).

Barrett, M. (1980). *Women's Oppression Today: Problems in Marxist Feminist Analysis*. London: Verso.

Barron, R.D. and Norris, G.M. (1976). 'Sexual Divisions and the Dual Labour Market' in Barker, Diana L. and Allen, Sheila (eds), *Dependence and Exploitation in Work and Marriage*. New York: Longman.

Beck, E.M.; Horan, Patrick M. and Tolbert II, Charles M. (1980) 'Industrial Segmentation and Labor Market Discrimination', *Social Problems*, 28 (2), pp. 113–30.

Becker, Gary (1965). 'A Theory of the Allocation of Time', *The Economic Journal*, LXXX (20), pp. 493–517.

Beechey, V. (1977). 'Some Notes on Female Wage Labour in Capitalist Production', *Capital and Class*, 3, pp. 45–66.

——— (1987). *Unequal Work*. London: Verso.

Block, Fred (1977). 'The Ruling Class does not Rule', *Socialist Revolution*, 33, pp. 6–28.

——— (1980). 'Beyond Relative Autonomy: State Managers as Historical Subject', *Socialist Register*, 14, pp. 227–42.

Bock, Gisela and Thane, Pat (eds) (1991). *Maternity and Gender Policies: Women and the Rise of the European Welfare States, 1880s–1950s*. London: Routledge.

Borchorst, Anette (1994). 'Welfare State Regimes, Women's Interests, and the EC' in Sainsbury, Diane (ed.), *Gendering Welfare States*. London: Sage.

Boris, Eileen and Bardaglio, Peter (1983). 'The Transformation of Patriarchy: The Historic Role of the State' in Diamon, Irene (ed.), *Families, Politics and Public Policy: A Feminist Dialogue on Women and the State*. New York: Longman.

Bouillaguet-Bernard, Patricia and Gauvin, Annie (1988). 'Female Labour Reserves and the Restructuring of Employment in Booms and Slumps in France' in Rubery, J. (ed.), *Women and Recession*. London: Routledge and Kegan Paul.

Bowles, Samuel and Gintis, Herbert (1986). *Democracy and Capitalism*. London: Routledge and Kegan Paul.

Brenner, J. and Ramas, M. (1984). 'Rethinking Women's Oppression', *New Left Review*, 44, pp. 33–71.

Bruegel, I. (1979). 'Women as a Reserve Army of Labour: A Note on Recent British Experience', *Feminist Review*, 3, pp. 12–23.

Bryson, Lois; Bittman, Michael and Donath, Sue (1994). 'Men's Welfare State, Women's Welfare State: Tendencies to Convergence in Practice and Theory?' in Sainsbury, Diane (ed.), *Gendering Welfare States*. London: Sage.

Bulmer, Martin (1984, reprinted 1992). *Sociological Research Methods: An introduction*. 2nd edn. London: Macmillan.

Bureau of Central Trust (1995). *Statistics of Government Employees' Insurance* (in Chinese).

Bureau of Labour Insurance (1995). *Statistics of Labour Insurance* (in Chinese).

Bureau of Small and Medium-sized Companies (1996). *White Paper on Small and Middle-size Companies* (in Chinese).

Burstein, Paul (1991). 'Legal Mobilization as a Social Movement Tactic: The Struggle for Equal Employment Opportunity', *American Journal of Sociology*, 96 (5), pp. 1201–25.

Bussemaker, Jet (1998). 'Rational of Care in Contemporary Welfare States: The Case of Childcare in the Netherlands', *Social Politics*, 5 (1), pp. 70–96.

Callender, Claire (1979). *The Role of Women in the Development of the Sex Discrimination Act, 1970–75*. Master's Thesis, University of Bristol, England.

Castle, Francis (1993). 'Introduction', in Castle, F. (ed.), *Families of Nations: Patterns of Public Policy in Western Democracies*. Aldershot: Dartmouth.

CEPD (Council for Economic Planning and Development, Executive Yuan)

—— (1971). Four-year Economic Plan, 1965–8 (in Chinese)

—— (1982). *The Fourth Phase of the Four-year Economic Plan*. Taipei: CEPD.

—— (1990). *Social Welfare Indicators* (in Chinese).

Chan Hou-sheng (1989). 'Let the Budget for Social Welfare Have True Meaning', *State Policies*, 2, pp. 100–11 (in Chinese).

Chang Henry Hwa-bao (1986). 'The Impact of Social Change upon the Sex Role of Chinese Women: A Social Exchange Interpretation', *Journal of Tung-hai University*, 27, pp. 269–84.

Chang Hsiao-chun (1976). 'Housewives' Roles in Urban Areas in Modern Society', *Symposium of Institution of Anthropology in Academic Sinica*, 37, pp. 39–84 (in Chinese).

Chang Hsiu-ching (1988). 'The Development of the Childcare Business in Taiwan within Forty Years', *Journal of Educational Data,* 13, pp. 147–76 (in Chinese).

Chang, J.T. (1995). *Research on the Contemporary Women's Movement and the Practice of Feminism in Taiwan*. Master's thesis, College of Humanities and Social Sciences, National Tsing-hwa University, Hsin-chu, Taiwan (in Chinese).

Chang Kuang-liang (1994). 'Evaluation of Parental Leave', *Journal of Personnel Matters*, 19 (1), pp. 74–83 (in Chinese).

Chang Li-yun (1987). *The Current Situation and Development of Female Public Officials*. Research Paper of Ministry of Personnel (in Chinese).

Chao, S.B. (1985). 'Current Status and Future Prospects for Mothers' Classrooms', *Social Welfare*, 18, pp. 8–13 (in Chinese).

—— (1993). 'The Import and Strategy of Foreign Workers', *Labour Administration*, 57, pp. 3–11 (in Chinese).

Charles, Nickie (1993). *Gender Divisions and Social Change*. Hemel Hempstead: Harvester Wheatsheaf.

Chen Feng-chih (1993). *Research on Welfare for Women Workers – A Feminist Perspective*. Master's thesis, National Chung-jen University, Chia-yi, Taiwan (in Chinese).

Cheng, Lucie and Hsiung, P.C. (1994). 'Women, Export-Oriented Growth, and the State: The Case of Taiwan' in Aberbach, J.D.; Dollar, David and Sokoloff, K.L. (eds), *The Role of the State in Taiwan's Development*. New York: M.E. Sharpe.

Cheng Yu-jui (1995). 'From Open the Import of Foreign Workers to Discuss the Problems of Them', *Labour Administration*, 81, pp. 38–41 (in Chinese).

Chia, Rosina; Chong, C.J.; Cheng, B.S.; Castellow, W.; Moore, C.H. and Hayes, M. (1994a). 'Attitude towards Marriage Roles among Chinese and American College Students', *Journal of Social Psychology*, 126 (1), pp. 31–5.

—— (1994b). 'Cultural Differences in Gender Role Attitudes Between Chinese and American Students', *Sex Roles*, 31 (1/2), pp. 23–30.

Chian Chien-Yi (1967). *The KMT Women's Movement and Women's Work*. Taipei: The KMT Central Women's Department (in Chinese)

—— (1968). *Explanation for the Work of Madam Chiang – A Letter for Young Women*. No. 8, Speech Paper from the KMT Central Women's Department (in Chinese)

Chiang, F.F. (1988). 'Gender Wage Gap of Junior High School Graduates in Taiwan: A Study of Human Capital Theory', *Economical Journal Series*, 16 (3), pp. 323–47, Department of Economics, National Taiwan University (in Chinese).

Chiang Nan-hung (1990). *Research on the Quality of Life and Welfare Needs of Women Workers in the Taiwan Area*. Research paper commissioned by the Council of Labour Affairs (in Chinese)

Chirot, Daniel (1984). 'The Social and Historical Landscape of Marc Bloch' in Skocpol, Theda (ed.), *Vision and Method in Historical Sociology*. Cambridge: Cambridge University Press.

Chou Pi-o (1987). 'Changes in Political Participation of Taiwanese Women.' *Community Development*, 37, pp. 14–24 (in Chinese).

Chou Wen-chi (1994). *Research on the Factors of Household Division*. Master's thesis, Department of Sociology, National Taiwan University, Taipei (in Chinese).

Chu Chih-hung and Hsieh Fu-sheng (1989). *The Participatory Process of Interest Groups in Politics*. Research Report of Commission of Research, Development and Assessment (in Chinese).

Chu Hsiao-yu (1968). 'From the Development of Women's Activities in Taiwan to the Improvement in Women's Status', *Taiwan Literature*, 19 (2), pp. 55–72 (in Chinese).

CLA (Council of Labour Affairs) (1979–95). *Annual Report of Inspection on Working Conditions* (in Chinese).

—— (1988). *Labour Legislation and Regulations in the Republic of China* (in Chinese).

—— (1991). *Survey on Welfare Provision and Policies in Business Units* (in Chinese).

CLA (1992). *Survey on Working Conditions and Opinions on the Labour Standards Law in Business Units not covered by the Labour Standards Law in the Taiwan Area* (in Chinese).

———— (1993). *Survey on Working Conditions and Opinions on the Labour Standards Law in Business Units covered by the Labour Standards Law in the Taiwan Area* (in Chinese).

———— (1994a). *Survey on Vocational Training and Career Development* (in Chinese).

———— (1994b). *Employment Service Law* (in Chinese).

———— (1994c). *Record of a Conference on Evaluating the Work Guideline for Part-time Workers* (in Chinese).

———— (1995a). *Statistics on Women Workers in the Taiwan Area* (in Chinese).

———— (1995b). *Survey of Working Conditions of Part-time Workers in the Taiwan Area* (in Chinese)

———— (1995c). *Report on the Special Investigation on the Single Article Event (Marriage Discrimination) in the Credit Cooperative Bank* (in Chinese).

———— (1995d). *Report on the Management of Foreign Maids in the Taiwan Area* (in Chinese).

Cockburn, Cynthia (1991). *In the Way of Women: Men's Resistance to Sex Equality in Organizations*. London: Macmillan.

Cohen, Miriam and Hanagan, Michael (1991). 'The Politics of Gender and the Making of the Welfare State, 1900–40: A Comparative Perspective', *Journal of Social History*, 24, pp. 469–84.

Commission on Population Policies, Ministry of the Interior (1995). *Data for Population Policies*. Taipei: Ministry of the Interior (in Chinese).

Coombs, Lolagene C. and Sun Te-hsiung (1981): Familial Values in a Developing Society: A Decade of Change in Taiwan', *Social Forces*, 59 (4), pp. 1229–55.

CEPD (Council of Economic Planning and Development) (1971). *Four-Year Economic Plan*. Taipei: CEPD (in Chinese).

———— (1978). *How to Promote Family Subsidiary Work through Community Development*. Taipei: CEPD (in Chinese).

———— (1986). *Middle- and Long-term Plans for the Manpower, Department for Economic Development*. Taipei: CEPD (in Chinese).

Dahlerup, Drude (1987, reprinted 1989). 'Confusing Concepts – Confusing Reality: A Theoretical Discussion of the Patriarchal State', in Sassoon, Anne S. (ed.), *Women and the State*. London: Routledge.

Dale, Jennifer and Foster, Peggy (1986). *Feminists and State Welfare*. London: Routlege and Kegan Paul.

DBAS (Directorate-general of Budget, Accounting and Statistics) (1982). *Report of a Survey on Attitude towards Family Life and Social Environment* (in Chinese)

———— (1990). *Report of a Survey on the Trends of Employed Workers in 1989* (in Chinese).

———— (1992). *Survey of a Survey on the Status of Elderly People* (in Chinese).

———— (1994a). *Report on Fertility and Employment of Married Women* (in Chinese).

———— (1994b). *Yearbook of Manpower Survey Statistics in the Taiwan Area* (in Chinese).

———— (1994c). *Yearbook of Earnings and Productivity Statistics* (in Chinese).

———— (1994d). *Report of a Survey on the Trend of Employed Workers* (in Chinese).

———— (1994e). *Report of a Survey of the Status of Disabled People* (in Chinese).

DBAS (1995a). *Survey of the Status of Elderly People* (in Chinese).
—— (1995b). *Report of a Survey on the Manpower Utilization* (in Chinese).
—— (1995c). *Report of a Survey on the Labour Force in Business in 1991* (in Chinese).
—— (1995d). *Report of a Survey on the Time Utilization* (in Chinese).
—— (1995e). *Report of a Survey on Business Labour Force in 1994* (in Chinese).
—— (1995f). *Report on Fertility and Employment of Married Women* (in Chinese).
—— (1996). *Survey of Family Income and Expenditure* (in Chinese).
—— (1993–96). *Budget of the Central Government* (in Chinese).
Democratic Progressive Party (DPP) (1995). *Constitution and Platform of the Democratic Progressive Party* (in Chinese)
Department of Examination (1996). *Statistic on Examination in the ROC* (in Chinese).
Department of Health (1996). *Annual Report on the NHI* (in Chinese).
Department of Statistics, Ministry of the Interior (1994). *Statistical Yearbook of the Interior* (in Chinese).
Diamond, Norma (1979). 'Women and Industry in Taiwan', *Modern China*, 5 (3), pp. 317–40.
Duncan, K.C. and Prus, M.J. (1992). 'Starting Wages of Women in Female and Male Occupations: A Test of the Human Capital Explanation of Occupational Sex Segregation', *Social Science Journal*, 29 (4), pp. 479–93.
Eisenstein, Hester (1990). 'Femocrats, Official Feminism and the Uses of Power' in Watson, Sophie (ed.), *Playing the State*. New York: Verso.
Eisenstein, Z.R. (1979). 'Developing a Theory of Capitalist Patriarchy and Socialist Feminism' in Eisenstein, Z.R. (ed.), *Capitalist Patriarchy and the Case for Socialist Feminism*. New York: Monthly Review Press.
—— (1983). 'The State, the Patriarchal Family and Working Mothers' in Diamond, Irene (ed.), *Families, Politics and Public Policy: A Feminist Dialogue on Women and the State*. New York: Longman.
England, Paula (1984). 'Wage Appreciation and Depreciation: A Test of Neoclassical Economic Explanations of Occupational Sex Segregation', *Social Forces*, 62 (3), March, pp. 727–45.
England, P.K.; Dou, T. Farkas, G. and Kilbourne, B.S. (1988). 'Explaining Occupational Sex Segregation and Wages: Findings from a Model with Fixed Effects', *American Sociological Review*, 53 (4), pp. 544–58.
Equal Opportunity Review (1996). 'Parental and Family Leave in Europe', *Equal Opportunity Review*, 66, pp. 22–9.
Esping-Andersen, Gosta (1990). *The Three Worlds of Welfare Capitalism*. Cambridge: Polity.
—— (1997). 'Hybrid or Unique?: The Japanese Welfare State between Europe and America', *Journal of European Social Policy*, 7 (3), pp. 179–89.
Fan Pi-ling (1989). 'Taiwan Economy and Women'. Paper presented at a 'Conference on the New Generation in Taiwan', Taipei (in Chinese).
—— (1990). *Analyzing Taiwanese Women: the Characteristics of the Civil Women's movement*. Master's thesis, College of Humanities and Social Sciences, National Tsing-hwa University, Hsin-chu, Taiwan (in Chinese).
Fei, J.H. (1982). 'Research on Gender Discrimination and Wage Differentials' in *Symposium of Institution of Three Principles on People*. Academic Sinica, Number 45. Taipei: Centre Research Bureau, pp. 1–27 (in Chinese).

Feng Yen (1995). 'Management System of Childcare Provision in Taiwan'. Paper presented at the 'Conference on the Changes of Women's Role and Child Welfare', Taipei (in Chinese).

Fillmore, C.J. (1990). 'Gender Differences in Earnings: A Reanalysis and Prognosis for Canadian Women', *Canadian Journal of Sociology*, 15 (3), pp. 275–99.

Folbre, Nancy and Abel, Marjorie (1989). 'Women's Work and Women's Households: Gender Bias in the US Census', *Social Research*, 56, pp. 545–69.

Forbes, Ian (1989). 'Unequal Partners: The Implementation of Equal Opportunities Policies in Western Europe', *Public Administration*, 67, pp. 19–38.

Freeman, Jo (1975). *The Politics of Women's Liberation*. New York: Longman.

Frohmann, Alicia (1978). 'Daycare and the Regulation of Women's Work Force Participation', *Catalyst*, 2, pp. 5–17.

Fu Li-yeh (1995). 'Constructing a Welfare State for Women' in Liu Yu-hsiu (ed.), *White Paper on Women in Taiwan*. Taipei: Shih-pao (in Chinese).

Gallin, Rita S. (1984). 'The Entry of Chinese Women into the Rural Labour Force: A Case Study from Taiwan', *Signs*, 9 (3), pp. 382–98.

———— (1990). 'Women and the Export Industry in Taiwan: The Muting of Class Consciousness' in Ward, Kathryn (ed.), *Women Workers and Global Restructuring*. Cornell: ILR, Cornell University, pp. 179–92.

Gannicott, Kenneth (1986). 'Women, Wages and Discrimination: Some Evidence from Taiwan', *Economic Development and Cultural Change*, 34, July, pp. 721–30.

Gauthier, Anne Helène (1996). *The State and the Family: A Comparative Analysis of Family Policies in Industrialized Countries*. Oxford: Oxford University Press.

Gelb, Joyce (1990). 'Feminism and Political Action' in Dalton, R.J. and Kuechler, M. (eds), *Challenging the Political Order*. Oxford: Polity.

George, Vic and Wilding, Paul (1994). *Welfare and Ideology*. Hemel Hempstead: Harvester Wheatsheaf.

Goodman, Roger and Peng, Ito (1997). 'The East Asian Welfare States: Peripatetic Learning, Adaptive Change, and Nation-Building' in Esping-Andersen, Gosta (ed.), *Welfare States in Transition*. Cambridge: Polity.

Goodman, Roger; White, Gordon and Kwon, Huck-ju (eds) (1998). *The East Asian Welfare Model*. London: Routedge.

Gordon, Ann D.; Buhle, Mari Jo and Dye, Nancy S. (1976). 'The Problem of Women's History' in Carroll, Berenice A. (ed.), *Liberating Women's History*. Champaign: University of Illinois Press.

Gordon, David M. (1972). *The Theories of Poverty and Underemployment*. Lexington, MA: D.C. Heath

Gough, Ian (1979). *The Political Economy of the Welfare State*. London: Macmillan Press.

———— (1996). 'Social Welfare and Competitiveness', *New Political Economy*, 1 (2), pp. 209–32.

Government Information Office (1994). *Selective Speeches of President Lee in 1993*. Taipei: Government Information Office (in Chinese)

Grant, Wyn (1987). *Business and Politics in Britain*. London: Macmillan.

Gregory, Jeanne (1987). *Sex, Race and the Law*. London: Sage.

Haas, Linda (1990). 'Gender Equality and Social Policy: Implications of a Study of Parental Leave in Sweden', *Journal of Family Issues*, 11 (4), pp. 401–23.

Harrison, Bennett (1974). 'The Theory of the Dual Economy' in Silverman, Bertram and Yanowith, M. (eds), *The Worker in Post Industrial Capitalism*. New York: The Free Press.

Harrison, John (1973). 'The Political Economy of Housework' in *Bulletin of the Conference on Social Economist*. Brighton: CSE, University of Sussex.

Hartmann, Heidi I. (1979). 'Capitalism, Patriarchy and Job Segregation by Sex' in Eisenstein, Z.R. (ed.), *Capitalist Patriarchy and the Case for Socialist Feminism*. New York: Monthly Review Press.

——— (1981). 'The Unhappy Marriage of Marxism and Feminism: Towards a More Progressive Union' in Sargent, Lydia. (ed.), *Women and Revolution: The Unhappy Marriage of Marxism and Feminism*. London: Pluto.

Hartsock, N. (1987). 'The Feminist Standpoint: Developing the Ground for a Specifically Historical Materialism' in Harding, S. (ed.), *Feminism and Methodology*. Bloomington: Indiana University Press.

Harvey, Lee (1990). *Critical Social Research*. London: Unwin Hyman.

Hernes, Helga (ed.) (1987). *Welfare State and Women Power*. Oslo: Universitetsforlaget.

Hernes, Helga (1987). 'Women and the Welfare State: The Transition from Private to Public Dependence' in Sassoon, Anne S. (ed.), *Women and the State*. London: Routledge.

Holter, Harriet (1984). 'Women's Research and Social Theory' in Holter, Harriet (ed.), *Patriarchy in a Welfare Society*. Oslo: Universitetsforlaget.

Hsiao Hsin-huang (1989). 'A Frame for Analyzing the New Social Movement in Taiwan' in Hsu, Cheng-kuang and Shung, Wen-li (eds), *The Newly Social Movement in Taiwan*. Taipei: Chu Liu Press (in Chinese)

Hsieh Hsiao-ching (1995). 'Education: From Patriarchal Reproduction to Women's Emancipation' in Liu Yu-hsiu (ed.), *White Paper on Women in Taiwan*. Taipei: Shih-pao (in Chinese).

Hsieh, T.M. (1985). 'Let's Promote Mothers' Classrooms', *Social Welfare*, 18, pp. 4–6 (in Chinese).

Hsiung Ping-chun (1996). *Living Rooms as Factories: Class, Gender and the Satellite Factory System in Taiwan*. Philadelphia: Temple University Press.

Hu Tai-li (1985). 'The Impact of Rural Industrialization on Women's Status in Taiwan' in Population Studies Centre, NTU (ed.), *Proceedings 2 of the Conference on the Role of Women in the National Development Process in Taiwan*. Taipei: Population Studies Centre (in Chinese).

Hu Yu-hui (1995). *Three Generations Living Together*. Taipei: Chu-liu (in Chinese).

Hu Yu-hui and Chang Chueh (1995). *Research on Policies for Women Workers*. Research Paper Commissioned by the Council of Labour Affairs (in Chinese).

Huang Chi-lien (1977). *Research on the Need of Women Workers in the Manufacturing Industry*. Research Paper of the Research, Development and Assessment Commission, Executive Yuan (in Chinese).

Huang Yih-jyh (1992). 'The Influence of Education over Occupational Status Attainment in the Process of Economic Development in Taiwan', *Bulletin of the Institute of Ethnology, Academic Sinica*, 74, pp. 125–61 (in Chinese).

Huang Hu-san (1977). *Women Workers and Industrialization in Taiwan*. Taipei: Ju-tung (in Chinese).

Humphries, J. (1988). 'Women's Employment in Restructuring America: The Changing Experience of Women in Three Recessions' in Rubery, J. (ed.), *Women and Recession*. London: Routledge & Kegan Paul.

ILO (1995). *Yearbook of Labour Statistics.*
Jary, David and Jary, Julia (1991, reprinted 1995). *Dictionary of Sociology.* Glasgow: Harper Collins.
Jayawardena, Kumari (1986). *Feminism and Nationalism in the Third World.* London: Zed Books.
Jessop, Bob (1990). 'State Theory – Putting Capitalist States in Their Place'. Cambridge: Polity Press.
Jones, Catherine (1993). 'The Pacific Challenge: Confucian Welfare States' in Jones, Catherine (ed.), *New Perspectives on the Welfare State in Europe.* London: Routledge.
Journal of China Discussion Group (1988). 'The Flourishing Women's Movement in Taiwan', *Journal of China Discussion Group*, 25 (11), pp. 12–24 (in Chinese).
Journalist (1995a). *29 Millionaires Enter the Legislative Yuan.* 456A, pp. 110–2 (in Chinese).
———- (1995b). *Hidden in an Advert Supporting Lee (Ten-hui) is a list of Chen's (Lu-an) Supporters.* 442, pp. 76–7.
———- (1995c). *The Real Story of the KMT's business.* 418, pp. 14–17.
———- (1996a). *Exposing the Property of the Sun-Kung Club.* 482, pp. 90–2.
———- (1996b). *Whether at Breakfast, Lunch or on the Golf Course, Officials Always Listen.* 491, pp. 97–8.
———- (1996c). *'Big Worm' Golf Tournament Is Still the Number One, James Sung Is Still the Leader on the Golf Course.* 503, pp. 71–2.
———- (1996d). *A Superb Cottage with Strange Proportions.* 481, pp. 94–5 (in Chinese).
Kao Chang (1993). 'Empirical Research on Women's Employment and Gender Discrimination in Taiwan', *Quarterly Journal of the Taiwan Bank*, 44 (4), pp. 223–48 (in Chinese).
Kao Chang; Polachek, Solomon W. and Wunnava, Phanindra V. (1994). 'Male-Female Wage Differentials in Taiwan: A Human Capital Approach', *Economic Development and Cultural Change*, 42 (2), pp. 351–74.
Kao, Feng-hsien (1994). 'Gender Equality in Marriage – From a Perspective of Legislation'. Paper presented at the 'Conference on Marital Systems and Sex Roles'. Taipei, Institution of Social Research (in Chinese).
Kao, Shu-kuei (1987). 'The Ideology of Married Working Women on Maternal Roles', *Community Development*, 37, pp. 40–6 (in Chinese).
——— (1989). 'The Ideology of Married Working Women towards Family and Career' in Journal of China Discussion Group (ed.), *Female Intellectuals and the Development of Taiwan.* Taipei: Journal of China Discussion Group (in Chinese).
Kao Shu-kuei and Yi Chin-chun (1986). *Research on the Attitudes of Married Working Women towards Sex Roles.* Taipei: Acadamia Sinica (in Chinese).
Kaohsiung City Government (1995). *Annual Administrative Report* (in Chinese)
The KMT (1976a). *Revolutionary Document. No. 76. The KMT Constitution.* Taipei: Central Historical Relic Company (in Chinese).
——— (1976b). *Revolutionary Document. No. 69. Announcements of the KMT.* Taipei: Central Historical Relic Company (in Chinese).
——— (1976c). *Revolutionary Document. No. 80. Important Resolutions of the KMT Central Convention.* Taipei: Central Historical Relic Company (in Chinese).

The KMT Central Women's Department (1968). *Record of the Ninth Working Meeting of the KMT Central Women's Department* (in Chinese).
—— (1979). *The Introduction of the KMT Central Women's Department.*
Kim Kyung-ai (1996). 'Nationalism: An Advocate of, or a Barrier to, Feminism in South Korea', *Women's Studies International Forum*, 19 (1/2), pp. 65–74.
Koven, Seth and Michel, Sonya (1990). 'Womanly Duties: Maternalist Politics and the Origins of the Welfare State in France, Germany, Great Britain and the United States, 1880–1920', *American Historical Review*, 95, pp. 1076–108.
—— (1993). *Mothers of a New World: Maternalist Politics and the Origins of the Welfare States.* London: Routledge.
Ku Yen-lin (1988). 'The Changing Status of Women in Taiwan: A Conscious and Collective Struggle Toward Equality', *Women's Studies International Forum*, 11 (3), pp. 179–86.
—— (1989). 'The Development of Female Consciousness and the Women's Movement' in Journal of China Discussion Group (ed.), *Female Intellectuals and the Development of Taiwan.* Taipei: Lien-ching Press (in Chinese).
Ku Cheng-fu (1983). 'How Business Groups can Participate in Official Economic Affairs', *Social Construction*, 49, pp. 155–9 (in Chinese).
Ku Yeun-wen (1995). *Welfare Capitalism in Taiwan: State, Economy and Social Policy 1895–1990.* Ph.D. dissertation, Department of Social Policy and Social Work, University of Manchester.
Kung, Lydia (1976). 'Factory Work and Women in Taiwan: Changes in Self-image and Status', *Signs*, 2 (1), pp. 35–58.
Labour Force Research Centre in Taiwan Province (1973). *Research on Women Workers* (in Chinese).
Lai Ching-hui and Chang Chin-fen (1993). 'Occupational Segregation between Gender in the Labour Market in Taiwan'. Paper presented at the 'Conference on Women's Employment and Education Training,' Taipei.
Lai Tse-han (1982). 'Changes in Household Composition, Power Structure and Women's Status in Chinese Society' in Chen, C.N., Chiang, Y.L. and Chen, K.C. (eds) *Social Science Integration Symposium.* Taipei: Sun Yat-sen Institute for Social Sciences and Philosophy, Academic Sinica (in Chinese).
Langan, Mary and Ostner, Ilona (1991). 'Gender and Welfare' in Room, Graham (ed.), *Towards a European Welfare State.* Bristol: SAUS, pp. 127–49.
Lee, Annie (1994). 'Gender Difference in the Social Security System'–'Analysis of the Old Age Benefits of Labour Insurance'. Paper presented at the 'Population Change, Citizen Health and Social Security International Conference' in Academic Sinica, Taipei (in Chinese).
Lee Chien-chang (1991). *Labour Movements in the 1980s in Taiwan.* Master's thesis, Department of Sociology, National Taiwan University, Taipei (in Chinese).
Lee Ching-erh (1994). *The Role and Status of Married Women in the Cloth Industry in Wu Fen Pu, Taipei.* Master's thesis, Department of Ethnography, National Taiwan University, Taipei (in Chinese).
Lee Chiung-yueh (1987). 'Give Them Reasonable Working Protection Back', *Awakening*, 64, p. 1 (in Chinese).
Lee I-yuan (1982). 'Changes in the Modern Chinese Family', *Bulletin of the Institute of Ethnology, Academic Sinica*, 54, pp. 7–23 (in Chinese).

Lee Ree-king (1995). *Research on Women's Policy*. Taipei: Ministry of the Interior (in Chinese).

Lee Yun-chieh (1992). *Political Economy Analysis of Trade Union Policies in Taiwan*. Taipei: Chu-Liu (in Chinese).

Levin, Peter (1997). *Making Social Policy: the Mechanisms of Government and Politics and How to Investigate them*. Buckingham: Open University Press

Lewis, Jane and Astrom, Gertrude (1992). 'Equality, Difference and State Welfare: Labour Market and Family Policies in Sweden', *Feminist Studies*, 18 (1), pp. 59–87.

Lewis, Jane and Davies, Celia (1991). 'Protective Legislation in Britain, 1870–990: Equality, Difference and Their Implications for Women', *Policy and Politics*, 19 (1), pp. 13–25.

Lewis, Jane and Ostner, Ilona (1994). *Gender and the Evolution of European Social Policies*. Working Paper, University of Bremen.

Li Yeueh-tuan and Ka Chih-ming (1994). 'Sexual Division of Labour and Production Organization in Wu Fen Pu's Small-Scale Industries', *Taiwan: A Radical Quarterly in Social Studies*, 17, July, pp. 41–81 (in Chinese).

Liang Shuang-lien (1988). *Women and Political Participation*. Paper presented at the 'Conference on Sex Role and Social Development'. Taipei: National Taiwan University (in Chinese).

Liang Shuang-lien and Ku Yen-lin (1995). 'Taiwanese Women and Political Participation – Observed Outside and Inside Systems,' in Liu Yu-hsiu (ed.), *White Paper on Women in Taiwan*. Taipei: Shih-pao (in Chinese).

Lin Ching-tung; Tsai, Tun-min; Cheng, Yu-po and Ku, Teng-mei. (eds), (1996). *The Compendium of Laws*. Taipei: Wu-nan (in Chinese).

Lin Chung-cheng (1988). *Wage and Employment Differentials between Genders at the Beginning of Entering the Labour Force*. Paper presented at the 'Conference on Sex Role and Social Development'. Taipei: National Taiwan University (in Chinese).

Lin Tsung-ming (1996). 'The Present and Future for Promoting the Employment of Particular Persons', *Employment and Training*, 14 (2), pp. 56–63.

Lin Ta-chun (1987). 'The Expectance of Labour on Labour Movements', *Labour's Friend*, 435, pp. 7–13 (in Chinese).

Lin Wang-fu (1992). *The Effect of on Women's Wages*. Master's thesis, Department of Economics, National Cheng-chih University, Taipei (in Chinese)

Lin Wan-i (1995). *Welfare State – A Historical Comparative Analysis*. Taipei: Chu-liu (in Chinese).

Lipset, S.M. (1968). 'History and Sociology: Some Methodological Considerations' in Lipset, S.M. and Hofstadter, R. (eds), *Sociology and History: Methods*. New York: Basic Books.

Lister, Ruth (1997). *Citizenship: Feminist Perspective*. London: Macmillan.

Liu Ching-leng (1976). 'Farm Housewives' Roles in Changing Rural Areas in Taiwan', *Quarterly in Taiwan Bank*, 27 (1), pp. 216–38 (in Chinese)

Liu Ko-chih (1975). 'The Growth and Utilization of Human Resource in Taiwan' in Li, Chen (ed.), *Human Resource in Taiwan*. Taipei: Lien-ching (in Chinese).

Liu, Paul K.C. (1983). 'Trends in the Female Labour Force Participation in Taiwan: The Transition to Higher Technological Activities', *Academic Economic Papers*. 11 (1), pp. 293–323.

Liu, Y.L.; Yu, H.M. and Chang, P.C. (1984). *Analysis of the Female Labour Force in the Taiwan Area.* Taipei: Council for Economic Planning and Development (in Chinese).

Lovenduski, Joni (1986). *Women and European Politics: Contemporary Feminism and Public Policy.* Hemel Hempstead: Harvester Wheatsheaf.

Lu Yu-hsia (1980). 'Women's Attitudes towards Career Roles and Family Roles in Changing Taiwan', *Bulletin of the Institute of Ethnology, Academic Sinica*, 50, pp. 25–66 (in Chinese).

—— (1983). 'Relations between Women's Employment, Family Roles and Power Structure', *Bulletin of the Institute of Ethnology, Academic Sinica*, 56, pp. 111–43 (in Chinese).

—— (1992). 'Married Women's Informal Employment in Taiwan', *Proceedings of the National Science Council*, 2 (2), pp. 202–17.

—— (1994). 'Economic Development and Married Women's Employment in Taiwan – A Study of Female Marginalizaton', *Journal of Population*, 16, pp. 107–33 (in Chinese).

—— (1996). 'Research on Women's Role in Family Businesses in Taiwan' in Chen, C.M. (ed.), *Population, Employment and Welfare.* Taipei: Economic Institute, Academic Sinica, pp. 177–211 (in Chinese).

Ma Hsin-yun (1992). *Women's Policies in the Three Principles of People and Women's Status in Politics.* Taipei: Cheng-Chung Pub (in Chinese).

Madden, Janice G. (1987). 'Gender Differences in the Case of Displacement: An Empirical Test of Discrimination in the Labour Market', *American Economic Review*, 77 (2), pp. 246–51.

Mallier, A.T. and Rosser, M.J. (1983). *Women and the Economy.* London: Macmillan Press.

May, Tim (1997). *Social Research: Issues, Methods and Process.* 2nd edn. Buckingham: Open University Press.

Measures for Promoting Female Employment (1994). *Employment and Training*, 12 (6), pp. 85–7.

Meehan, Elizabeth M. (1985). *Women's Rights at Work.* London: Macmillan.

Mei Chia-yu (1993). *Research on the Relationship between the Government and Business Groups – A Case Study of the Business Promotion Association.* Master's thesis, Department of Public Administration, University of Chung-hsing, Taipei, Taiwan (in Chinese).

Meyer, D.S. and Whittier, N. (1994). 'Social Movement Spillover', *Social Problems*, 41 (2), pp. 277–98.

Mies, Maria (1991). 'Women's Research or Feminist Research? The Debate Surrounding Feminist Science and Methodology' in Margaret, Fonow M. and Cook, Judith A. (eds) *Beyond Methodology.* Bloomington: Indiana University Press.

Mincer, Jacob and Polachek, Solomon (1980). 'Family Investments in Human Capital: Earnings of Women' in Amsden, Alice H. (ed.), *The Economics of Women and Work.* New York: St Martin's Press.

Ministry of Education (1995–96). *Statistical Indicators of Education in the ROC* (in Chinese).

Ministry of Finance (1995). *Statistics on Finance in the Taiwan Area* (in Chinese).

Ministry of the Interior (1982–93). *Vocational Training in ROC* (in Chinese)

—— (1987). *Research on Social and Business Groups* (in Chinese)

—— (1990). *Six-Year Administrative Plan of the Ministry of the Interior* (in Chinese).

Ministry of the Interior (1993a). *Report of a Survey on Women's Life in the Taiwan Area* (in Chinese).
—— (1993b). *Survey Report on Children's Status in the Taiwan Area* (in Chinese).
—— (1993c). *Nursery Survey Report in the Taiwan Area* (in Chinese).
—— (1993d). *Social Indicators in the Taiwan Area* (in Chinese).
—— (1994a). *Survey Report on the Status of Disabled People in the Taiwan Area* (in Chinese).
—— (1994b). *Survey Report on the Status of the Elderly People in the Taiwan Area* (in Chinese).
—— (1994c). 'The Practical Situation of Women's Welfare in Taiwan', *Community Development*. 67, pp. 154–6 (in Chinese).
—— (1995). *Report on Community Development in the Taiwan Area* (in Chinese).
Ministry of Personnel (1995). *Statistics on Personnel in the Government Department* (in Chinese).
Moghadam, V.M. (1992). 'Development and Women's Emancipation: Is There a Connection?', *Development and Change*, 23 (3), pp. 215–55.
Morrow, R.A. and Brown, D.D. (1994). *Critical Theory and Methodology*. London: Sage.
Nanneke, R. and M.T. Sinclair (1991). *Working Women: International Perspectives on the Labour and Gender Ideology*. London: Routledge.
Nash, June and Fernandez-Kelly, Maria Patricia (1983). *Women, Man and the International Division of Labour*. Albany: State University of New York Press.
New Party (1995). *The White Paper on the Policy of the New Party* (in Chinese).
Norris, Pippa (1987). *Politics and Sexual Equality: The Comparative Position of Women in Western Democracies*. Brighton: Wheatsheaf Books.
Oakley, Ann (1990). 'Interviewing Women: A Contradiction in Terms' in Roberts, Helen (ed.), *Doing Feminist Research*. New York: Routledge, pp. 30–61.
O'Connor, James (1973). *The Fiscal Crisis of the State*. New York: St Martin's Press.
O'Connor, Julia S. (1993). 'Gender, Class and Citizenship in the Comparative Analysis of Welfare State Regimes: Theoretical and Methodological Issues', *British Journal of Sociology*, 44 (3), pp. 501–17.
OECD (1995). *OECD Economic Surveys*. Luxembourg: OECD.
Orloff, Ann Shola (1991). 'Gender in Early U.S. Social Policy', *Journal of Policy History*, 3 (3), pp. 248–81.
—— (1993). *The Politics of Pensions: A Comparative Analysis of Britain, Canada, and the United States, 1880–1940*. Madison: University of Wisconsin.
—— (1996). *Gender and the Welfare State*. Working Paper of the Instituto Juan March de Estudios e Investigaciones.
Pai, H.H. and Kuo, C.H. (1988). 'Report on the Neighbourhood Childcare Scheme', *Community Development*. 41, pp. 22–44 (in Chinese).
Pao, Chia-lin (1979). *The History of Chinese Women*. Taipei: Tao-hsiang (in Chinese).
Pascall, Gillian (1986). *Social Policy: A Feminist Analysis*. London: Tavistock.
Pateman, C. (1988). 'The Patriarchal Welfare State' in Gutmann, A. (ed.), *Democracy and the Welfare State*. Princeton: Princeton University Press.
Patton, M.Q. (1987). *Qualitative Evaluation Methods*. Beverly Hills, CA: Sage.
Pierson, Christopher (1991). *Beyond the Welfare State*. Cambridge: Polity.
Pillinger, Jane (1992). *Feminizing the Market*. London: Macmillan.

Bibliography 271

Piore, M.J. (1975). 'Notes for a Theory of Labour Market Stratification' in *Labour Market Segmentation: Conference on Labour Market Segmentation*, Harvard, 1973 (Edwards, R.C. et al. (eds)). Lexington: D.C. Heath.

Piven, F. Fox (1984). 'Women and the State: Ideology, Power, and the Welfare State', *Socialist Review*, 14 (2), pp. 14–17.

Ramazanoglu, Caroline (1989). *Feminism and the Contradictions of Oppression.* London: Routledge.

Rees, T. (1992). *Women and the Labour Market.* London: Routledge.

Reich, Michael; Gordon, David and Edwards, Richard (1973). 'A Theory of Labour Market Segmentation', *American Economics Review*, 63 (2), May, pp. 359–65.

Ronalds, Chris (1990). 'Government Action Against Employment Discrimination' in Watson, Sophie (ed.), *Playing the State: Australian Feminist Interventions*. London: Verso.

Rubery, J. (1988). 'Women and Recession: A Comparative Perspective' in Rubery, J. (ed.), *Women and Recession*. London: Routledge and Kegan Paul.

Rubery, J. and Tarling, R. (1988). 'Women's Employment in Declining Britain' in Rubery, J. (ed.), *Women and Recession*. London: Routledge and Kegan Paul.

Ruggie, Mary (1984). *The State and Working Women: A Comparative Study of Britain and Sweden*. Princeton: Princeton University Press.

Sainsbury, Diane (1994a). 'Introduction' in Sainsbury, Diane (ed.), *Gendering Welfare States*. London: Sage.

––––––– (1994b). 'Women's and Men's Social Rights: Gendering Dimensions of Welfare States' in Sainsbury, Diane (ed.), *Gendering the Welfare States*. London: Sage.

––––––(1996). *Gender, Equality and Welfare States*. Cambridge: Cambridge University Press.

Scott, Joan W. (1988). *Gender and the Politics of History*. New York: Columbia University Press.

Scott, John (1990). *A Matter of Record*. Cambridge, MA: Polity Press.

Shiu Chuen-min (1992). *The Ideology and Schemes of Child Welfare in a Changing Society*. Master's thesis, National Taiwan University, Taipei (in Chinese).

Sheu Lin-hui (1991). *Research on Wage of Married Women in the Taiwan Area – A Human Capital Theory Approach*. Master's thesis, National Taiwan University, Taipei (in Chinese)

Siaroff, Alan (1994). 'Work, Welfare and Gender Equality: A New Typology' in Sainsbury, Diane (ed.), *Gendering the Welfare States*, London: Sage.

Siim, B. (1987). 'The Scandinavian Welfare State – Toward Sexual Equality or a New Kind of Male Domination?', *Acta Sociologica*, 30, pp. 255–70.

Skocpol, Theda (1984). 'Emerging Agendas and Recurrent Strategies in Historical Sociology' in Skocpol, Theda (ed.), *Vision and Method in Historical Sociology.* Cambridge: Cambridge University Press

––––––– (1985). 'Bringing the State Back In: Strategies of Analysis in Current Research' in Evans, P. et al. (eds), *Bringing the State Back In*, Cambridge: Cambridge University Press.

––––––– (1992). *Protecting Soldiers and Mothers*. Cambridge: Harvard University Press.

Skocpol, Theda and Ritter, Gretchen (1995). 'Gender and the Origins of Modern Social Policies in Britain and the United States' in Skocpol, Theda, *Social Policy in the US*. Princeton: Princeton University Press.

Stake, Robert E. (1994). 'Case Studies' in Denzin, Norman K. and Lincoln, Yvonna S. (eds), *Handbook of Qualitative Research*. Thousand Oaks: Sage.

Stanley, Liz and Wise, Sue (1983). *Breaking Out: Feminist Consciousness and Feminist Research*. London: Routledge and Kegan Paul.

Stanley, Liz and Wise, Sue (1993). *Breaking Out Again: Feminist Ontology and Epistemology*. London: Routledge

Sun Te-hsiung (1995) 'The Changes of Fertility Attitude and Behaviour in the Taiwan Area' in Liu, K.C. (ed.), *Essays on Human Resource in Taiwan*. Taipei: Lien-ching (in Chinese).

Taipei City Government (1993). *Social Welfare in the 1980s in Taipei City* (in Chinese).

———— (1995). *Annual Administrative Report* (in Chinese).

Taiwan Provincial Government (1966). *Important Events in the Bureau of Social Affairs* (in Chinese).

———— (1982–86). *A Report on Social Administration* (in Chinese).

———— (1985–89). *Statistics on Women in Taiwan* (in Chinese).

———— (1989). *A Survey on Women's Lives* (in Chinese).

———— (1992). *Annual Report on Social Administration* (in Chinese).

———— (1993). *A Survey on Women's Lives* (in Chinese).

———— (1995a). *Annual Report on Social Administration* (in Chinese).

———— (1995b). *Annual Administrative Report* (in Chinese)

Tan Sho-ying (1952). *Forty Years of Women's Movements*. Taipei: Ko-ta (in Chinese).

Thomas, Janet (1988). 'Women and Capitalism: Oppression or Emancipation? A Review Article', *Comparative Study of Society and History: An International Quarterly*, 30 (1), pp. 534–49.

Trade Department of the KMT (1964*). A Decade of Party Matters in the Taiwan Sugar Company*. Taipei: Trade Department of the KMT (in Chinese).

———— (1976). *Summary of Regulations Related to Social Movements*. Taipei: Trade Department of the KMT (in Chinese).

Tsai Hung-chao (1989). *Labour Welfare Policy*. Taipei: Chu-Liu Press (in Chinese).

Tuan Cheng-pu (1992). *The Economy in Taiwan after the War*. Taipei: Jen-chien Pub (in Chinese).

Twenty-first Century Foundation (1995). *An Analytical Report of a Survey on Women's Attitudes*. Taipei: 21st Century Foundation (in Chinese).

Vocational Training Bureau, Council of Labour Affairs (1996). *Research on the Model for Estimating Reasonable Numbers of Foreign Workers*, Research Report of the Vocational Training Bureau (in Chinese)

Walby, Sylvia (1986). *Patriarchy at Work: Patriarchal and Capitalist Relations in Employment*. Cambridge: Polity.

———— (1989). 'Flexibility and the Sexual Division of Labour' in Wood, S. (ed.), *The Transformation of Work*. London: Unwin Hyman.

———— (1990). *Theorizing Patriarchy*. Oxford: Basil Blackwell.

Wang Cheng-huan (1993). *Capital, Labour and State Mechanism*. Taipei: Tung-sun (in Chinese).

Wang Lih-rong (1992). *Research on the Need for Women's Employment and Child Welfare in Taipei City*. Research paper commissioned by the Taipei City Government (in Chinese).

———— (1995). *Women and Social Policy*. Taipei: Chu-liu (in Chinese).

Wang, L.R.; Lin, H.C. and Hsueh, C.T. (1994). *Initial Evaluation of the Welfare Needs of Women in the Taiwan Area*. Research paper commissioned by the Ministry of the Interior (in Chinese).

Watson, Sophie (ed.) (1990). *Playing the State*. New York: Verso.

Wen Chung-i (1989). *Industrialization and Social Change in Taiwan*. Taipei: Tong-ta Press (in Chinese).

Widerberg, Karin (1991). 'Reforms for Women – On Male Terms – The Example of the Swedish Legislation on Parental Leave', *International Journal of the Sociology of Law*, 19, pp. 27–44.

Wilson, Elizabeth (1977). *Women and the Welfare State*. London: Tavistock.

Yang Chung-fang (1988). 'Feminism and Development: An Examination of the Role of the Family in Contemporary Mainland China, Hong Kong and Taiwan' in Sinha, Durganand and Kao, Henry S.R. (eds), *Social Values and Development: Asian Perspectives*. New Delhi: Sage, pp. 93–123.

Yang Tsui (1993). *Women's Liberal Movement in Taiwan during Japanese Colonization*. Taipei: Shih-pao (in Chinese).

Yang Yin; Chen Chao-lung and Wu Ming-ju (1991). *Research on the Welfare Needs of Women in Urban Areas of the Taiwan Province*. Research paper commissioned by the Taiwan Provincial Government (in Chinese).

Yi Chin-chun and Chang Ying-hwa (1994). *A Study of the Change of Family Structure in Taiwan*. Paper presented at the 'Conference on Family, Human Resources and Social Development', Taipei.

Yi Chin-chun and Tsai Yuay-lin (1989). 'An Analysis of Marital Power in Taiwan Metropolitan Area: An Example of Familial-making' in Yi, C.C. and Chu, R.L. (eds), *An Analysis of Taiwanese Society*. Taipei: Academic Sinica.

Yin, Robert K. (1994). *Case Study Research: Design and Methods*. 2nd edn. Thousand Oaks: Sage.

Young, I. (1981). 'Beyond The Unhappy Marriage: A Critique of the Dual Systems Theory' in Sargent, L. (ed.), *Women and Revolution: The Unhappy Marriage of Marxism and Feminism*. London: Pluto.

Yu Chien-min (1992). 'Observing Taiwanese Women's Education during Japanese Colonization', *Bulletin of Taiwan History Field Research*, 23, pp. 13–18 (in Chinese).

———— (1994). 'New Taiwanese Women during Japanese Colonization', *Bulletin of the Women's Research Program*, 32, June, pp. 2–5 (in Chinese).

Yu Han-i; Chan Huo-sheng and Wu Sen-i (1991). *Research on Gender Employment in the Taiwan Area*. Research paper of the Council of Labour Affairs (in Chinese).

Yu May-nu (1993). *The Legal Status of Taiwanese Women*. Paper presented at the '1993 International Women's Conference', Taipei (in Chinese).

Zhan, Heying J. (1996). 'Chinese Femininity and Social Control: Gender-Role Socialization and the State', *Journal of Historical Sociology*, 9 (3), pp. 269–89.

Index